"In *I Must Remember This*, George Youngblood paints portraits of his coming of age during the Great Depression and World War II. Those struggles and others, such as race relations, will pull young readers into those periods of history. Older audiences can find an easy chair and take a trip down memory lane."

Idella Bodie, South Carolina author

"In his memoir, *I Must Remember This*, George Youngblood captures the spirit and the soul of America as it faced economic disaster and social injustice and then found itself fighting World War II. Humor, warmth, sadness, and fear play themselves out in the eyes of a child growing into a teenager and then a young man. It's a literary journey worth taking."

Cliff Hollingsworth, celebrated screenwriter, famous for "Cinderella Man."

"George Youngblood is truly one of the best Southern writers to emerge in a long time. His memoir, *I Must Remember This*, brings together all the charm, intimacy, and mystique of the South in a tale only a Southerner could tell."

W. Thomas Smith Jr., author, columnist, executive editor of World Defense Review

I MUST REMEMBER THIS

I MUST REMEMBER THIS

A SOUTHERN WHITE BOY'S MEMORIES OF THE GREAT DEPRESSION, JIM CROW, AND WORLD WAR II

George Thomas Youngblood

iUniverse, Inc.
New York Lincoln Shanghai

I Must Remember This
A Southern White Boy's Memories of the Great Depression, Jim Crow, and World War II

Copyright © 2006 by George Thomas Youngblood

All rights reserved. No part of this book may be used or reproduced by any means, graphic, electronic, or mechanical, including photocopying, recording, taping or by any information storage retrieval system without the written permission of the publisher except in the case of brief quotations embodied in critical articles and reviews.

iUniverse books may be ordered through booksellers or by contacting:

iUniverse
2021 Pine Lake Road, Suite 100
Lincoln, NE 68512
www.iuniverse.com
1-800-Authors (1-800-288-4677)

ISBN-13: 978-0-595-39512-5 (pbk)
ISBN-13: 978-0-595-67721-4 (cloth)
ISBN-13: 978-0-595-83911-7 (ebk)
ISBN-10: 0-595-39512-0 (pbk)
ISBN-10: 0-595-67721-5 (cloth)
ISBN-10: 0-595-83911-8 (ebk)

Printed in the United States of America

THE DEDICATION

To the mostly wonderful people
In these pages who made my life
And made it mostly happy.
George Youngblood

PROLOGUE

I MUST REMEMBER THIS is a collection of family memoirs reflecting the warmth, the sadness, the humor, the excitement, and the shocks of white boys coming of age in the rural south in the 1930's and 1940's. We moved five times during this period. Each time we lived near a creek that would become a stream of memories with echoes and visions of the family.

It's about family and friends and neighbors struggling with the Great Depression in South Carolina. Poverty, the Boll Weevil, cotton failures, bad water, and poor sanitation aggravated Depression's blight. Deadly disease was rampart. Pneumonia terrified everybody, as did typhoid fever, polio, tuberculosis, and other killers.

The Depression gave little reason to hope, but our people hoped. With little cause to smile, they laughed. It didn't even make sense to try, but they tried. With little to celebrate, they celebrated because they had a life to live and they lived it with relatives, friends, and neighbors. They lived through The Depression, survived, and grew stronger. They did it with basic honesty, charity, respect for others, and an astounding sense of humor.

These memories are about our absurd reactions to our first awareness of death, sex, race, and the truth about Santa Claus. They're about smoking rabbit tobacco, trembling at ghost stories, dreading snakes, watching haircuts for excitement, getting baptized, and gawking at locomotives and alligators. They're about school, fishing, football, and adolescence in the 1940's with a few adult memories thrown in. They're about confusion on segregation because our favorite playmate, work associates, our beloved housekeeper, and neighbors were black.

Segregation had crystallized around laws, customs, and public opinion. Some people made a science of it—unwritten but widespread views about what to do under various conditions. Jim Crow was harsh and we saw some horrible things making these memories all the more melancholy and all the more precious because we did some things right.

It was the sober time of the Great Depression and general want, but it was also a time to live and enjoy life as much as possible. The memories include Lang Roland and Bub Waters, two black men who worked for my father. Lang and his wife Nell were our nearest neighbors and they had a son, Lang, Jr. The hard times drew us together. Lang couldn't get a job and Bub was a deaf mute. My father was trying to succeed with his sawmill and store so he hired Lang and Bub to look after his farm. Mama often helped in the store and or in the church so Nell was often our housekeeper, cook, and second mother. Lang, Jr. was our playmate so the color line was often indistinct and we lived on both sides of it.

Segregation was strictly enforced but we lived in a kind of symbiotic relationship with the black people that lived and worked on our place. The relationships were still unequal but these black people were part of a life that can never be relived. Subsequent legal and social changes disallow such lives. Now by law we must accept them as equal, but we don't. These stories are about a time when by law we could not consider them equal, but we did. Our experiences with these people in those times are precious to me and hopefully to others.

Then The War came. We knew it was coming, but December 7, 1941 still left us in shock. Then for four years, visits and letters from our kin in military service, the news, rationing, and prayers in the churches reminded us of the war. Uncles and cousins served as did friends and people we knew. We lost no kin but some men we knew didn't come home. Still life went on.

This is a collection of personal stories of things I experienced or knew about. It does not try to be politically correct, does not point fingers, does not apologize, and does not condemn. It's what I saw, heard, smelled, tasted, felt, and lived.
George Youngblood

I MUST REMEMBER THIS

Memories of Hardemore Creek 5

Memories of Bee's Creek (1) 121

Memories of Black Mingo Creek 141

Later Memories of Bee's Creek (2) 199

Memories of Noxborough Creek 217

Memories of Rosemary Creek 247

PART ONE

MEMORIES OF HARDEMORE CREEK
1932–1938

GUIDE TO THE MEMORIES

The Memoirs	Page Number
THE ELKO COMMUNITY AND THE CHARACTERS	9
THE OLD PLACE	13
THE COLLAPSE OF THE WATERMELON WAGON	15
GRANDMA	16
POSING FOR THE PICTURE	17
MY FIRST SCIENTIFIC EXPERIMENT	18
MOVING TO GRANDMA'S HOUSE	20
ME AND LANG	22
OLD CROP	24
CHOCOLATE MILK	25
LANG, JR.'S SNAKE LECTURE	27
THE COTTON BARN	32
MY FOREST FIRE	34
THEY DIED HARD	36
PICKING FIGS	37
PUPPY LESSONS	38
WAITING FOR THE BUTTER TO COME	40
THE BLACK BASEBALL GAME	43
THE SEVENTEEN-YEAR LOCUST	45
ANGEL?	47
BAPTISM	51
FALL FROM GLORY	55
SYRUP CANDY	58

THE POOR HOUSE	60
YEAH, RIGHT	64
MUDDYING THE WATER	68
PICNIC AT HEALING SPRINGS	76
PICKING COTTON	78
GOING TO THE GRIST MILL	80
UNEQUAL JUSTICE	82
SANDY CLAWS	84
THE BEE SWARM	88
LANG'S OLD CAR	89
ENTRAPMENT	91
GOING TO CHARLESTON	92
THE BEST FRIEND	94
GETTING PUNCTURED	98
THE CHAIN GANG	100
THE FOURTH OF JULY	103
HAIRCUTS	107
MAKING SYRUP	109
THE ELKO SCHOOL BELL	111
FROGS IN THE WELL	113
GRANDFATHER WOODWARD	115
TWO ELIZABETHS—DIXIE HEROINES GRANDMA MCNAB AND GRANDMA WOODWARD	117

THE ELKO COMMUNITY AND THE CHARACTERS

Mama chased the cat with her broom as angry as I ever saw her. "You Hessian!" she yelled. "You Sherman! Oh, Lord, forgive me. It slipped out. I didn't mean to cuss."

The cat had jumped on the table, spilled a glass of milk that rolled over, fell to the floor, and broke. Her reaction said a lot about our heritage. Our part of South Carolina was bitterly divided during the Revolution between Patriots and Loyalists. The British, Tories, and their allies—the German mercenaries predominantly from Hesse—occupied Charles Town and major outposts like Camden, Orangeburg, and Ninety-Six. The Hessian and Tory raids for food and supplies infuriated our Patriot ancestors even more than similar deeds by the British. The feelings died hard. During the Revolution, my German ancestors anglicized their names. Jungblut became Youngblood. That's why a century and a half later, Mama called the feline miscreant a Hessian.

The other swear word was engendered in the Civil War. Sherman sent two columns of troops through our area and wrought such devastation on private citizens his very name became profane. Mama sometimes called us Hessians but never Shermans. That was a swear word by which none of us deserved to be addressed—except the cat.

Our people had been there for a long time. Every ancestor family we have discovered came to this land prior to the Revolutionary war. Seven men were Patriot soldiers and others were just Patriots. They were early settlers. They came before the towns and villages were established. Records to indicate when Elko, South Carolina, was first settled have eluded us. Perhaps none remain.

Before the Revolution, the backcountry of South Carolina was a lawless place. Settlers tried to farm and ranch the area, but bands of thieves and murderers kept things in turmoil. The royal government on the coast did nothing until the settlers took their security in their own hands and formed the Regulators, a vigilante force to "regulate" the thieving, raping, and murdering raiders. Then the royal government considered the Regulators the lawbreakers and sent troops to capture or kill them. The Regulator War ended with the Battle of Alamance in which nine Regulator leaders who surrendered were hanged. Our trouble with the English royal government started well before the Boston Massacre.

During and after the Revolution, our people still struggled to survive and weren't all that interested in records. The British, Tories, and Hessians burned most public buildings, anyway, and few records escaped. Then Sherman's torches got most of those remaining. But we know this—shortly after the Revolution, our great-great-great-grandfather, Joseph Youngblood, got a land grant for his service in the Patriot cause. The grant was located on Spur Branch about five miles east of the village site. Another great-great-great-grandfather, James Mims, son of a Revolutionary Patriot, owned the site that would become the village in the early 1800's.

It was already a village in 1832 when the South Carolina Canal and Railroad Company inaugurated traffic on the first commercial railroad in the United States. The train ran through the hamlet that lay ninety-six miles from Charleston, so they called it Ninety-Six Station. If it had a prior name, we have not discovered it.

But a district and town farther north had already taken that name because it was ninety-six miles from somewhere else. So to avoid a local civil war, they looked for another name. The hamlet, station, and rail siding stood on land purchased from one of our ancestors, Eleanor Mims, widow of James Mims, Jr., so they called the village Mims Turnout. The trains often went off the line there on a siding because they couldn't see to travel at night. Nobody complained—the passengers needed food and lodging and the village needed the business.

But folks up in Darlington County already had a town named Mims and the hardheaded people of our village weren't about to share a name with anybody. Then after years of calling the village the village or town, they came up with Elko, a strange name for a plantation located nearby. That name stuck—who else wanted it?

Elko, South Carolina, lies three miles southeast of Williston. When we lived there, the two towns shared schools, kinfolk, cotton, the train, and many other things. Although the twin towns were about as non-Dickensian as they could be, this is a tale of two towns where we grew up in the worst of times and where we spent our childhood in the best of times. It was the time of the Great Depression, the time of Jim Crow, the time of Boll Weevil poverty, and the time of our mostly happy childhood.

It was the time of active local politics and Confederate heroes because we still had some living. It was the time of Baptist revivals, fish fries, Fourth of July picnics with barbecued pig, Sunday dinners with ambrosia and coconut pie, fresh peanut boils, baptisms in the creek, watermelon cuttings, Confederate Memorial Day, and catfish stew.

Things changed after I was born in 1929. My father said it was all my fault—how could any nation so conceived and so dedicated long endure the troubles that came with George Thomas Youngblood (me). He was right—the market crashed, we were depressed by the Depression, the stock market smelled like the stockyard, brokers went broke, the New Deal got dealt, fascism flourished in Europe, and prohibition got prohibited.

Things were awful. This was Elko, South Carolina, in the thirties. We saw some of it firsthand and heard about more: ruined crops, herds devastated with cholera, good crops with no markets, bank failures, separate and unequal justice, unemployment, soil erosion, empty pantries and stomachs, and almost total despair. We knew living on homegrown food was better than nothing because we had tasted both. Roosevelt tried to float us out of indigence on the National Recovery Act (NRA) and his alphabet soup of acronyms, but we were almost swept away and drowned in his flood of organizational abbreviations.

Things were wonderful. We had fields and streams to play in and woods with trees to climb. We lived near two of my father's brothers and their families. Mama's grandfather and her aunt lived near Williston so we had plenty of company and often visited back and forth with these people. My father had a close friend and we could go swimming and fishing in his pond.

It was a time without indoor plumbing, running water, or electricity. The REA (Rural Electrification Administration) couldn't find us for a long time. Then the house had a line attached to it, but no power came before we moved. Indoor plumbing was for the towns and cities. For us, it was a time of drawing water from the well, using the new outdoor privy built by the WPA (that's the Works Projects Administration), and washing clothes and ourselves in No. 3 galvanized tubs, the standard size for washing clothes.

But we had more to fear than just fear itself, Mr. Roosevelt. We were afraid of dying and going to hell, hog cholera, typhoid fever, falling in the well, rattlesnakes, pneumonia, lightning, going broke, polio, and the big alligator in Tom Willis's pond.

We depended on my father and mother, God, the Southern Railroad, the Elko cotton gin, Good Gulf Gasoline, the Augusta Chronicle, Octagon Soap, Sears Roebuck, and no bank at all.

The women were a romantic and loyal bunch and they revered the memory of Reverend Peacock, Robert E. Lee, Wade Hampton, Stonewall Jackson, and all Confederate soldiers, mothers, and grandmothers.

The men were good old boys who liked Senator "Cotton Ed" Smith, Prince Albert Tobacco, state Senator Edgar Brown, other people's white lightning, ready-made cigarettes, and old man Charlie Bates, everyone's adopted grandfather.

We, the children, disliked school, hot-dry weather, and cold-wet weather, and without knowing why, we hated William Tecumseh Sherman, the Bowl Weevil, and Republicans.

Those bad/good times forced us to become self-sufficient on the little farm. For companionship, Joe, Richard, and I had each other to play with and Mama had us and our little sister, Helen. We harvested cucumbers, cantaloupes, asparagus, cotton, and watermelons to sell and about everything else to eat. It was the time for hog-killing and fresh liver, brains and eggs, chitterlings, backbone and rice, fresh sausage, and liver pudding. From the orchard came figs, peaches, pears, pecans, and apples. The gardens yielded green peas, string beans, butter beans, field peas, okra, onions, collards, tomatoes, sweet corn, potatoes, sweet potatoes, and rutabaga turnips. It was the time of pickled peaches, sour kraut, fig and pear preserves, and apple butter and jelly. We produced our own corn and wheat for meal, grits, and flour, and my father planted sugarcane for syrup.

The Still family lived across the creek and up the hill, but we seldom saw them. In the other direction at about the same distance lived Uncle Clint and his family. We saw them often. About once a month we got together with them and Uncle Norman's family for Sunday dinners.

Down the hill just three hundred yards from our house stood an unpainted tenant house where Lang and Nell Roland lived. Lang worked for my father on the farm and Nell worked in our house that was also unpainted and not much better than theirs. In one of the ironies of the period, we saw the Rolands all the time—at work and at play. They are frequent actors on memory's stage.

Another black man, Bub Waters, appears from time to time. Bub was a deaf mute whose name came from his efforts to talk. He was the butt of many jokes and pranks from both blacks and whites, but he took it all in stride with a good nature. My father would help those he could and he could help Bub. The Rolands and Bub were the only people he hired on a permanent basis.

As a consequence, my father had to understand Bub and somehow he learned. To everyone else, Bub's attempts were gibberish, but my father knew just what he said and their frequent communications made them close. My father did a lot for Bub and Bub would do anything for my father.

Lang was a strong man and a hard worker. A veteran of World War I, he was my father's right arm on the farm. My father depended on him to keep the farm going while he worked at the store and the sawmill. We felt as safe with Lang around as when my father was home. Lang's wife, Nell, was something else. In the language of the times, she was "a mess," but that's getting ahead of the memories.

The dialect used in these stories is the speech I remember speaking and hearing. Most of our friends and kin spoke that way, too. The black people who lived near us had the same dialect. Over the years, we probably taught each other because some of the sayings go back to old English and others came from West Africa by way of Barbados and other islands with huge slave populations in colonial times. Words are often omitted but sometimes we used even more words than our present-day speech employs for the same thought. This too, I want to remember.

THE OLD PLACE

My parents were living with my father's mother when my brother Joe was born. My father and his mother had some differences a few years before, but she went to the same church that Mama attended in those days. They knew and respected each other. When they got married, Grandma welcomed her daughter-in-law and her son back home. The differences were settled and they were reconciled.

Grandma's house was located about forty yards north of the Elko/Spur Branch Road about two miles east of Elko. After a few months, my parents moved across that dirt road to another unpainted wood frame house where I was born and spent my first four years. Our baby sister, Eleanor was born there, too, but she died when she was six weeks old. Joe said he remembered her but I was only two. Mama used to tell us about Joe wondering at the funeral, "Why they put our little baby in that box, Mama?"

Brother Richard was also born in that old house when I was three years old. I remember when he was a baby. Trying to be a kind older brother, I tried to make him something to play with out of cardboard, but Mama took the knife and scissors away from me.

That old house is gone, the well is gone, the trees are gone, and even two tombstones marking the graves of some distant relatives are gone. The site now lies in the middle of somebody else's field. No one knows exactly where the house stood and almost no one cares.

One of my early remembrances is about one of my father's friends or associates who slipped on snow in the front yard. He fell on his back and his head made a depression in the rare snow. Mama, a rather strict Southern Baptist, said it served him right because he had been drinking. The incident impressed me but I don't remember whether it scared me or made me laugh. Maybe I remember it because of the snow.

But I remember well the time I pulled the radio crashing to the floor in the living room. It didn't work anymore so I asked Joe to help me fix it. I had heard people blaming radio troubles on the aerial so I asked Joe if the aerial was the problem. He looked at the thing lying on the floor in the shattered glass and said he didn't think so. Then we went outside to see if the radio was still grounded, but despite our technical efforts, the radio wouldn't play.

We had an open well with a chain, pulley, and bucket to draw water for the house and farm animals. We were scared to death of the well because we might fall in. My cousin used to bully Joe by holding his head over the well and threatening to drop him in—until Mama saw him do it.

The old house was about a quarter mile from the Elko/Spur Branch Road and sometimes Joe and I had to take a path to the road, cross it, and walk to Grandma's house for milk and eggs. I was a year and a half younger than Joe, so he drifted away from me and I cried because I felt deserted. He fussed at me, but he always came back for me. He was a good brother.

THE COLLAPSE OF THE WATERMELON WAGON

My first keen memory of the old place is the collapse of the watermelon wagon that happened when I was three years old. That morning when my father was leaving to go to the store, Bub Waters, his deaf and mute worker, asked with his gestures if he could take me with him when he went to gather watermelons. Bub liked to have Joe and me around and I think he thought it would pay my father back for some of the favors he did for him.

My father agreed and went back inside and told Mama what I would be doing and where I would be. She came to the porch and looked at Bub and me. She said nothing but her blazing eyes and her frown broadcast her disapproval. Mama's frown always portended trouble. I knew things were not right, but Bub lifted me and set me on the Jersey Wagon seat. A Jersey Wagon is a small one that was pulled by one horse or one mule. We had only mules.

Bub climbed in and we drove off. In my obscure and uncertain memory, I was sitting beside Bub, thrilled and proud—I was getting a ride in the wagon. Bub drove along a two-rut dirt road to the watermelon field. When we reached the field, Bub got down and gathered watermelons he had already picked and laid in rows. Then he pulled the mule's bridle to move the wagon forward between the rows of melons. Every few feet, he stopped, lifted and carried the melons, and loaded the wagon.

Then in a vivid recollection, I was gripping the edge of the wagon seat and holding on in desperation. Evidently the frame connecting the rear axle and wheels with the front became disengaged and I was left sitting on the slanted seat with watermelons strewn behind me and Bub was making strange sounds of distress about the disaster. Then Mama came storming across the field yelling at Bub and took me home.

GRANDMA

Grandma, pronounced "Grandma" (as in "mass") not "Grandmaw", was Mary Estelle Youngblood nee Mims. She's one of the heroines of my family tree because she met the Depression head on and beat it. She worked and managed her farm for almost two decades and made a profit each year. Our grandfather, James Thomas Youngblood, died in 1915, so Grandma had to do it alone. She worked her five sons and several black workers from sunrise to sundown and she worked right beside them. She never had to go to work—she woke up every morning in the middle of it.

Grandfather left her about two hundred acres, a solid but unpainted house, a stable, several mules, barns, planting and harvesting equipment, and a shop with various kinds of equipment. She made the most of it and actually saved a little, but lost it when the Bank of Williston failed. After that she kept her money to herself. Some of it may still be buried on the old place.

Grandma planted cotton, asparagus, cucumbers, cantaloupes, and watermelons, as well as corn and oats for the livestock. In addition to three mules, she kept two cows, chickens, and hogs. She had a large peach orchard, apple trees, pear trees, walnut trees, and pecan trees.

Grandma tolerated no foolishness. She was a strict disciplinarian but when work was done she was pleasant and kind. She was nicknamed "Miss Sweet." I never found out why. But I remember her with affection because she talked to Joe and me as though we were grownups. She knew our limitations, but she expected us to do what we could when she had charge of us.

We had a time of grief and dread in 1933 when Grandma got real sick. My father and Uncle Clint took her to the hospital in Aiken where we visited her several times. I remember being in a car parked on a hill near the hospital when my father and mother came back looking real sad. Then they told us she was dead. I remember Grandma's coffin in the east front room of her house. I've been to her grave in Elko many times, but I don't remember her funeral.

POSING FOR THE PICTURE

Joe and I seemed to fascinate our many relatives and friends—not because we were children—everybody had lots of children. It was probably because we were so young and close in age. Math Bolen, my father's old friend and associate, asked for a picture and said he'd pay for it. So he took my father and mother and us to Denmark in his Buick to get our picture taken. It was a long ride of almost twenty miles to a drug store that had a photography shop in the rear.

When we arrived, things were busy and while we waited, a man brought in a puppy and asked the proprietor to cut off its tail. I don't know what kind of dog it was that had to have its tail taken off, but the men acted like it was a normal thing to do. The dog's owner held the little animal under its stomach and stretched its tail out over a wooden block and the proprietor chopped the tail off. I cringed and cried.

The little dog yelped and yelped while the men wrapped the tail stump to stop the bleeding and then they bandaged it. The dog was still whining when they took it out of the store.

Then the tail chopper, who may have been the pharmacist as well, took us in the back and set us on a large old chair. Mama wiped my eyes and combed my hair and Joe's. The tail chopper joked to make us comfortable and unafraid, but we were uncomfortable and we were afraid. Then he held up toys and shook things trying to make us smile for our picture, but I didn't smile at the mean man. If he were that cruel to puppies, what would he do to children? I couldn't smile. Then he did things he thought was funny, but I didn't think anything was funny because he had just chopped off the puppy's tail.

We still have the picture that shows Joe trying to get down from the chair and me about to break into tears again. Otherwise, it's a good picture. It's in color and it's on the front cover.

MY FIRST SCIENTIFIC EXPERIMENT

My father had a long series of old cars and trucks—rusty, smoky, clattering things. They ran some of the time, but he couldn't brag about them or depend on them. Then one day, several cars brought several families into the yard and everyone was impressed with a shiny new one. They had come for some social thing and after a time of examining the new car and oohs and ahs by all the adults, they went inside.

The visitors brought their children but released them to the freedom of our yard. I saw Mama blink and my father frown. Joe and the older children ran screaming and yelling to the fields and the barns and played things like hide and seek, leaving me on the porch by myself. I didn't mind that so much. I was a curious four-year old and there was a fascinating thing in the yard—a new car. I was almost afraid of it, but it drew me down the steps into the yard. I looked to be sure no one was looking and crept up on the beautiful, scary thing.

The black car's chrome work dazzled me, especially the headlights. Those early models didn't hide the lights inside the front fenders as they did later. In those days, they mounted them in shiny housings on top of the front fenders. The housings looked like giant shiny chrome eggs cut in half and the shape and the mirror-like finish drew me like ripe figs draw June bugs.

I walked around the shiny car several times then halted beside a headlight because my image flashed in it as I passed by. I sneaked up close and stared at it. My facial image was distorted in the curved shiny surfaces and that mesmerized me. The juvenile noise faded. I became aware of only the headlight housing. Everything and everybody else disappeared from my mind.

I tilted my head and my eyes seemed farther apart. I tilted back and my chin was smaller and odd shaped. I moved closer and the image grew and changed shape again. I stood there tilting my head, moving it toward then away from the shiny surface and marveling at the changes.

Then I began to make faces at the slanderous thing that was deceitfully reflecting my image. I frowned at it but it returned a worse frown. It didn't do justice to my smiles, either. I showed my teeth and almost ran from my own image peering back at me. I screwed up my courage and tried to look ugly back at it—I pulled my lips apart, squinted my eyes, and wrinkled my nose all at the same time. My likeness was dreadful to behold, but I caught my breath and sneered on one side and then the other, all the time observing the changes in my image in the headlight housing. Then a burst of laughter interrupted those scientific observations. All the adults had gathered on the porch to watch me perform.

When I saw them, blood rushed to my head, my face warmed up, and I ran lickety-split to the barn. I hid there until Mama came and told me it was all right. She was glad I had given her guests a show, but I was still too embarrassed to go back with her. I waited until the company went home.

MOVING TO GRANDMA'S HOUSE

While Grandma was alive, Joe and I spent a lot of time with her. We knew Grandma's place as well as the Old Place where we lived. A few months after Grandma died, my father and mother moved us into her house, but we had misgivings. Joe, Richard, and I slept in the room where Grandma's coffin had been set up for visitation and viewing prior to her funeral. The room disturbed us—we found it disquieting to sleep in a place where she lay dead only a few months before. I worried. "What we gonna do if Grandma comes back home, Joe?"

"Why don't you jes' shut up?" he said.

Grandma's house was a tall one-story farmhouse, tall because it had high ceilings and a huge, high attic. Like most houses of the period, it was built off the ground and rested on joists supported on brick pillars about three feet high. It boasted a wide front porch and a long back porch. Lightning rods with sharp spikes projected from the roof and connected to insulated cables that ran to the ground. "What them things, Joe?" Richard asked.

"Lightning rods. We have to have 'em because some of us might make God mad."

"How you make God mad, Joe?" Richard asked.

"Whole bunch of ways. I don't know them all."

We kept an icebox, firewood, and stove wood on the back porch. At the end of the long back porch was a well from which we drew water with a galvanized bucket, pulley, and chain. The well was an essential part of Grandma's place and I believe Melvin Youngblood dug it. He was our great uncle and a well digger. Don't ask. I never learned how cold his backside was. The well was our source of water for the house, the animals, and the farm.

North of Grandma's house and opposite the stables lay the garden that was fenced for protection and to provide vine support for Kentucky Wonder Beans and climbing butter beans. On the northern edge of the garden was an old house where our father was born. Our father used the old run-down house to store cotton and corn. We thought it was haunted.

A path from the back yard led past the chicken house to the outdoor privy. It was sixty yards from the house. On most days that was far enough, but when the wind came from that way…

The path continued through a field about three hundred yards to an unpainted house where Lang and Nell Roland lived with their son, Lang, Jr. The path led beyond the Roland house to the sugarcane mill equipped with a two-roll mill and a shed-covered syrup kettle. A lane that crossed the Elko/Spur Branch

Road also led to the sugarcane mill and to my father's sawmill that lay across the Elko/Spur Branch Road on that same lane.

Beyond the syrup mill, the lane became a path that continued through the woods to Tom Willis's pond where we kept a boat. I'm not sure who owned the boat, but my father and Uncle Clint used it as did Bo, Uncle Clint's son.

ME AND LANG

I was too young to know much about what was going on in 1933 because I lived in the shell of the immediate and things I could see and touch. I thought the life I lived and the things I saw were common to everyone. One day I found out they weren't.

Twice a day Lang came to the back porch and drew water from the well and poured it into a square basin that drained down a pipe about eighty yards to a water trough in the lot. He had to pull about fifty gallons of water each time for the mules and the cows. The creaking pulley always told us when someone was drawing water so we knew when Lang was watering the stock.

A board siding about eight feet high protected us little ones from the well on the ground and on the porch where it was over four feet high. The porch roof extended out over the well to protect it from falling debris and to cover the water drawer if it rained. Water came from a pool at the bottom of the well about thirty feet down. That's why we weren't allowed to go near the well.

The well was an essential part of the place because it was our only water source. Grandma had even used it as a hiding place for money when the Bank of Williston took Roosevelt's bank holiday and never re-opened. She lost most of her money in the failure. From that time, she put her money in jars and buried them several places in the yard. She kept some in a special jar, tied a string to the jar top, and hung it in the well. She mistrusted banks until she died.

Lang came up on the porch to do this twice-daily watering chore. One day while he drew water, I sat on the porch steps striking and playing with wooden matches. Lang stopped and looked at me. "Miss Gladys know you playing with them matches?"

I nodded my lie and kept striking matches and watching them burn out. When the top part burned, I waited until the charred portion cooled and then held it up while the remainder burned. "Better watch out you don't burn your fingers, Georgie," Lang warned.

I could tell Lang didn't believe my lie about Mama's permission, but he kept drawing water.

I kept burning the matches. I was impressed with the way the white wooden matches turned black when they burned. I had several black sticks laid out. "What you doing anyways?" Lang asked.

"Making niggers," I said in my four-year old innocence.

Lang looked at me and frowned and his eyes narrowed. "Take more'n a match to make a nigger, Georgie."

Lang went on drawing water and said no more about it, but I felt rebuked although I didn't know why. I knew I had hurt Lang or made him angry and I didn't want to do either. It was my first exposure to the terrible situation and the tension between the races. I didn't understand it, but I knew it was somehow my fault and I felt bad about it.

I talked to Mama about it and she said colored people (the preferred description in those days) didn't like that word so I shouldn't use it. I don't know how I learned it in the first place, but I didn't make it up. My parents didn't use it so I must have heard it from our friends or kinfolk.

Lang and I continued to be good friends for many years after that, but I still regret the incident even though I was too young to know what I said or what it meant.

OLD CROP

There was not much for us to laugh at and plenty to feel sad about in 1934. Grandma had died and her house and farm seemed destined for sad times and sad events. Like Old Crop's death.

Old Crop was one of Grandma's mules that my father and his brothers had rescued from a stable fire while they still lived at home. The animal's long ears had been badly burned and when they healed, they stayed crumpled. Someone named him Crop because he was a crop-eared mule. Everybody likes survivors so everybody liked Old Crop.

Crop was old because my father plowed with him when he still lived at home. The mule had to be at least seventeen years old, and he was probably more than twenty years old. After we moved to Grandma's house, my father still used Old Crop for light work like garden plowing, but most of the time, he just grazed in the pasture. Then he came down with some sickness.

My father called in the veterinarian but Old Crop got worse. The veterinarian said the mule had to be destroyed. My father didn't have the heart to shoot Old Crop himself so he asked Lang to end his suffering. He went to the store early that day to be away when it happened. He didn't even want to be there.

Joe went to school but I was home when it happened. Nobody said anything as they got things ready. Bub hitched two other mules to the large wagon and tied a rope to the rear of the wagon to drag Old Crop away when he was dead. Lang stood by the gate hiding my father's Marlin pump gun and waited for Old Crop to come close. That was when I left the stables and went home. I was young but I knew what was happening. I expected it but I was crushed when I heard the gun shot. I felt sad for Old Crop and Mama did, too. "Poor old mule," she said.

A few minutes later, Mama and I watched the wagon leave with Bub and Lang on board dragging Old Crop to the place my father told them to bury him. We knew where it was—a place in a sandy field over by the gully, a washout that destroyed a portion of a good sandy field every time it rained hard. We didn't see them bury Old Crop, but we know they did a good job. Bub Waters and Lang Roland were good workers.

But about a week later, Joe and I went by that field and smelled something awful. Then we saw buzzards circling over the spot and dropping down and knew Old Crop had somehow been uncovered. Maybe the rain washed the sand off. At any rate it smelled so bad our father decided to let the buzzards eat the body and then they reburied the skin and bones. The whole episode made me sad and it still does.

CHOCOLATE MILK

During the Depression, my father and most farmers produced much of their own food. Orchards, gardens, cows, chickens, and hogs made most farms in Barnwell County almost self-sufficient. To make sure there was enough, there was sometimes too much—especially the milk. We used some and the Rolands used some, but when we were milking both cows, there was plenty left. Then Mama tried to sell the excess milk in my father's store. Each evening, my father told Mama how much milk to bottle based on sales that day. She always sent more than he asked for and he brought it back if it wasn't sold.

Lang milked the cows in the morning and in the evening. Mama strained the raw milk through muslin, but we didn't have equipment to pasteurize or homogenize the milk. She simply poured the evening milk into pans for kitchen use and put it in the icebox. The cream would rise during the night and she would skim it off for butter or whipped cream.

When Lang brought the morning milk, Mama strained and bottled it in sterilized pint and half-pint bottles, the usual refreshment sizes. She sealed them with cardboard caps that had a tab for removal, then the common way to sell milk. By the time we got the milk to the store, the cream had risen to the top. If the customer wanted the milk and cream mixed again, he had to shake his own bottle, but many people liked to drink the thick cream right off the top.

My father had to leave early in the mornings whether he was going to the sawmill or the store so he couldn't take the milk. We had to get the milk to the store another way. The Arthur Still family lived up the hill across Hardemore Creek, and Cornet Still, a young single man who still lived at home, owned a car. He had a job or route that sent him by Grandma's house going toward Elko every morning. My father asked him to look for me on the way and to take the milk to the store.

On those days, I waited in the break in the hedge bordering the road until I heard Cornet's car climbing the hill. He stopped, picked up the milk, and took it to my father's store in Elko. If my father was working in the store that day, I went with Cornet and came back with my father for dinner. If my father went to the sawmill, Cornet took the milk to the store and gave it to my father's partner, Hugh Bert.

Sometime in 1934, Mama expanded her business to include chocolate milk. That put her in local competition with the Coca-Cola trade then sweeping the south. The customers would come in and ask for a cold "Dope" meaning a bottle of the soft drink. Mothers and fathers would rarely force a child to drink milk rather than a Dope, but the chocolate milk gave them something to bargain with when they tried to persuade their children out of a Dope. My father's store sold more of Mama's chocolate milk than regular milk.

My father always closed the day at the store so that he could relieve his partner who had worked since morning. When he closed, he brought back the unsold milk and chocolate milk for us. One day we sent twenty-four bottles of chocolate milk in the carrying crate and expected my father to bring some of it back home. But that day a school bus with children on some excursion or school event stopped by the store and bought it all as well as all the regular milk. We didn't have chocolate milk for supper that night.

If Mama wasn't ready with the milk when Cornet Still came by, all was not lost. An older gentleman usually came by about an hour later in his buggy. I don't remember his name, but it must have been Old Man Charlie Bates, everybody's adopted grandfather. When I waved for a ride, he always smiled and helped me up in the buggy. He seemed to enjoy the company on the way to Elko, but he probably wanted someone to listen to his singing. He was quite good, but I don't remember any of the songs. I do remember him waving and speaking to everybody we met along the Elko/Spur Branch Road when I went with him to deliver Mama's chocolate milk.

Mama's milk business produced little income, but every bit helped in 1934.

LANG, JR.'S SNAKE LECTURE

Mama hated snakes. She lived on farms all her life. She was used to the hard life and the dangers, but she never got used to snakes—they terrified her. "Just looking at the squirmy things makes my skin crawl," she said.

My father hated snakes even more than Mama did and he may have been afraid of them, too, but his reaction was to kill them. He killed every poisonous snake he could as well as snakes that raided our chicken house for eggs and biddies (baby chicks). He would hunt or track down those snakes, sometimes to their holes and kill them if he found them.

But my father tolerated rat snakes in the fields and in the barn. He said they kept the rodent population down. He also ordered us not to kill king snakes because they killed other snakes. Mama did not discriminate—any snake would terrify her. She probably never heard the word ophiophobia, but her perspective and reactions defined it well. Whenever we went out in the fields or the woods, she would always warn us. "Look where you're walking so you don't get on a snake."

My brothers Joe and Richard and I inherited Mama's fear of snakes so we were just as afraid of them as she was. So was Lang, Jr. who was always praising my father and his own father, Lang, another champion snake killer. "My Daddy see a snake," he said, "that snake's go die sho as the sun go set. And if Mr. Seece see a snake, he gone quit what he doing, track it down, and kill it."

"Our Daddy don't chase down every kind of snake, Lang, Jr." Joe said, "just them chicken snakes and poison snakes. He says some snakes is good."

"I ain't never seen no good snake," I said, "but maybe them garden snakes is good snakes."

"Naw. Ain't no such of thing as a good snake," Lang, Jr. said. "Look all the trouble they caused in the Bible and histry. Eve got Adam in a heap of trouble on account she took up with a snake that ruint the garden God made for 'em. Then God run them all off and Adam and Eve felt real put out about it. But, man, God wuz some kinda mad. That's when He made Adam sweat. There wasn't no sweating before Adam et the apple, don't you know?"

"You sho about that, Lang, Jr?" Richard asked. "God didn't make him sweat, he sweated on account of the heat."

Lang, Jr. nodded. "But God's the one who makes it hot or cold, and He made it hot for Adam. He jes' give us a little taste of heat. He's got a real hot place for them that don't behave—all because of that garden snake. And the thing made

Him so mad, He made Eve have babies and made the snake crawl on his belly without no legs."

"But there's different kinds of snakes, Lang, Jr." I said. "I hear tell some people hold snakes in their hands and pet 'em."

"Yeah? Well, a woman way back yonder named of Cleo Patro tried to hug a snake and nurse it like a baby. But he bit her and she died. Ain't no such of a thing as a good snake. Best we think all them snakes is poison snakes. If Adam and Cleo Patro hada kilt them snakes, things woulda been a whole lot different now."

"But some them poison snakes are worse'n other poison snakes," I said.

Lang, Jr. nodded. "That's right, Georgie, and the worst poison snake is the Carl snake."

"Carl snake?" Joe asked. "I ain't never heard nothing about no Carl snake. You sho that's what they call it? What kind of a snake is it?"

Lang, Jr. shrugged. "I ain't never seen one myself, but I hear tell that there's a real strong poison snake. It ain't too big and they call it the Carl snake."

"They musta named him after that mean old Mr. Carl Ramsey," Richard said.

"They mighta. Anyhow, that Carl snake's kinda purty, but he's a mighty strong poison snake. Daddy said a man that lives on the other side of Blackville claims that a Carl snake bit a mule and the mule fell and was dead before he got to the ground. Never kicked or moved no more. When the mule started stinking, then the buzzards swarmed in and et him up and they all died, too. That man said there was no buzzards in the county for years, but they started sneaking back in and now we got plenty of them."

"You don't believe that trash, do you, Lang, Jr.?" Joe asked.

"Sho' I do. Ain't got no reason not to believe it. That man don't lie much, Daddy said."

"But that snake's a poison snake," I said. "How about them that ain't poison?"

"Them unpoison snakes can kill you, too, Georgie. You know all 'bout them coachwhip snakes, don't you."

I shook my head. "Coachwhip snakes? Naww. I ain't never heard nothing about no coachwhip snake. How it kill you?"

"He run you down and grab a hold to your pants leg and then he starts to whipping you with his tail and keeps on whipping till you dead."

"Huh," Joe snorted. "How the coachwhip snake gonna know if you done died?"

"The coachwhip snake sticks the end of his tail in your nose to feel if you still breathing. If he feels air, he beat you some more until he don't."

I frowned at him. "I ain't never heard nothing like that before, Lang, Jr."

"Well, they's a lot you ain't heard, Georgie, but you know all about them rattlesnake pilots, don't you?"

I shook my head. "I ain't never heard nothing about no rattlesnake pilots, neither," I said. "What they do?"

"Rattlesnakes don't see too good, don't you know. They crawl around sticking their tongues out trying to figure out which-a-way to crawl. So there's this little ole snake that guides him. He looks like a rattlesnake, but he ain't. He stinks up the air where he's at and smells strong like a dirty goat. Rattlesnakes stink that-a-way, too, so they don't mind following the pilot snake."

Joe frowned. "The rattlesnake follow right behind the pilot snake or a little ways off? If I was a pilot snake, I wouldn't want no rattlesnake following me too close."

Lang, Jr. nodded. "You right, Joe. Rattlesnakes like to eat mice and rats and warm little animals, not other snakes, but the rattlesnake pilot, he don't know nothing about that. He don't trust no rattlesnake neither. He crawls a whole day ahead so the rattlesnake can't eat him. Sometimes you can smell a rattlesnake pilot cross a road and wait a day and kill the rattlesnake when he come the next day. Your daddy hunt rattlesnakes that-a-way?"

"You ain't telling the truth no more, Lang, Jr." Joe said. "That's a tall tale."

"Trouble with y'all is y'all don't know nothing. Mr. Seece hunts rattlesnake ever which a way he can so I jes' wondered if he hunts 'em with rattlesnake pilots."

"You right about that, Lang, Jr." Joe said. "My Daddy kills rattlesnakes all kinds of ways, but when there's a lot of 'em, he uses hogs to get rid of 'em."

Lang, Jr. laughed. "Ain't no hog go run no rattlesnake off."

"I ain't never said nothing about running them off," Joe said. "The hogs eat them rattlesnakes up. They sniff out the snakes in their holes and then root 'em out and eat 'em up."

Lang, Jr. laughed. "Ain't no way. All the rattlesnake got to do is haul off and bite the hog and the hog'll die."

"Won't do him no good to bite a hog. Hog's got thick fat all around so if a snake was to bite him, the snake's poison ain't go git in his blood."

"Now you the one ain't telling the truth," Lang, Jr. said. "I can see all y'all don't know much about snakes. Bet y'all don't know nothing about milk snakes."

Joe squinted, I shook my head, and Richard gave him a blank look. "What in the world is a milk snake, Lang, Jr.?" Richard asked.

Lang, Jr. squinted. "There's this snake that likes to milk cows. That's how come they call him a milk snake. He sneaks up on a cow when she's out in the pasture eating grass and then he slips up close when she ain't looking. First thing the cow knows, he jumps up and bites one her tits and hangs on. He sucks the milk but he don't get much milk before the cow kicks him off and if he's lucky, she don't cut him in half with her hooves."

"You just making all this up, Lang, Jr., that ain't so," Joe said.

"Naw, I ain't. That there's the truth. And the milk snake ain't got nothing on the cannonball snake."

"Cannonball snakes? You trying to fool us again, Lang, Jr.? Ain't no such of a thing," I said.

"Sho there is. They call 'em cannonball snakes on account of they eat one another."

"You musta meant to say cannibal snakes," Joe said.

"That's what I said. Cannonball snakes. I didn't see it happen, but my daddy swears to it. Said two of them cannonball snakes got in a fight and they twisted and wrassled a long time, but they couldn't swallow one another's head like they supposed to. Then they started swallowing one another's tail and they had to eat fast so they could eat up the other before they got et up their selves. So they et and they et. My daddy said first thing he knowed, they done et each other up and there was nothing left on the ground."

"Huh. How you 'spect us to believe that tale, Lang, Jr." Joe asked.

"Don't believe it then. I ain't go tell y'all nothing else."

"Aw, come on Lang, Jr. I wuz jes' teasing," Joe said.

"You don't believe what I said 'bout them cannonball snakes, you sho ain't go believe nothing 'bout the hoop snakes."

"Yeah, we will, Lang, Jr. Tell us," Joe said.

"Well. A hoop snake is a long black snake. He looks like a reglar black snake, but some of them is hoop snakes."

"How they different, then, Lang, Jr.?" I asked.

"Reglar black snake crawls along trying to catch frogs and mice and things, don't you know. But if the hoop snake sees a mouse or something he wants to eat, he bites his own tail and makes a stiff ring. Then he throws hisself up in a hoop and rolls hisself so fast that he catches it, turns loose his tail, and gobbles up what he's been chasing."

I shook my head. "I know that ain't so, Lang, Jr."

"All right, then. I ain't gone tell y'all nothing about them joint snakes."

"Aww, come on, tell us."

"All right, but y'all better quit saying it ain't so. Y'all making me tired saying it ain't so. Well, joint snakes is strange snakes, too. They looks like reglar chicken snakes but they ain't as big."

"Then how come they so strange, Lang, Jr.?" I asked.

"Most the time when a snake see somebody coming, he crawls off as fast as he can so he don't get killed. Most people kill snakes with a hoe, don't you know? First they chop the snake's head off and then they chop him up in little pieces. But you chop at a joint snake, he breaks his own self up and makes little joints out of his own self. That way the man with the hoe won't cut him up. When the man thinks he killed the joint snake, he walks on off proud, but the joint snake gathers hisself back together and slips on off in the grass."

"You done gone to lying now, Lang, Jr." Joe said.

"I ain't never go tell y'all nothing no more."

He didn't have to. I had already heard enough to make me scared to death of snakes. If I had not already inherited ophiophobia from Mama, Lang, Jr. gave me a strong exposure to it.

THE COTTON BARN

When my grandfather lived and worked the place, it was a vibrant, working farm. He was good with machinery and building and he seemed to pass these talents on to my father. My grandfather was clever in his imagination and good with his hands. He played the fiddle and shaved with a straight razor, but my father never attempted those things.

My grandfather left several old wooden outbuildings like the shop, the barns, the stables, the chicken houses, the asparagus shed, the smokehouse, and the privy. One special old unpainted building stood opposite the lot and almost directly behind Grandma's house. My father used it as a barn. I believe he was born in that old house, but I don't remember if I ever asked him the straight question. I remember the old house having only two large rooms, but my father or someone may have taken out some interior walls. Perhaps the old structure was partially demolished before it was converted into a barn.

We used the smaller room to store and work corn. That's where we each earned ten cents a week shelling a bushel of corn to take to my father's gasoline-powered gristmill in Elko. The other room was much larger, and my father used it to store cotton to keep it out of the weather until he could get it baled and hauled to the covered Elko depot shed.

When freshly picked, cotton smelled good to me, almost sweet. The pickers wrapped their day's work in wide, square burlap sheets that had a distinct oily smell of their own. Then they tied the opposite corners to form a bundle. My father paid the pickers by the pound, so he or Lang weighed the cotton to determine each picker's daily contribution. Then it went into the old barn.

When the cotton dried it took on a musty smell and Lang tossed it with a pitchfork about once a week to make it dry evenly. We used to play in the loose cotton, but not much and not too long. The stuff made you hot in a few minutes because it was such a good insulator.

At first the cotton went in through the front door of the old house, but as the cotton pile in the house grew, the front door couldn't be opened without some falling out. The house didn't have a porch—just a wooden block to step up into it. When the cotton got too high for the front door, Lang threw the cotton in through two windows on the east side.

The cotton stayed there only until it was dry, then Lang and Bub hauled it to the Elko gin. The bales never came back to Grandma's place—they all went to the covered Elko depot beside the railroad tracks. Farmers could get better prices if they waited, but most farmers needed the money right away. My father was no exception.

The loose cotton in the old cotton barn was ginned, de-seeded, and pressed into tight bales. Then it would sit on the Elko depot waiting for the train to take it to Charleston or Augusta. I often wondered what the cotton was used for and what kind of fabrics it was processed into. I supposed shirts, dresses, pants, sheets, towels, pillow cases, diapers, and God only knows what had their origins in our cotton fields and spent a few days drying in our cotton barn.

MY FOREST FIRE

I tried to hide my anxiety. "Mama, quick. I need a jar of water for my house."

Mama got a jar down and filled it for me. "What you need the water for?" she asked.

"Playing," I said

I ran back to our playhouse in the woods, a stand of second growth pine trees that grew across the road in front of Grandma's house. We played there a lot. We couldn't climb the tall, straight trees, but we had a lot of fun pulling down saplings and releasing them to watch them spring back up. When we could pull down a fairly large one, one of us would ride it up, hanging on for dear life. Sometimes when the sapling righted itself, it would snap the rider off and he would fall. I was a frequent victim but I enjoyed being catapulted. The fall was not too bad because several inches of pine straw had accumulated over the years.

We also played in that pine straw and made a playhouse from sticks and straw. It was like a house to my five-year old mind, and I enjoyed playing in it. But I was not playing that day; I had to put out the fire.

That morning Joe was in school and I had to play alone. I went to the playhouse and noticed the lack of furniture. Then a notion came over me to make furniture. I made chairs and beds from twigs and sticks and straw. It still seemed incomplete because it didn't have a fireplace. Then I made a fireplace from some old bricks. All houses need pots and pans so tin cans soon served as pans and small nails became forks and knives.

Matches were easy to find so I had made a fire and set a can of water on the bricks beside the fire and the water had soon boiled away. Everything was play, but the fire was real.

The floor of the house was some of that accumulated pine straw. In a short time, the fire spread from the fireplace to the straw floor. I watched in horror. Soon the little playhouse was in flames. I was only five, but I knew how to fight fires—you pour water on it to cool it off.

That's why I asked Mama for the jar of water. I ran with it to the fire and found a fiery circle of flames ten feet across. It was hot but I poured the water on the flames. The water worked well—for the few inches it covered.

Then Bub saw the smoke and came running and went into a tirade with his sounds and gestures. I knew what he was excited about, but I did not understand a single sound he made. I never did but my father and Bub communicated about as well as people without his handicaps, and that day I learned the hard way how well Bub could communicate with my father.

Bub assessed the fire, ran back, drew water from the well furiously, and filled some five-gallon buckets we used for feeding the animals. Mama stopped Bub and asked him what he was doing. Bub gestured his excitement, unloading a barrage of his expressions—bub, bub—bub, bub—utterances from which he got his nickname. Mama understood none of it until he pointed to the woods boiling with smoke. Then he pointed at me. She saw the flames, she saw me, and she saw red.

Bub took two buckets of water at a time to the fire until he stopped it from spreading. Then with a rake and shovel, he isolated the area from the rest of the woods and got the fire out. Mama cut a peach tree switch and started another fire on my backside.

I was still in jeopardy. Playing with fire in the woods was such a serious thing, my father might punish me, too. My parents would never punish us more than once for an offense, but for something so serious, who could be sure? So I worried.

But then reason assured me that Bub couldn't tell my father what happened or who did it. I began to feel better about the thing. Mama would tell my father and explain that I had already been punished and it would be over. My only worry was that my father would find out before Mama could tell him what happened. But that was unlikely because Bub was the only other person who knew and how in the world could the deaf-mute tell my father anything? I never understood a thing he tried to say.

About sundown, my father's truck rolled into the yard, and Bub was right there, pouring out his monosyllabic expressions and waving his hands. In about twenty seconds, my father leveled furious eyes at me. "Bub said you set the woods on fire."

I thought I faced another switching, but Mama appeared and reduced my father's fury to simple anger and wrought my deliverance. Even facing possible punishment, I was amazed at how my father understood as soon as Bub made his sounds and moved his hands. I didn't have the courage to ask that day, but a few days later I had to know.

"How do you understand Bub, Daddy. Nobody else can make out his mumbles."

"Look at him, son, and listen to what he says and watch his hands. You really want to understand somebody, you can."

My father and mother and Bub are dead. Like Melville's Ishmael, I alone am left to tell of that forest fire and that remarkable communication.

THEY DIED HARD

Uncle Norman nodded. "She died hard, real hard."

My father jerked his head to one side in affirmation, and Uncle Clint waved his head. Dying hard was their expression for accidental death and killings. Uncle Norman was referring to a woman in Elko who died in a house fire started by lightning. Hopefully the lightning killed her before the fire, but in any case, she died hard.

We knew about people who died hard by accident and through angry acts of others. They were all tragic—like the cousin who was crushed by the cotton press in the Elko cotton gin and my father's first cousin, Cleve Youngblood, a train conductor, who was scalded to death in a spectacular wreck of two locomotives. He died very hard.

Skeletons from our family closet sometimes emerged like the duel fought by one of my great-great uncles and another man. Two witnesses said the opponent shot my great-great uncle first—with a shotgun in the stomach at a distance of six feet as they discussed the dueling rules. The blast knocked my great-great uncle down, but he was still conscious and unloaded his revolver into the man's head. My cousin died an hour later. They both died hard.

Great Uncle Chester Woodward was a good horseman until he raced under a low oak limb and didn't duck low enough. It cracked his skull and he died. Another great uncle, Melvin Youngblood, was a well digger and he died in a well cave-in. Both died hard.

Dying hard seemed almost common place, but things happened now and then in Elko and Barnwell County that sobered us, frightened us, or sickened us. The hanging did all of those things. I don't know much about it. As far as I know, no one ever found out who did it. I refer to the discovery one morning of a black man hanging from a tree limb near the Elko cotton gin.

I didn't see the man myself but I heard about him. I know they found him, cut him down, and buried him, but I don't know if he had a family or if the county buried him. Rumors circulated that he had enemies among the black people and some of them hanged him. That may be, but I never before or since heard of a black man being killed that way by his own people. They did some killing, but it was usually with knives or axes and, if they could afford or borrow them, with guns or pistols.

I never learned what happened—I only remember the thing saddened and frightened me. Whoever he was and whatever the reason for his death, he died hard.

PICKING FIGS

The lane leading to Grandma's house continued across the Elko/Spur Branch Road through Black Jack oaks and pine saplings. About five hundred yards from the road, the lane came to an old wooden house that lay collapsed in ruin. Huge climbing rose vines spread over the edge of the caved-in roof. An untrimmed privet hedge paralleled the lane and enclosed the yard. It must have been a pleasant old home for someone, but when Grandfather bought the place in 1902, it was already dilapidated.

When I passed the old ruin, the sweet smell of so many roses almost made me pass out. I never found out anything about the people who had lived there, but judging from all the roses, the privet hedge, and a huge fig tree that spread out on one side of the yard, they must have been gentle people. We thought the old place was haunted, but we never heard any stories about it. We didn't know who had lived there, but we felt connected to them through the sweet smell of the roses and the fig trees.

In summer when the figs began to ripen, Japanese Beetles—we called them June bugs—came in by the hundreds to eat the fruit. Mama sent us to catch as many bugs as we could in an effort to save the figs. Since the bugs were trying to eat our figs and were going to be killed anyway, we didn't have much feeling for them. The bugs were so intent on eating they didn't try to fly away when we put our fingers on them to pick them off the figs.

In those days in that part of the country, we had a game we played with June bugs. I heard since those early years about other boys and girls tying sewing threads to the June bugs' legs. We tied a few and tried to get them to fly around, but they didn't cooperate. Then we tried to see how strong they were by how much they could pull. They were not good at that either so we went back to killing them.

Even with all our work with the bugs, they ate or ruined most of the figs. They seemed to attack fig after fig without finishing them, but we managed to save several gallon buckets of the fruit and Mama made fig preserves from them. The preserves were delicious on her hot fresh biscuits, but so was about anything else.

PUPPY LESSONS

"They tell me puppies know how to swim soon's they're born," Joe said. "Let's throw Cora's puppies in the creek and see."

On our farm, everybody and everything had several functions. Our routine duties were to go to school, hoe the garden, pick the vegetables, and help Lang feed the cows, mules, and hogs. Special duties could be almost anything from helping with the hog killing, picking chicken feathers, shoveling mule, chicken, and cow droppings to spread on the fields, picking cotton, making asparagus crates, and things like that.

The animals had several duties as well. We had a sweet old English Setter named Cora, as good a pet as we ever had. Her other duty was hunting—she was the finest bird dog my father ever owned. We played with her and my father hunted with her. I saw her in action a few times.

Cora crisscrossed the field ahead of my father, sniffing the ground. When she froze and pointed, my father knew he was close to quail or partridges, as he called them, and he knew about where the partridges were hiding. Then my father raised his old Marlin pump gun, and Cora waited for him to walk toward the place she pointed. Cora froze in place on her point and my father flushed the birds and fired.

The first time I saw a bird fall, I wondered how my father would ever find it in all that tall grass. Cora to the rescue. "Dead bird, Cora," my father said.

Cora swept through the area where the bird fell, scooped it up with her mouth, and brought it to my father.

One day Cora "found" three puppies. That's one of the understatements my parents used—this one referred to animal births. I never heard of a woman finding a baby, but it may have been used that way, too. I was familiar with terms like the cow found a calf, the sow found some pigs, and a hen stole a nest and found some biddies, our word for infant chickens.

Anyway, Cora found her puppies and we were delighted with all the little Coras to play with. We carried the puppies when we romped in the fields with Cora, and she seemed glad we included her puppies. We watched her nurse her babies and then we all played again.

Somewhere Joe heard about a dog's natural instinct to swim and now he wanted to test that preposterous theory. That's why we were on the Hardemore Creek bank. "Just shove 'em in," Joe said. "See if they can swim."

So we shoved the puppies into the creek and we were amazed to see the little things paddle their legs in the stream, come back, leave the water, shake off, and go to Cora. She licked them and went out in the sun to nurse them and warm them.

A few weeks later, I heard my father tell one of his friends he had some healthy puppies from a good bird dog. He offered to give the friend one to raise, teach, and train. I knew my father was trying to find good homes for Cora's puppies, so I tried to help. "They already know a lot, Daddy. They already know how to swim. They're smart puppies."

WAITING FOR THE BUTTER TO COME

Some of our kinfolk and friends went to church whenever the doors were open. My father and mother went most of the time and took us boys. Joe and I liked the children's programs, but we dreaded the sermons. Maybe that's why we didn't go as regularly as some wished—certainly not as often as the preacher and the deacons wanted. But when it came to practicing and living their faith, our parents were better Christians than some of the more pious ones.

They would have been good members no matter what flavor of religion they followed or what kind of church they attended. They were kind to the less fortunate like their poor relatives, friends, church members, neighbors, and the occasional tramp who stopped by for a meal. They were even compassionate toward suffering animals. They didn't have much to give, but their lives were patterns of generosity, fairness, compassion, and honesty.

It was not a matter of education. Mama only completed the sixth grade and my father finished the seventh and started the eighth but never finished it. They didn't mention the gospel often because they were not learned in the scriptures or in theology. Later as they became more consistent about church attendance, they both taught Sunday school and learned much more. They often asked Mama to play the piano, but they never asked my father to sing. He sang anyway—so far off key that people near him couldn't stay in tune either.

But their lives indicated something more than knowledge—the way they lived and treated people shouted faith, strength, and love so when they died we were as certain of their transport to Heaven as anyone can be about those matters.

We saw them work the family, the store, and the farm with these principles. Like most South Carolina farms of the period, our farm was almost self-sufficient. We grew vegetables and grains for flour and meal and grits. We raised hogs and chickens and kept two cows for milk, cream, and butter. Our neighbors and friends shared in this bounty and we in theirs. When a cow went "dry," neighbors helped with milk until the cow was "fresh" again. When a family butchered hogs, the ham, shoulders, and middles could be "cured" by salting and smoking, but the sausage and liver pudding couldn't be kept with as much confidence. So the sausage and pudding—known locally as "fresh"—was distributed among neighbors and relatives.

My brothers and I tended and gathered the vegetables, shelled the corn, collected the eggs, killed the chickens, and helped butcher the hogs. For some reason, I was usually the one who had to churn the butter.

We had two butter churns, both powered by hand—my hand. One had a crank assembly that screwed down into a wide-mouth gallon jar. When I turned the crank, a paddle beat the cream and that made it the easiest churn to use. The second churn was an old-fashioned type with a wooden plunger fitted with blades to agitate the cream. Mama told me to push down and twist at the same time, but usually I just pushed. I didn't like that churn. Mama didn't either because it was too much trouble to clean.

These churns had another drawback—they needed about a gallon of cream, and Mama didn't often wait to collect enough cream for these machines. She wanted fresh butter everyday. She filled a quart jar with cream, screwed the lid on tight, and gave it to me wrapped in a kitchen towel. "Here, shake it until the butter comes," she would say.

Those orders confined me to the chair for a time and to a chore that was a thorn in my side—it takes a lot of energy to break down the emulsion we call cream into butter and buttermilk. I didn't have to shake the jar hard, but I had to shake it a lot. I first got tired of shaking and then irritable. I'd beat the jar against my lap. Then I'd change back to shaking because I was hurting my thighs with the beating. I'd stop now and then to look at the cream and wonder why the butter wouldn't come. Mama would notice and smile. "The Lord's trying to teach you patience, George Thomas."

But sometime Mama would be impatient, too, and come and ask if the butter had come. "Well, keep shaking. I need to mold the butter and put it in the icebox so it will set hard. Your father'll be here for dinner soon."

Now dinner meant the noon meal. If you talked about having dinner as the evening meal in South Carolina in those days, people would look at you funny and walk away. Some might suggest psychological or even spiritual counseling for you.

But by icebox, Mama meant icebox. It was a safe-like contraption lined with galvanized sheet metal. It stored a block of ice in a tray on top and the tray had a hose that took the water from the melting ice to a collecting pan. Below the ice tray, several shelves were available for food storage. That was where Mama would put the butter mold—if only the butter would come.

I shook and I beat the jar in my lap, often with juvenile violence because the butter wouldn't come. I sometimes imagined it was the bully at school and my sin nature took over. I pictured myself beating his head against something until I realized it was my thigh. Mama would stop me and tell me to pitch it forward gently and pull it back and repeat. This reciprocal agitation (that's not what she called it, though) was the best way to get the butter to come.

After a few minutes of shaking that seemed like hours at hard labor, I would see the cream change. Pale yellow globules of butter floated in the buttermilk. "Mama, the butter done come!" I would yell.

After I shook it a few more times, the butter coagulated into a mass. Mama strained off the buttermilk and gathered the butter with a fork, salted it, pressed it into the mold, and set it in the icebox.

I didn't care much for buttermilk, but after fighting the cream in the jar, I could hardly wait to taste the butter. On those summer days we had fresh vegetables like butter beans, field peas cooked with smoked hog jowl meat, rice, fresh corn sliced off the cob and slow cooked, and maybe some okra, and everything came with Mama's biscuits.

Most people never got the chance to taste Mama's hot biscuits dripping with fresh butter and I'm sorry about that. They have my sympathy. They've got a lot to learn about good eating and the best way I know for them to catch up on their learning is to trust the Lord and be good so they can go to Heaven and find out. Mama's there and she's going to make her biscuits and have her butter and she'll have a multitude of angels waiting to enjoy them. And I'll be there, my sin nature bleached out, shaking the jar for her, waiting for the butter to come.

THE BLACK BASEBALL GAME

The black population of our county far exceeded the white numbers when we were growing up. The races were separated by law, custom, and emotion; we saw few black people most of the time except for the Roland family. The black people were probably some other place working or playing with others of their race, but for some activities, they didn't have facilities for some of the things the white people did.

Later the concept of separate but equal treatment and privilege was espoused and sometimes followed, but equality was not then present. It was not even considered by lawmakers and most of the white population. Jim Crow was the law and the practice of the community.

When the black community around Elko had their social events in the churches and schools, they attended in large numbers. They had their neighborhood meetings and Saturday night social gatherings in town, but I never saw where they met. Some of them participated in sports, too, primarily with their amateur baseball league. Nothing excited them so much as these teams.

The black families near us used a field on the southern side of the Elko/Spur Branch Road on the Old Place where I was born. It lay across the road from Uncle Clint's land. I don't know who owned it then, but my father or Uncle Clint helped them get the use of it. That field was never farmed in my memory because some kind of carpet grass was dominant there. It was hard to plow and keep crops hoed. It was not ideal for baseball, either, but it was adequate.

They had no stands or backstop. The spectators crowded the first and third baselines. Others mobbed the area behind home plate. They couldn't afford a backstop or maybe the owner didn't want one erected on his property. Having no backstop was not a usual matter of concern, but sometimes with passed balls or wild pitches, the ball would disappear into the crowd never to be seen until the play was over. That was the reason for the rule that a lost ball entitled the runners to only one base.

One day, a wild pitch wound up in the crowd and it couldn't be found. Everybody looked for it for a few minutes. Then a young woman held a baseball up. "I ain't seen your ball," she said, "but I brung this one from home. I'll let you have it for a dime."

Nobody had a dime to spare so she gave the ball to the pitcher on credit.

The large number of people helped stop foul tips, wild pitches, overthrows, and passed balls. This hurt a few spectators but benefited the teams because baseballs were expensive and they had only a few. My father helped the team with money for the balls and bats, but the men had to furnish their own gloves. A few played with no glove and sometimes had to catch a hard throw or hit ball with their bare hands.

Lang sometimes took us to the games with Lang, Jr. That way, Joe, Richard, and I got to see several games. I remember most the enthusiasm of the players and the spectators. The local black people came by the hundreds to see their favorites. I don't remember much of the games except that none of the players were men we knew. Lang knew some of them. One of them was his younger brother. He also knew another man—a large man who was evidently their big hitter. That man would pound the plate and shake his bat at the pitcher and taunt him. "The bell go ring. The bell go ring."

Then the crowd picked it up and they all shouted: "The bell go ring. The bell go ring."

Sure enough the man hit the ball and his people went wild. "Run, man, run."

He ran around the bases before they could find the ball in the field. I didn't know much about the sport then so I can't judge how well they played. I do know they were amateurs. They met for each game, somehow picked the players, and played. There was little organization. They didn't have a coach and I never heard of them practicing. I remember the large man hitting the ball, but there must have been more because there was a lot of yelling at the games we saw.

I don't know what they thought of us. They either accepted or ignored the little white boys sitting beside Lang.

THE SEVENTEEN-YEAR LOCUST

"Look all them locust," Lang, Jr. said.

He was referring to cicada shells on the pine trunks in our yard. "Let's find a bag and pick them," I said.

Joe stared. "Then what we go do with them?" he asked.

Joe was always being practical.

"Can I pick, too?" Richard asked.

Joe nodded. He was always being protective of Richard.

"We can't do nothing with 'em," I said. "Just put 'em in a bag and look at 'em."

Lang, Jr. blinked and looked at me funny. "Well, all right, then," he said.

Joe, Lang, Jr., Richard, and I picked the shells we could reach and soon we had a bag full, but Lang, Jr. wanted one he couldn't reach. He looked all around for some way to get it down.

We always found things to do. Sometimes we went bird hunting with our Red Ryder BB-guns, but Lang, Jr. used a slingshot. We let him use our BB-guns, but he preferred the sling shot because he was good with it. Lang, Jr. would hold the forked handle in his left hand in front of him and concentrate on the target while his right hand pulled back the pebble in the small pocket at the end of the rubber strips. I watched in wonder as he held the fork up at arm's length and stretched his other hand behind him to put power in the shot. He either had a natural ability with the slingshot or he had practiced a lot.

Most of the time we were busy with our chores or engaged in a game. Sometimes we were bored and had to devise things to do. Then we did weird things like collecting dried locust shells. We didn't know anything about the complex life cycle of the cicada, but we had heard them called the seventeen-year locust. That day we looked for shells abandoned by cicada adults and found some within reach.

But the shell that intrigued Lang, Jr. was about eight feet off the ground and he looked around for something to throw at it to knock it off. He searched in the old shop and found a mower guard, a heavy piece of molded metal in the shape of a fat dagger. The flat base had a hole with which it was bolted onto the mower. A series of these guards protected the reciprocating mower blades on our mule-drawn mower.

Armed now with heavy metal, Lang, Jr. took aim and threw the mower guard at the locust several times attempting to knock it off. On his last throw the guard hit the tree, glanced off, and hit Richard in the head. We screamed and the blood poured. We ran to Mama who came out and saw her child bleeding from the head. She screamed, too, and Lang came running to see what was the matter. He learned that his son had thrown the thing that hit Richard in the head and caused the bleeding.

Lang took Lang, Jr. to the cornfield and beat him unmercifully, we thought. We heard Lang, Jr. squalling, but Mama said he wasn't getting hurt. Lang was beating him with a dried corn stalk that made loud cracking sounds but inflicted little pain.

Lang, Jr. had injured a white boy and he was punished with a lot of noise and cries for our benefit. That was the expected response under the system. No one said anything.

Richard didn't suffer a serious hurt, but he still carries a long scar. The incident and the whipping disrupted our play—for about half an hour.

ANGEL?

"Seese, I'm sorry as I can be but I can't help you with Sarah's grocery bill no more," Mr. Martin said.

My father, Cecil Youngblood, said nothing. Mama blinked. She was about to cry. "How will Sarah feed them children then?" she asked.

Mr. Martin waved his head. "I don't know. I feel sorry for 'em. I been giving 'em money and stuff from the garden for years and meat when I kill hogs, but I'm tired of it."

My father still said nothing. "Well," Mr. Martin said, "I got be going. I didn't see y'all in church last Sunday. Y'all better quit backsliding and come on to church like ya supposed to. Got go feed the hogs now and pull Lizzie some rutabaga turnips before I start plowing."

Mr. Martin was a hardworking man, but his patience had been exhausted on Sarah. She had married my father's first cousin who was killed in a cotton gin accident in 1924 leaving her with four boys and a girl, all less than ten years old. She had sued the gin and won, but the gin went bankrupt and didn't pay. For twelve years she had lived on help from her kin and friends. The three oldest boys joined the Civilian Conservation Corps, the CCC as we called it, and sent home what they could. At least they were no longer a drain on Sarah.

My father watched Mr. Martin walk up Elko/Spur Branch Road toward his own cotton farm and shook his head. "Sarah's youngest boy comes to the store everday asking for work and I give him odd jobs for money and groceries to take home. It's a lot more than he's worth, but I can't let Sarah and them children starve. They've run up bills in the store to where they'll never be able to pay, but I let them keep on charging. I don't keep the books on them no more, but it makes them feel better when they charge it. That way it don't seem like it's an outright gift."

"Keep feeding them," Mama said. "Someday, maybe there'll be work and wages so people don't have to beg. I'm going inside and work on that dress for Sarah's little girl some more. You be home before sundown? That old mule's been lying there since yesterday. It's liable to die."

My father sighed, nodded, and got in the old truck. Joe worked the spark lever for him while he cranked. He finally got the old thing started and looked at Mama. "It won't last much longer, Gladys. Then I don't know what I'll do for a truck."

He clattered his way toward town and the store. Mama went inside to sew and Joe and I climbed the white oak tree on the edge of the front porch. We had a good view of the Elko/Spur Branch Road on our observation limb up in the tree.

We didn't see anyone. Most people using the road walked and a few came by in wagons and even fewer in buggies. Automobiles were not common then in rural South Carolina where we lived. Then the rickety old school bus topped the hill and we climbed down. We walked through the gap in the privet hedge to the road where we met the bus and went to school.

There was no lunch at school in those days. When we got back home Mama gave us each a biscuit to hold us until supper. Then we climbed up into our tree and looked to see if any people were on Elko/Spur Branch Road. No one came for about ten minutes, and then I spotted a stranger coming up the road from the Springfield direction. We stared and wondered about him. "Where you reckon he's going, Joe?" I asked.

"He's going toward Elko," he said. "Then he might go any whichaway. Ain't no sense in guessing."

Then that tall man made a quick turn off Elko/Spur Branch Road. I couldn't believe my eyes. He walked through the gap in the privet hedge and came into our yard, walking towards our house. "I ain't never seen him before," Joe whispered. "Reckon he's a tramp?"

I was terrified. Joe was eight, one year older than I was. Mama was in the house cooking supper and taking care of our four year-old brother and baby sister. "Daddy won't be home until supper," I stammered.

We scampered down the tree and wondered what to do.

"I'll watch him," Joe whispered. "Go tell Mama."

I ran to the back porch and into the kitchen to tell her.

"Mama," I gulped, "a strange man's in the front yard. Joe stayed out there to watch him, but he's liable to get hurt."

Mama looked at me and blinked. "Go get Lang."

Mama knew she could depend on Lang's protection, but he wasn't there, either. "Daddy sent him and Bub to cut logs for the sawmill," I said.

She blinked faster. "Then I got to go see what that man wants."

She folded her butcher knife in her apron and walked to the front door. I followed but she turned. "If anything happens, run to Lizzie's house and tell her. Maybe Mr. Martin's there but he's likely still plowing. Lizzie might know where help is."

"Yessum."

Lizzie was our cousin on my father's side. She and Mr. Martin were our nearest neighbors and lived about a mile away. I hung back, ready to run to Lizzie's house. I followed Mama out on the porch where we found the stranger talking to Joe.

When he saw Mama, the man smiled and gave her a deep nod. "I was telling your boy I'm mighty hungry. I asked him if you could spare me something to eat. Anything. I'll work for it."

Mama kept on blinking. When Mama blinked, she was thinking. She looked at the stranger and nodded to a rocker on the porch. "Have a seat. I'll fix you a plate, but it'll be a few minutes."

She signaled me back inside with a nod and walked fast. "We got to hurry. He's probably all right so I'm going to feed him. You got to help. Run out and get me an armful of stovewood. Remember. If anything happens, run to Lizzie's."

I came back with the wood and Mama handed me a quart jar full of cream to shake to make butter. After I shook it a while, the butter coagulated into a mass. My mother strained off the buttermilk and gathered the butter with a fork, salted it, pressed it into the mold, and set it in the icebox.

That day Mama was simmering some dried lima beans in a pot of water. She didn't use fatback like most women did in that section so the beans would need butter, but the collards she was cooking with smoked hog jowl meat wouldn't. She also had rice that could use some butter. There were also some baked sweet potatoes—they demanded butter. Every meal came with Mama's biscuits. She cooked them to matchless perfection and the butter made them divine.

Mama prepared the stranger a big plate of food and took it to him with a glass of ice tea. I followed with another plate with three biscuits and a big dab of fresh butter. Mama couldn't wait for the butter to set hard. She handed the plates to the tall man and called us inside so he could eat on the porch in privacy. We would eat later when my father came home.

After a few minutes the stranger knocked. He handed Mama two empty plates. "That was mighty good, ma'am."

I couldn't believe it. The stranger had eaten it all. "Now what can I do for you. Cut some wood? Shuck some corn? Anything."

I could tell the man scared Mama. "That's quite all right. I'm glad you enjoyed it. Where you going?"

"Barnwell. I heard there's work over there. I left my wife and children in Springfield and I'm walking to Barnwell for work. I thank you, ma'am. Them's the best biscuits I ever et. It was a privilege to meet you."

Mama gave him half a dozen biscuits in a paper bag to take with him. "If you was to take the time to do some chores around here, you wouldn't be in Barnwell soon enough tomorrow to work and you might miss out on the job altogether. The best thing you can do for everybody is to get that job and take care your family like you're trying to do. God bless you."

"God bless you, too, ma'am," he said and left.

Joe and I were full of questions. "Weren't you scared, Mama? What would you do if he attacked us or you?"

She didn't answer. She pulled the butcher knife from her apron folds and put it away. "The Bible says we should be kind to one another and hospitable to strangers. If we're good to strangers, we might be entertaining angels unawares. That mean angels in disguise."

Joe and I looked at each other. "Reckon he was an angel, Mama?" Joe asked.

She smiled. "I doubt it. But he's a good man. He's trying to take care of his family. That's angel enough these days."

The sun was getting low and Joe looked at me. "Time to feed up, George," he said.

We went to the stables to feed the cows and mules. "Lookee yonder," Joe said. "That ole mule's up and chasing the others."

The mule that had been sick was running and kicking at the others because it wanted to get to the oats first. "Mama thought it was going to die," I said.

The western sky was getting red, but we climbed back in the hickory nut tree to watch the road. "I hope no more angels or tramps come," Joe said.

"I hope not, too," I said, "both of 'em scare me."

Then Joe saw our father's truck coming up the lane toward the house. It had already turned off the road, but we didn't hear it. Our father got out and looked at the truck. "Beats all I ever seen," he said. "That old truck's running better than when I bought it."

Joe's eyes got big. "Maybe he wuz an angel."

Our father stared. "What you talking about?"

Joe told him about Mama feeding an angel and he smiled and shook his head. "She gets the funniest notions sometimes."

That was a long time ago. My father and mother and Joe are dead. The stranger angel probably is, too, but he might have just gone on back to Heaven. We never saw him again. He's probably there waiting with the other angels for some more of Mama's biscuits.

BAPTISM

"Josephus! George Thomas!"

Mama wanted us and she wanted us NOW. Mama's compelling call for Joe was Josephus and she sounded out each syllable and made a summons impossible to misunderstand or ignore. "Jo—see—fus!"

She called me by my first _and_ middle names to make the call imperious. "George" just didn't say enough, but "George Tom—mus!" sent me running to her.

We rushed to Mama who stood on the back porch waiting. "Yessum, Mama?" Joe said.

"Need to talk to y'all about baptizing. Last Sunday, the preacher said them that wanted to be baptized had to sign up. Your daddy and I put both your names down. Time y'all got baptized."

"What's bab tithing, Mama?" I asked.

"Bap-tizing, George Thomas. It's what you have to do to join the church. You're seven years old and Joe's eight so it's time. The good Lord gave us you two boys and we're supposed to look out for you and make sure you go to heaven."

The Southern Baptists practiced total immersion the old Anabaptist way. Our parents had scheduled us for that kind of baptism—the only kind of baptism they knew. All we knew was that we were going to be ducked all the way under the water and we didn't really know why. We only knew that baptism was the right and holy thing to do and you had to do it to join the church. Anyway, Mama said we had to.

Our religious lives started in Mount Cavalry Baptist Church in Barnwell County, South Carolina. The church building stood about three miles east of our house on Elko/Spur Branch Road. We had several ancestors who helped start that church in the 1850's, and our mother and father as well as Grandma and my uncles were baptized and held membership there.

Mama enrolled Joe and me in the Little Sun Beams, the Baptist program for preschoolers.

We liked the Little Sun Beams but not the main service because the singing and preaching went on and on. The preacher would get hot and sweaty, but the words kept coming. He was excited about his messages so they must have been good and important, but I understood nothing.

But a young man sat up front in a wheelchair and he must have understood because he shouted "Amen!" every few minutes. One day I counted sixteen amens from that wheelchair and I might have missed one or two. The young man had been crippled by polio and couldn't move his arms or his legs. His head sagged when he talked. He couldn't even make his wheel chair go by himself—his father had to push him. But his faith was strong, his piety sincere, and he could shout "Amen" with the best.

The young man's father rolled him into the church and found a place for him up front on the aisle. After his proclamations of "Amen" and the services were over, they took him down the ramp where he waited at the exit with the preacher. Everyone exited with praise for the preacher's sermon and kind words for the young man.

I didn't really know why we went to church—I didn't understand the gospel until a soldier explained it to me when I was in the army years later. As a child, I knew church services had something to do with God and Jesus and preaching and singing and stuff, but the reasons weren't clear. In my juvenile mind, it didn't make a lot of sense to sit on a hard bench while the preacher preached, the men took up money, people sang, and several men prayed. I was relieved when we stood, but soon grew tired of standing in one place to sing five long verses of several long hymns. Then we'd sit for the sermon and my bottom would go to sleep even if I didn't.

It was hard on some men, too. They had to wait for more than an hour without smoking. They seemed to be in as much torture as we suffered in not moving or talking for that extended period. Some put cigarettes in their mouths as soon as they got to the door and lit up as soon as they were outside.

The women seemed to have it easier. Some of them kept looking around probably to see what the others wore. Meeting in the little rural church was the week's high social event and the way they looked around, you'd think they wanted people to see them, too. Or maybe they wanted to see which backsliders didn't come—they always needed something to talk about after church.

Most people in the county went to church. They came in buggies because few could afford automobiles. We usually went to church and everywhere else in my father's truck. He, Mama, and Helen, the baby, rode in the cab, but the three boys had to ride on the flat bed. We got pretty dusty getting to church sometimes, and Mama would dust us off and try to make us look neat.

One hot summer the church called a visiting evangelist to preach revival. The evening services started late so the men could finish farm work and feed the livestock before they came to the preaching. The summer night air further heated by the flames of the carbide lights inside the church and the hellfire messages from the pulpit made for warm sessions indeed. Men fanned wives frantically to try to keep some from fainting and all of them from sweating. Those were about the longest sermons I ever heard. I would have joined the church right then if it would have shut that preacher up. He probably preached the precious words of life, but it all went over my head.

Then for some reason my parents changed churches and we attended the Elko Baptist Church. They enrolled us in the Sunday school classes, but I remember nothing they taught me there either. The sermons were still beyond me, but the teachers and the preacher were probably good at their ministries. I was rather young to be learning so much about religion.

My father and mother didn't talk much about salvation at home because they weren't learned in the Scriptures, but they put us in Sunday school and made sure we sat through the sermons. They expected us to get it from more spiritual and informed people. I'm sure we heard the gospel in church and at home, but it didn't register or sink in.

Joe and I were scheduled for baptism so we could be members of Elko Baptist Church. They made that sound pretty important and we regarded it as a part of growing up. They convinced us that we should be baptized, but neither of us had any idea what it meant.

It was a big event. Many of our kin and my parents' friends came to see us baptized. Mama dressed us in white short pants and our best shirts so we concluded that baptism was not only important, it was to be done in great formality.

We rode for a long time in Math Bolen's car—the thing was too dignified and holy to go in the truck. We kept going and I had no idea where. We drove past the church building and that surprised me. Church stuff was supposed to be done in the church, wasn't it?

But we kept going and finally came to a line of cars stopped on the side of a road at a creek bridge. We walked to the bridge and then down the creek bank to a sandbar where the preacher stood with a number of white-clad boys and girls who were to be baptized. A few women and one man also waited to join the church.

Joe and I joined those on the sandbar and trembled while we waited for other candidates to arrive. Then the preacher scared me further when he waded out into the stream and read from the Bible and prayed. The people sang and then to my horror he called for the first to be baptized. I don't remember how many there were, but I suffered every time the preacher pushed somebody under the water.

If the candidate for baptism brought a handkerchief, the preacher used it to cover his or her nose and mouth when he plunged his or her head under the water. Most of the boys, including Joe and I, didn't bring handkerchiefs so the preacher used his hand to cover our noses and mouths to make sure we didn't breathe any water.

When a person had been baptized the folks on the bank said "Amen." Then he had to walk out of the creek to the sandbar and then to friends who were waiting to pull him up on the bank. Friends and/or parents had towels ready to dry off the newly baptized person and to make sure the car seat did not get wet on the way home.

The preacher finally called Joe and I watched him walk out in the water, scared for him and for me because I was next. Then I saw the preacher push him under the water and terror took possession of me. When my turn came I was so afraid I don't remember any of the ceremony, not even getting wet. I couldn't have been more terrified. Mama said later that I was as white as my short pants.

But something impressed me. I remember feeling that some great spiritual thing had happened to me, and I felt a kinship with the pious young man in the wheel chair. I don't remember getting dried off or the drive home, but I remember going to the bed and kneeling and praying. I was still confused about it. We did it because we were supposed to do it to join the church. It was twelve years later when a soldier in Korea told me about the Gospel.

He made it so simple it was hard to believe but I do believe I'll see the Lord. The first thing I want to ask him is to give me the lowdown on baptism. I also believe that Mama's up there worrying we might not have made it. She's probably looking for us and calling for us. The saints are probably doing all they can to get us in so Mama will stop yelling.

"Jo—see—fus! George Tom—mus!"

FALL FROM GLORY

The names in this story have been changed to protect the guilty and the exact time and location are nebulous for similar reasons.

We were waiting for the school bus to go home and I had to listen to Joe growl again. "The principal come to your class again today?"

"He sure did," I said.

"Mr. Williams don't never come to our room. Why y'all so special?"

I shrugged and that made him even more jealous because the most important person in the school seemed to favor my class. Joe didn't like being left out of anything.

Joe probably felt this way because our mother and father had instilled in us a profound respect for teachers because teachers had knowledge, training, and a special gift. They could read, write, and do arithmetic. Some were even smarter than that and some of them had gone to college. They knew more than anyone else in town and we had to honor them. Teaching was an admirable profession and a fervently sought career because teachers were usually paid, even in the Great Depression when all this happened.

Everybody seemed to feel that way about teachers—the whole community respected good teachers, often through several generations. It took a lot to shake that kind of admiration, but I remember one school year when there was some shaking going on.

I was in Miss Brown's class when it happened, but I don't remember much except the large door to the cloakroom and her desk centered in the front of the room. What I remember clearest is that Mr. Williams, our principal, often came to our room. And almost everyday, Joe asked if he came. "I don't see why your class is so special."

But we must have been. Once he started, I doubt Mr. Williams missed coming a single day. He never looked at us students but came in, bent over, and whispered to Miss Brown. Then they looked over papers on her desk and whispered some more. We tried to hear but they just whispered.

Then Miss Brown would smile a little. After a while, she would get up and squint at us and warn us to behave and keep quiet. She and the principal had to discuss something and she would wear us out if we misbehaved or got noisy. Then she and Mr. Williams would go into the cloakroom and close the door.

I don't remember how long they stayed in there, but it seemed like a long time. Then Mr. Williams would come out—he always came out first. He looked us over and left. Then we waited until Miss Brown came out and went to her desk, looked over things, and then started teaching again.

We were scared to death of both of them, especially Mr. Williams. We didn't dare disobey him. The other boys said he was born mean and got worse and worse until he finally got so bad they didn't know what to do with him. Somebody that bad had to be a school principal or sent off to the penitentiary.

Joe told me that the other boys said Mr. Williams had a bad temper and a paddle about two feet long with holes bored in it. It would produce polka dots where the paddle struck. Others said he used rough wooden paddles so the splinters could stick in your bottom when you got paddled. If you were real bad, they said, he had a special paddle with tacks sticking out. The message was clear—you didn't want to get on the bad side of Mr. Williams.

Most of us didn't like to read so while Miss Brown and Mr. Williams stayed in the cloakroom there wasn't much to do. We didn't dare talk or play. Some children like me sat there bored and oblivious while others looked at each other and burst into giggles. I didn't see any humor in the thing and wondered what they thought was so funny.

I just squirmed and looked around wondering what Mama fixed me for lunch and what they were doing in there. Everybody else was ignoring them or giggling about them, but I was curious. I thought about going to the door and listening, but I was a coward when it came to dealing with Miss Brown or Mr. Williams.

One day while Miss Brown and Mr. Williams were in the cloakroom, some boys got bored. Two or three started whispering and soon everyone was buzzing, but the door stayed closed. Then the boy who sat in front of me turned and began whispering to me. I whispered back as nervous as if I had gone into the girls' restroom by mistake. The noise level rose. The cloakroom door loomed larger and larger. I expected it to burst open and Miss Brown to fly out breathing fire with Mr. Williams fuming and waving paddles. Nothing happened. They didn't come out.

Then two of the braver boys got up and paraded around. More boys and some girls joined them, whispering and giggling. No response from the cloakroom. Then they started throwing chalk and erasers and that made even more noise, but nobody in the cloakroom seemed to care. I stayed out of it until an eraser hit me in the back of my head. I jumped up intent on revenge and threw back at the running boy who hit me, but he ducked and the eraser thumped the cloakroom door with a loud thud. We all scooted to our seats. I tried to appear innocent and studious, but I could feel my hot, blushing face radiating my guilt.

The door still didn't open. I kept squirming in my seat. I don't know how long I squirmed, but the waiting was agony. They were certain to find out I threw the eraser and I would have to face Mr. Williams alone. Then the door opened and Mr. Williams blasted out and closed it behind him. My heart jumped into high gear and tried to break through my rib cage, but he left the room without even looking at me.

I no sooner had my breath back than Miss Brown came out, sauntered about, smiled at us, picked up the eraser, and put it back in place. Once again, I couldn't breathe for fright, but she didn't say anything. I thought she would ask who did it because two girls, eager little tattletales, thrust up their treacherous little hands. They tickled the air with their fingers trying to get Miss Brown's attention. My red face still proclaimed my guilt and anyone could see that I did it. Miss Brown probably knew but she said nothing.

She ignored the little female traitors and went to the blackboard. There with sweeping hands, she showed us how to make cursive A's and B's and C's. I tried but I never got the hang of writing cursive because I was terrified the first day they taught it.

Later, while we waited for the bus, one of the girls who tried to tell on me acted as if I had not noticed her treachery. She cocked her head and stared at me. "You know why Mr. Williams and Miss Brown stay in the cloakroom so long?"

I didn't even acknowledge the little traitor's existence, but she kept on. "Cursive is hard to learn. He's the head teacher, so he had to show her how. See how long it took her to show us?"

I couldn't let that go so I snapped back. "They go in there everyday. She don't teach cursive everyday."

"Miss Brown's just learning, but Mr. Williams is smart. He knows everything, and that's why he spends so much time with Miss Brown. He has to teach her all the lessons."

I don't know when it started or what was said or who said it, but people began to ask questions about Mr. Williams and Miss Brown. I heard my mother and her friends say their names now and then, but they always stopped talking when I came near.

Those in authority must have talked also. The inherent respect and honor due teachers must not have been enough because both Mr. Williams and Miss Brown taught somewhere else next year. And Joe had to find something else to growl about.

SYRUP CANDY

Nell was already singing when Mama walked down the back porch steps to the truck.

"If that golden ring turns brass,
"Daddy's gonna buy you a looking glass.
"If that looking glass gets broke,
"Daddy's gonna buy you a billy goat…

Mama turned and went back up the steps. "You near 'bout ready, Gladys?" my father called.

He was waiting in the old truck and he was almost out of patience with Mama, but she went back to be sure she and Nell understood each other. Then she finished primping and went with my father to help in the store. They didn't worry about leaving us with Nell because Lang was always near doing farm chores. They were as protective of us as our own parents. They knew we could depend on Lang and Nell if we needed help and we often did.

Nell helped Mama several times a week with the washing and ironing. We always liked to see her come because Lang, Jr. would come, too, and we could play with him. When Mama had to be away helping in the store, working in the church, or visiting a sick neighbor, Nell came in, took over, and cared for us. We loved her except when she gave us our Saturday baths.

On a typical Saturday, Nell came in the morning just before my father and mother left for the store. She cleaned the house and made dinner (the noon meal) for us. She ate with us and insisted that we observe table manners. That was interesting but Nell wasn't as permissive as Mama was about such things. Eating with Nell was not much fun. But things were about to get worse.

As we ate we began to get premonitions of pain and discomfort because after dinner, it was bath time. We dreaded being washed because Nell was a woman and she would see us naked. Mama was a woman, too, but she was Mama.

Nell could scrub your hide off, but we had to get into a No. 3 galvanized wash tub and submit to her hard rubbing. Then she told us to close our eyes and poured warm water on our hair. It flowed down our bodies taking away the soap and the dirt. We were clean.

Nell was rough even when she dried us, especially rubbing our hair and gouging in our ears to get the water out. Then she made us stand while she dressed us. I didn't like to be dressed in anything but my dirty, torn overalls, but to be finished with Nell's cleaning operations I was only too willing to be dressed in anything.

Nell always surprised us in some way when the baths were over. She often made a cake she called sweet bread and sometimes candy—peanut brittle or syrup candy, a kind of taffy from sugarcane syrup. That made the Saturday bath more acceptable and memorable, but the most unforgettable thing was her singing.

> "Hush, little chillun don't you cry,
> Daddy's go be home by and by.
> Know them old shoes you can't wear?
> He gonna bring you a brand new pair.
> If them new shoes pinch your feet,
> He's gonna give you a candy treat.
> If that candy don't taste good,
> Daddy's done done the best he could.
> Now lemme tell you what else I heard
> Daddy might give you a mocking bird.
> If that mocking bird don't sing,
> Daddy's gonna give you a golden ring
> If that golden ring turns brass,
> Daddy's gonna give you a looking glass.
> If that looking glass gets broke,
> Daddy's gonna give you a billy goat.
> If that billy goat runs away,
> Daddy's gonna give you a bale of hay,
> If that bale of hay gets wet,
> That's the last thing you ever gonna get.

Then Nell would get herself ready and call Lang to bring Lang, Jr. We would all wait for my father to come back in the truck to take us to town and to the store. It was Saturday and we were clean. That was seventy years ago. My father, mother, and Nell have been dead a long time, but the memories still come and make my eyes moist, but they also make me smile.

THE POOR HOUSE

"Reckon we gonna get anything for Christmas?" Joe asked. "Daddy said the cotton didn't bring much money and the store ain't doing good."

I had just learned about Santa Claus so that bad news squashed my hopes. "I was wishing for a pocket knife like that one Uncle Norman's got."

Joe pointed. "Yonder it comes."

Joe and I were up in the white oak tree in our yard watching the road from our observation limb. Joe had spotted the Elko school bus. We shimmied down and ran to meet it. "Guess which Watson girl and boy gonna be on the bus," Joe said.

I carried my books under one arm. With the other hand, I carried a small cedar tree that I had cut for the class Christmas tree. The teacher had yelled at me and I thought she wouldn't be so mad if I brought a tree for the class.

The door opened and I had to answer before we got on. Joe made the challenge so I had to guess.

"Betty and Warren," I said.

That left Joe with Sally and Whitney. When we got on the bus, Joe whispered. "You're half right and half wrong. There's Betty and Whitney."

The two Watson boys had one old pair of shoes between them and the girls shared one presentable dress. They took turns going to school. Mama planned to make Betty and Sally a dress when she finished the one she was making for Cousin Sarah's girl. "We got to take care of kin first," she said.

When the bus arrived, Betty and Warren walked to their classes without talking. They were trying not to be noticed, but everyone knew they and other poor families had to share clothes and take turns going places. My teacher took the tree and we all helped decorate it. She smiled and told everybody that I brought it and I felt good about that. Betty was in that class but she didn't smile.

After school, we got back on the bus and started home. I looked at Warren and tried to smile, but he just looked away with his sad eyes. It made me feel awful. Sad people make everybody sad.

When we got home, we each took one of Mama's biscuits, punched a hole in it, and filled it with cane syrup to allay our hunger. We ate our syrup biscuits then went to feed the hogs, chickens, and the mules. We pulled water from the well to fill the water troughs and the chores were done. We climbed up in the tree to our observation limb and waited for our father to come home for supper. Then Joe pointed and we climbed down.

When the old truck pulled into the yard our father got out, but so did a man and a woman. Four children climbed down from the truck bed. I had seen this man and woman in church, but I didn't know their names. Then I saw Betty, Sally, Warren, and Whitney behind them. It was the Watson family. This time Sally wore the dress and Warren the shoes. Betty wore a gown made from a flour sack. Whitney was barefooted and he must have been cold; it was just five days before Christmas.

I ran and told Mama we had company. "How many?" she asked.

"Six," I said. "The Watsons and four children."

She blinked and sighed. "You and Joe make out like y'all already et. I'll make y'all some grits. You and Joe can eat when they finished and gone. Take this jar of cream out on the porch and shake it till the butter comes."

Mama welcomed the Watsons and invited them to sit down. My father didn't join them. "I just et some parched peanuts at the store. I might eat a little later."

Everybody seemed embarrassed as Mama and Joe set the table. My father talked to Mr. Watson and Mama to Mrs. Watson. I shook the cream while I listened from the porch and learned the Watsons had been evicted. Their house was an old unpainted wooden shack, but it had been their home. I took my anger out on the jar.

"We lost the farm when the cotton didn't bring much," Mr. Watson said, "and the sheriff come today and run us out of the house."

I pounded the jar on my thigh.

"They just threw you out of your own house?" Joe asked.

I choked the jar and gave it a furious shaking.

"Sheriff said we had to go," Mr. Watson said. "Somebody told your daddy and he come out in the truck. He got us and what little in that house was our'n and brought us home with him."

I kept slamming the jar against my thigh.

"What will you do?" Mama asked. "Where will you go?"

By this time, the butter had come. I brought the jar in and handed it to Mama.

"To the poor house, I reckon," Mr. Watson said. "Ain't got no other place to go."

Mr. Watson's face was drawn. Mrs. Watson firmed her lips. They didn't shed tears. I had seen adult tears before and I've seen a lot since, but I've never seen sadness like I saw on those Watson faces.

My father motioned Joe to follow him and Mama asked Mr. Watson to say grace. When he finished, Mama rose. "I got to fix this butter. We done et. Y'all go right ahead."

Mama had put on some grits and two pans of biscuits in the oven for us. She molded the butter and went back to the Watsons who were finishing up. "I wish

I had a cake or pie or something for desert, but all I can offer y'all is some cane syrup to go with them biscuits."

"That'll be just fine," Mr. Watson said. "You make the best biscuits in Barnwell County."

Mrs. Watson didn't say anything. She sniffed and blinked.

My father and Joe collected all the sheets, blankets, and quilts we had and made pallets so the Watsons could stay with us. My father came and made the announcement. "Y'all go spend the night with us," my father said. "We'll worry about tomorrow in the morning."

Mr. and Mrs. Watson would use our bed and the girls would sleep on the floor on pallets in the same room. The Watson boys would sleep on pallets with Joe and me in the hall. My father and mother would take our little brother and baby sister into their room.

The thing angered me so much I wanted to ask Mama why it happened and what could be done about it. I went to their room but they were talking. I stopped outside to listen. "The store go good today?" Mama asked.

"Sarah's boy come. He swept the floor and raked the trash out back. I give him a quarter for it. He brung a list of things Sarah needed and I packed them up for her. He asked me how much they owed and I told him something. It don't make no difference. They'll never be able to pay."

"You sell much?"

"A little but more people come in for them relief cans we give out for the government."

"Them black and white labeled cans?"

"They took more of that than my stuff and I had to charge most of what I sold."

Silence. Then Mama made a loud sigh. "We just got to keep trying and praying," she said. "That's all I know to do."

"If you try your best and mean what you pray, there ain't much more you can do."

Silence. Then Daddy said it. "We got to keep the Watsons, Gladys. At least for a while."

Mama sighed. "It'll be an awful Christmas for them, but maybe we can make things a little better for them. We'll have to think about it and see what we can do."

I still wanted answers to my questions, but my parents had made me proud with what they were going to do. It led me to go in and ask. "Daddy, can I go out in the woods and cut another cedar tree for the Watsons? Be nice if they can have their own tree while they're with us."

"All right, son. Take the Watson boys with you and let them pick it out."

"I'll help Mrs. Watson and the girls decorate it," Mama said.

The Watson girls were excited decorating their tree. Betty even smiled. Daddy bought each boy a pair of shoes for Christmas and Mama made each girl a new dress. Mrs. Watson helped her bake two hens with all the trimmings for Christmas Day, a fruitcake, and five sweet potato pies.

We kept Mr. Watson's family for several weeks until he got a job with the REA (Rural Electric Administration) and moved to town.

That was a long time ago. Everybody we knew somehow survived the Great Depression and some like the Watsons even became prosperous later. Those times, especially when we kept the Watsons, exemplified what my father and mother taught us about hard work, charity, and prayer.

My mother and father and Joe are dead. So are Mr. and Mrs. Watson. I lost track of their children. They may also be dead. There must be a whole bunch of people up there in Heaven enjoying Mama's biscuits.

YEAH, RIGHT

I heard it again and shivered. I was scared of ghosts and the floor of the old empty cotton barn groaned. I looked to Joe, my older brother. His eyes were wide open. We looked at each other and listened. Then the groaning stopped but the rafters creaked. A strong, dusty smell tickled my nose and made me sneeze. I could taste my terror. At that moment, the old barn door rattled open and my heart stopped. Joe eased over to see who was there. "Ain't nobody there," he said.

I didn't wait for Joe. I jumped out through that open door first and ran for the house and Mama, but Joe beat me there. "That haint's back in the cotton barn, Mama," Joe said. "Stinks like sulfur or something."

"The floor grumbled and the rafters creaked," I panted.

"Aw, y'all smelt something your daddy put out for rats."

"But the floor grumbled, Mama," Joe said. "How come the rafters creaked?"

"Old barn's just settling down, son. Ain't no such of a thing as a ghost."

She returned to the kitchen and we went to sit on the back steps. "I wish I could believe Mama," Joe said, "but I heard and smelt them things. I even tasted something in the air and my skin crawled."

I nodded. I had sensed many of those things that didn't exist—in that dusty old barn—down by the old wooden bridge over Hardemore Creek after the sun went down—even outside our bedroom window late at night.

That was years ago. We could make money on those sounds and smells today—ghosts and spirits have become commercial. People recall or fabricate claims that places and houses are haunted to embellish the charm and mystique of historic places—even historic places that are not too old—even new historic homes under construction. Those without indigenous ghosts have imported some because historic tour houses are nothing without ghosts. Bed and breakfast places that don't allow one to sleep in haunted rooms are losing out to those that do.

We heard many ghost stories when we were growing up. The black folk we knew told us most of the horror tales. Some were not so scary but others would make us tremble and pull the cover over our heads when we went to bed. "Don't believe them stories," Mama said. "Ain't no such of a thing as a ghost."

Mama told some of the stories herself but after she told them she would always say they weren't true. It was fun, she said, to be afraid of something and then learn that it wasn't true.

She had a trick she sometimes pulled on Joe, Richard, and me. She would pin one of her hats onto a pillowcase and stick the straw part of a broom into the pillowcase to spread it out. That made the hat ride the top like a tall lady was wearing it. Then she fitted the pillowcase with a blouse or coat and if it was cold she might tack a shawl under the hat.

Then she would wrap herself in an old chenille bedspread she cut eyeholes in and her whole body looked like the bottom part of a huge dress. When she lifted the broom handle, the illusion at a distance became a woman ten feet tall. Up close it must have looked funny, but we never got up close. When that tall thing appeared on the back porch, Joe, Richard, and I scattered like hens from a chicken hawk and ran to the cotton field or hid in the barns.

When the tall apparition went back inside, Mama waited a few minutes, came out, and called us. "Did y'all see Miss Blanche Carter? Y'all see my tall friend?"

We wouldn't go in the house until she assured us Miss Blanche was gone. Mama never admitted she was under the bed spread. "Y'all will just have to be more polite next time she comes."

Yeah, right.

She insisted there was nothing to fear outside or inside, in the daylight or in the dark. The creaks in the house came from timbers or floors settling or the wind pushing on the walls. Murmurs, screams, and wails that floated from the woods at night came from animals or the wind in the trees or some other real thing. But when I heard those sounds I pulled the covers over my head and repeated her words: "Ain't no such of a thing as a ghost. Ain't no such of a thing as a ghost."

I tried to tell others about what I heard and felt and smelled, but my friends all had better ghost stories. The old deserted academy building in town hadn't been used for years. It was about to collapse but some folk insisted that someone or something still held classes there in the late hours. Others said several old vacant houses were not deserted after midnight. Some even claimed they heard Confederate troops marching and cavalry hoofs pounding the road.

I didn't want to be outside after dark even at our own house unless someone was with me. I tried to tell myself I was too old to believe in ghosts and smart enough to explain what I might see or hear, but my courage was proportional to the ages, sizes, and number of my companions.

Mama had another frightening game she played on us that was supposed to be fun—when it was over. Sometimes when she put us to bed she told us to imagine some ogre was outside and the thing made its presence known. She did the vocals for whatever it was. "I'm on the porch," she said.

None of us knew what the scary thing was supposed to be, but it became terrible as Mama continued.

"I'm in the house," Mama said.

We began to giggle with apprehension. "I'm in the hall," she said.

The giggling stopped. Things were getting more serious. "I'm on the stairs," she said.

I imagined the hideous thing plodding up the stairs and Mama proclaimed each step as the demon climbed. "I'm on the third step."

"I'm on the tenth step."

By this time, I was trembling and I think Joe and Richard were, too. "I'm on the last step."

We snuggled close to Mama.

"I'm in your room."

Panic set in.

"I'm beside your bed."

Hearts raced and skins crawled.

"I gotcha," she shouted and grabbed us all in a hug.

Terror slowly gave way to normal breathing and yielded to the comfort of her hugs. She pursed her lips and smiled. "Ain't no such of thing as a ghost. Now y'all get to sleep."

Yeah, right.

Our black neighbors were another source of ghost stories Mama told us not to believe. Some tales were associated with the old barn and the Elko/Spur Branch Road that sloped down a modest hill in front of our house to Hardemore Creek. Ghosts were supposed to haunt that dirt road, the bridge, and the swamp.

Once when we were at the bridge about dark, a wail sounded out in the swamp. Richard and I ran up the hill like our souls were in jeopardy. Joe laughed at us when we ran into the yard. He insisted he wasn't afraid, but he beat us to the house.

It was a strange thing. I was afraid of the presence of the haints or ghosts, not what they would do to me. I couldn't remember ever hearing that they did anything. But they might come! That was enough. The terrifying things might come.

Two gravestones on the side of the house added to our concern about those things that Mama said didn't exist. Joe and I read the names and dates on the stones, but neither my father nor my mother knew anything about them. Most of their people who had passed on were buried in family and church burial grounds or in several nearby town cemeteries. Who were these people and why were they buried there? What did they think about people with other names living almost on top of them?

We weren't comfortable having gravestones just outside our bedroom window. We couldn't see the stones at night, but we knew they were out there. That was enough to raise all kinds of juvenile horror. We associated those gravestones with all the outside sounds we couldn't identify.

The things Mama insisted didn't exist weren't confined to the house, yard, and farm. A number of them might be encountered along the road itself. These road haints would come in groups and crowd around you, the story went. They wouldn't leave until you gave them some whiskey. The way to escape was to pour some whiskey on the ground. The haints would leave you alone to lick up or sniff up the whiskey while you escaped. We never encountered these ghosts and that was a lucky thing. We were far too young to carry bottled ghost defense like some of the men folk did.

Mama insisted there was no such of a thing as a ghost, but knowing so many men carried bottled ghost protection challenged our faith in her and that made us nervous. Some men carried the liquid anti-haint repellant in flat bottles in their back pockets. Others hid it under buggy seats and a few with cars had some in the glove compartments. It didn't help us to know so many grown men were prepared for ghosts.

On other occasions, I heard things or felt the presence of something or someone when I was alone in the hayloft, in the woods, or on the roads. Imagination is strong when you're seven years old and alone. I knew—I was almost certain—well, I thought what I imagined could be explained as natural phenomena if investigated because there ain't no such of a thing as a ghost.

Joe claimed one day that half the people in the country believed in ghosts. "Somebody did a count and that's what they found."

I wondered about that. "What you reckon them others would think if they heard what we heard outside the window or inside the old cotton barn?"

The old run-down structure used to be our grandfather's house and that's where my father was born. What would the unbelievers think about doors and windows opening by themselves? Or the smell of brimstone and the taste of sour milk? And the creepy feelings? And the dusty smell of age or something and the floor groaning and the rafters creaking. Their words might be different, but they would echo Mama's conclusion: there ain't no such of a thing as a ghost.

Yeah, right.

MUDDYING THE WATER

I jumped up from the hard wooden bench at the kitchen table without eating a bite, but Mama made me sit again. "The fish'll still be there when you're done eating," she said. "They'll probably still be there when you're done fishing, too, so eat your breakfast."

I took a bite of my flapjack soaked in cane syrup. It was sweet, strong, and greasy just like the air from the kitchen where the robust aroma of Mama's coffee declared many things. We were still too young to have that wonderful adult beverage, but that marvelous aroma gave comfort to our humble kitchen and our weathered clapboard house.

My flapjack disappeared with minimal chewing. I took it in a few large mouthfuls and washed it down with cold milk. Glad to get the sweet taste out of my mouth, I was too excited to eat anymore. When my two brothers were finished, we left the kitchen and ran to the shed. "Y'all be careful and don't get on no snake," Mama called.

"No, ma'am. We won't," Joe said.

Joe flexed several bamboo poles our father had cut and put under the shed to dry. He whipped them to see their stiffness and how they played. He handed me two. "Take them poles and run go see if Lang, Jr. can go fishing with us. Me and Richard will bring the rest of the stuff."

I grabbed the poles by their stout ends and started for the Roland house vibrating with excitement. My bones tingled and my skin prickled—I was going fishing.

I ran barefoot down the path dragging a pole in each hand. The grass still damp with the morning dew wet my feet then the loose sand coated them. The path penetrated a field and divided it into almost equal areas of cotton. I ran through blossoming stalks so tall I could see only cotton on either side of the path. I had often tried to smell cotton blossoms, but couldn't always detect the faint bouquet. That morning, row after row of flowering cotton released the perfume that collected over the field to give it a heavenly fragrance. I wanted to shout that it was wonderful to be alive, to breathe such scented air, to have such a good family, and to go fishing with Lang, Jr., but seven-year old boys don't say things like that. They just feel the thrills and tickles inside.

But things were not yet perfect; a possible pall loomed above my joy—did Lang, Jr. have to work that morning? Would Nell let him go? "I sho hope so," I told the air.

I ran on to the Roland's unpainted, weathered house, knocked on the backdoor, and Lang, Jr. came to the door. "Come on, Lang, Jr.," I whispered, "we going fishing in Hardemore Creek. We got you a pole if you ain't got one."

Lang, Jr. shot out of the house grinning. "Let's go," he whispered. "Mama's busy fixing collards so she won't know where I went. Y'all got any rabbit tobacco?"

While we quivered under our bubble of excitement, times were hard in the world outside. People were poor, banks were suspect, and cotton was king without a crown or even a prayer. Prosperity was a promise but a myth. Jim Crow was real enough but we boys didn't know enough about that to be bothered.

Joe was in the third grade. I was in the second but Richard hadn't yet started school. Lang, Jr., was about the same age as Joe. With Richard alway tagging along, we three older boys played and worked together, feeding the mules and the hogs and gathering vegetables. We shoveled manure, raked straw, pulled weeds, swept the yard, dug potatoes, and picked cotton.

When we had time to play, Joe and I chose up sides for games. The winner got Lang, Jr. and the loser got Richard. An older cousin had given me an old rubber ball we used to throw, catch, and hit with an old sawed-off pitchfork handle. From a similar source, Joe had the skin of an old football, but the rubber bladder was split. We stuffed the football skin with cloth scraps and old cotton wads and passed, kicked, and ran with it. We also had corncob fights and sometimes tomato wars. The pinecone battles were worse because the cones were sharp and could cut.

We were as tempted by the aroma of my father's roll-your-own cigarettes and Big Lang's pipe as we were by Mama's coffee. Both my father and Big Lang used Prince Albert tobacco that came in a red can. Just as we were prohibited from Mama's coffee, we were not supposed to smoke.

Sometimes we would sneak off and smoke rabbit tobacco. The weed grew everywhere and the silver-gray leaves could be harvested almost any time. We would tear off small sections of a newspaper page, wrap the rabbit tobacco in it, and roll it into cigarettes. Then we would light up. It smelled awful and tasted worse. We weren't supposed to do that either. That's why we did it.

Lang, Jr. and I waited until Joe and Richard arrived with the poles and the other stuff, but Joe looked troubled. "We got fishing cord, cork floats, hooks, and split lead weights, but we ain't got no dern bait, Lang, Jr."

The bad news dampened my fishing hopes until Lang, Jr. spoke. "Then we got to dig up some worms. I'll go get Daddy's hoe and a tin can."

Soon Lang, Jr. scurried around the house, but Nell's voice threatened the outing with disaster. "Lang, Jr. where you at? I need you to bring in some stove wood."

When Nell went out into the backyard looking for Lang, Jr. he ran into the house then darted out again and joined us three brothers. "Be right still for a few minutes," he said. "Make out like we ain't here. Mama just wants to be bossy. She got plenty wood. I done toted in three armfuls."

When Nell went back into the house, we walked the pine straw covered lane from the Roland house to the Elko/Spur Branch Road. We followed that dirt road to a wooden bridge where a little-used footpath led off the left side down to the small stream called Hardemore Creek. The shallow black water looked like dark tea as it flowed with its typical dank fragrance. But that day the sweet shrub was in bloom and a marvelous—almost holy—incense drifted about the bridge and enhanced the magic of our fishing outing.

"Where we go dig up them worms?" I asked.

"I'll find us a good place," Lang, Jr. said.

We pushed aside broom sedge and dog fennel and made our way through the brush to the stream's bank. "Best place is wet dirt close to the creek," Lang, Jr. said, "but don't go chopping up the dirt right off. We got to be smart about this."

Joe cocked his head. "Smart? How you be smart with worms, Lang, Jr.?"

"You got fool the worms so you turn the hoe over and tap all around where you go dig. When the worms crawl under the mud to get away from the tapping, then you surprise 'em. Just haul off and dig fast where you think they went. When you dig 'em up, they so scared they wiggle and try to crawl off and hide. You got snatch 'em up and put 'em in the can. Put a handful of mud in the can so they can hide under it. Then they won't try to climb out."

"Is it dinner time yet?" Richard asked.

"Ain't that a heap of trouble just for some dad blame worms?" I asked.

Lang, Jr. nodded. "But if them worms don't settle down, they be so nervous they won't smell good to the fish and you won't catch nothing."

"How you make them dern worms smell good, Lang, Jr." Joe asked

"Best to have a whole mess of worms so they can socialize and wiggle and wrap they selves round one another and go to sleep. Then when you wake 'em up they be just as fresh as morning dew on a watermelon and smell good to the fish."

So Joe tapped the mud all around rotten limbs where we thought the worms might live. Then he yanked a limb away and attacked the mud with the hoe blade in the center of his tapping. Sure enough, he unearthed many wiggling, squirming earthworms. Richard, Lang, Jr. and I snatched them up and put them into the can containing the moist earth, and they settled down under the mud just like he said.

Next we split the corks with Joe's pocketknife and forced the lines into the slits so we could adjust our fishing depths by moving the corks up or down. Then we tied hooks to the ends of the lines and just above the hooks we pulled the lines through ready-made slits in round lead weights Joe got from our father. When I had my lead weight where I wanted it, I bit down on it to squeeze it tight around the line so it wouldn't slip. Then I positioned and bit Richard's lead weight. The lead always tasted cold and funny, but I had never worried or even heard about lead poisoning. I was just moments away from catching fish.

Then we were ready, but Joe wanted some last minute counsel. "Big Lang's about the best fisherman in this dern county. How's he fish for perch?"

"My daddy say you want to catch perch, put a big worm on the hook. Don't hook him too much. You want him to wiggle. Just 'fore you throw him in, spit on him. Then the fish can't help himself. He's going after that worm with his mouth wide open. Of course, it helps if you chewing tobacco, Daddy said."

Joe and Lang, Jr. followed that ritual minus the chewing tobacco and cast their baited hooks into the deep pool of the shallow branch. I tried but I couldn't get the hang of hitting my worm with the spit. Richard couldn't get his out of his mouth, and mine always wound up on my shirt so we skipped that step. It didn't matter because no one caught anything. After a fruitless time, Joe frowned and threw down his pole. "Ain't no dern fish in this dern branch."

"How you say that?" Lang, Jr. asked. "Look all them pikes swimming yonder. See how they point upstream in the shallow water?"

"Well," Joe said, "let's catch them dern pike."

Lang, Jr. frowned. "You want to catch pike, you don't use no hook."

I had grown tired of Lang, Jr.'s overbearing nonsense. "Come on, Lang, Jr., you can't catch no fish without no hook."

"Yeah, you can. Just make a knot on the end of the line and roll a dough ball on it. Then when the pike bites, let him swallow it. All the way down. Then you jerk him out of the water before he can spit it out."

Lang, Jr. had just such a piece of dough in his pocket. "When I run back into the house I grabbed a finger pinch of dough outta Mama's dough bowl. Heah. Roll some into a little ball and wrap it around the end of the line. Let it in gentle so you don't scare the pike."

We tried it but that didn't work either. We could see the pike but they wouldn't bite worms and they darted from the dough balls. "Them dern fish making me mad," Joe said. "We got do something."

"Is it dinnertime yet," Richard asked.

I felt the tingle of inspiration. "Let's make us a trap," I said.

Lang, Jr. beamed. "Y'all got some chicken wire?"

"No," I said, "let's set out a net."

"This dern Creek's too dern shallow for a net," Joe said, "and Daddy's got the dern net set out in Tom Willis's pond. Let's muddy the water."

We had often heard that fishing technique discussed, but none of us had ever done it. The plan was to make the water so murky the fish would come to the surface and we could scoop them up with our father's dip net. We decided to do it.

We left the creek and went back to the shop to return the ineffective poles and lines and to get the dip net, a shovel, and another hoe. On the way back to the creek we passed the watermelon field and were briefly distracted from fishing. Joe thumped several of the larger melons with his middle finger. Then he selected and picked a large Curly Queen melon with dark green irregular stripes on a light green base. "How you go cut the watermelon, Joe?" Richard asked.

"Ain't nothing to it," Joe said.

Joe raised the large melon over his head and threw it on the grass. The watermelon almost exploded with a "splat" sound and it was easy to pull apart the shattered rind. We all reached for the center portion or the heart and left the rest. Joe pointed and laughed at me.

"Now you got sticky hands and watermelon juice on your shirt to go with the spit."

I had to endure my brother's ridicule because I couldn't think of anything to say. I turned my mind to rolling the crude rabbit tobacco cigarettes. My wet hands made the rolling easier, but when I tried to light up, the juice made the cigarette harder to light. After several attempts, I got it going and then we all had cigarettes burning. We huffed and coughed and stank up the field around the shattered watermelon.

Then Lang, Jr. frowned and pointed out a problem. "We can't let nobody see us muddy the water on account it might be against the law."

We didn't know that for certain, but it would infuriate Mama if we played in the mud—that we knew for certain. So we slipped through the woods behind the Roland house to the branch with hoes and shovel where Joe gave us the bad news. "We got to build a dam else the dern fish will get away downstream into Tom Willis's pond."

Few people were out and about during workdays and traffic on the bridge was uncommon, but someone might come by in a wagon or a buggy. A few people had cars but the most likely travelers would be on foot. Anyone crossing could see us from the bridge, so Joe assigned Richard bridge duty. "Richard, you keep watch while we make the dam," Joe said. "If somebody comes up or down the road, sing that 'I'm a little sunbeam' song you memorized in Sunday school. Then we'll hide the shovel and the hoes, then duck down in the tall grass."

We dug on the banks and pitched dirt into the shallowest part of the little stream and blocked it with a small earthen dam. When we had the water trapped,

I looked at the strange empty streambed and felt guilty about something, but I didn't know what or why.

The water kept rising so we had to keep adding dirt to the dam. When the water rose about a foot, my apprehension reached alarm proportions. The streambed could no longer contain the water so it rose up out of its banks and formed a small pool. We had to work even faster to keep adding dirt to make the dam longer and higher.

Then Joe took a hoe and stepped into the water. "Come on," he said, "let's do it."

We went in with hoes and shovels and our bare feet and made a muddy mess of the little lake. "Y'all look out for cottonmouth snakes while I dip the fish," Joe said.

The hard work and cottonmouth danger sapped my enthusiasm for fishing, but I waded about with the others. I stirred more mud into the water with the shovel while Lang, Jr. wielded the hoe. Joe sloshed around with the dip net looking out for snakes and waiting for the fish to show themselves. None surfaced and the morning wore on. "Wonder why them fish don't come up?" Lang, Jr. asked.

"Reckon what we done wrong?" I asked.

Then Richard yelled and pointed from the bridge. "Lookee yonder. The dam done bust!"

The pressure of the trapped water had forced a hole in our dam and the stream washed the dam away except for the edges above the branch. Defeated and dejected, we stood there in the captive water rushing and escaping around our feet. Then we sat down on the bank and watched the stream take our dam away, but Joe tried to inspire further efforts. "I ain't 'bout to give up. Let's figure out how to catch them dern fish."

We stared at the flowing water and thought, but no good ideas came until Joe stared at us. At first, I thought Joe was mad but he revealed his new plan. "Mud's good but green walnuts is magic. Can't no dern fish stay under water got green walnut juice in it."

"Is it dinnertime yet?" Richard asked.

"Green walnuts?" Lang, Jr. asked. "What you go do? Dye the fish green?"

"Makes the dern fish drunk. Sometimes they get so drunk they turn belly up and you can pick 'em up with your hand."

"When you see green walnuts work, Joe?" I asked.

Joe looked at me like I was crazy. "I ain't never," he said.

"Then how come you know about green walnuts, Joe. How come you know it's go work?"

"Ever dern body knows 'bout green walnuts. You don't know 'bout green walnuts, you don't know nothing."

I didn't think Lang, Jr. knew either but he nodded, so I wasn't about to admit my ignorance of green walnuts. We went upstream to clean water, played and splashed in the stream, washed the mud and dirt from their clothes, and spread them on bushes to dry. It was summer so we had time for these adventures and it felt good to play in the water.

"Is it dinner time yet?" Richard asked.

Joe looked up at the sun and nodded. Then he turned to Lang Jr. "Meet us at the walnut trees. We got to check in with Mama and eat. Reckon Nell go let you come back?"

"She don't, I'll sneak off."

We found the black walnut trees loaded with green balls. Joe and Lang, Jr. climbed the tree and picked a croker sack half full. Then we set out for the branch through the woods so no one could see. Lang, Jr. was certain this was against the law. "Got be," he said. "Else people catch all the fish in the county with green walnuts."

When they reached the creek, Joe picked up a shovel. "We got to fix our dam and make it stronger. We don't want them dern drunk fish swimming away. Richard, you watch the road again."

"I'll watch, Joe, but I ain't go sing. I'm too bashful to sing by myself."

"Then don't sing the dern song," Joe said. "If anybody comes, holler out and ask if it's dinnertime yet. You ain't too bashful to say that."

My skepticism yielded to Joe's enthusiasm and Lang, Jr.'s cheerfulness. I took up my hoe and helped build a higher, thicker, stronger dam. Once during the dam construction, we had to stop and hide our tools because Richard called out and asked if it was dinnertime yet. We scurried about hiding the bag and the tools. Soon an older man rode by in a buggy and looked at Richard, but he didn't notice us hiding in the tall dog fennel growth.

When the man passed, they went back to work and finished the dam. Then Joe beat the croker sack containing the green walnuts with the shovel blade until everything inside was crushed. He lowered the bag into the water and moved it around to spread the walnut juice. Lang, Jr. and I waded about with the dip net for the intoxicated fish to surface. We waited and waited but saw no fish bellies or any other fish part.

After a few minutes, the water broke through that dam also and washed our new efforts downstream toward Tom Willis's pond. We stood barefoot in the water feeling dejected until Lang, Jr. pointed downstream. "What you reckon that walnut juice go do to Mr. Willis's fish? Make 'em all drunk? Reckon it'll kill 'em?"

I felt a panic attack. Not only had we stretched our own limits of right and wrong, not only had we broken the law, we had jeopardized a whole pond of fish. "We got to go to the dern pond and see," Joe said.

We hid the bags and tools and ran down the narrow two-rut road under tall poplar, water oak, and pine trees. After about half a mile, we approached the dam at Tom Willis's pond. I heard the waterwheel rumbling before I saw it turning—it was the sound we wanted. Tom Willis's miller was grinding somebody's grain, and the rich, dusty smell of fresh ground wheat floated our way. He was busy so he wouldn't be watching.

We crept over the creaky wooden bridge above the millrace where the noisy, foaming water poured over a retaining board and rushed down to turn the creaking waterwheel. Then we walked out on the dam and looked along both edges of the pond, but we saw nothing but a large alligator in the still water. From our perspective, he had a better claim on the pond than even Mr. Tom Willis did. I was terrified. "That gator swallow you whole," Lang, Jr. said.

I looked around the pond for other alligators. "Reckon he got friends or kin folk?"

"People all over this dern county talk about the dern gator in Tom Willis's pond," Joe said, "but I ain't never heard talk about more than one."

We left Richard to keep his eyes on the gator and Joe walked one side of the pond and Lang, Jr. and I walked the other. If the gator moved toward us, Richard was to yell.

The lazy alligator's snubby nose never moved and we were relieved when we found no sign of fish damage. We were also exhausted and dragged ourselves home. "Let's do something else tomorrow," I said. "I had enough of fishing."

Joe nodded. "We got get another project. Fishing's too much trouble."

"I don't care much for fish no way," Lang, Jr. said.

"Can somebody tote me?" Richard asked. "I'm plumb wore out. Lang, Jr. let me ride your back. You reckon it's dinner time yet?"

PICNIC AT HEALING SPRINGS

"I don't know if God wants it," my father said, "but He owns that yonder piece of ground."

We had just arrived at Healing Springs, a community in the eastern part of Barnwell County, South Carolina, a few miles north of Blackville. The previous owner, L.P. "Luke" Boylston, had deeded the land to Him (Barnwell County Deed Book 10K, page 423).

"Some folks are nervous about God owning a piece of ground because the federal, state, and county guvments say He ain't a legal person. Some say there ain't no God at all. The One who made the whole universe and us, to boot, ain't got no legal rights."

Mama smirked. "When you in trouble, when you want things your own way, when some of the things you do make you nervous, what else can you do but say there ain't no God and that there never was one. Then you don't have to worry about Him, do you?"

My father smiled back at her. "Some folks talk about taking this place away from God through a legal trick. Something called Emmett's domain or something like that."

"That means the guvment could take it?" she asked.

"If they want to take it from God, that's what they have to do. If they didn't take ownership, the land would be sitting there with no owner. The land would own itself. There's been other places where people deeded land to itself. There's even some trees that own their own selves, but this here land's been deeded to God."

"This place would still be special even if they took it," she said. "Look at that flowing well."

The flowing well was named Healing Springs and it gave its name to the community. From the time the Indians lived in the area, Healing Springs water has been touted for it powers to restore health and prevent disease. Local legends claim the water miraculously healed some Revolutionary Tories wounded in the nearby Battle of Windy Hill where they defeated the Patriots and massacred them to the last man.

Years ago a sanitarium was located near the spring, and Mama's father, George Anderson Jowers, spent his last days there. When he died of tuberculosis, she was only two so she didn't remember it. We were always aware he died of the tragic disease that took several members of the Jowers family in spite of the curative powers of Healing Springs.

The flow of the spring has steadily declined over the years. Sometimes it offers only a trickle and sometimes no water at. But then heavy rains fall and restore the water table wherever the flow comes from and the curative water from Healing Springs issues forth again. People still come for miles trying to collect some of the healing waters.

But we boys didn't care about all that grownup talk. The weather had turned warm and we were at Healing Springs for a picnic. Mama had fixed fried chicken, biscuits, potato salad, slaw, and a cake. My father picked the biggest watermelon in the patch and we had come to Healing Springs in the truck.

In those days the spring flow was appreciable—enough to fill and maintain a small swimming pool. The water was ice cold and nobody swam in it for very long. It was great for cooling the watermelon and some brown bottles some of the other men lowered into the pool.

The pool was made of cemented stone and was rough in places. We were warned to be careful and not to run or play because we might stumble on the rocks. I ran and I stumbled and scraped my leg and it bled. Mama wrapped it in a piece of a towel and my father tied it around my calf.

Then it was time to eat. Mama sat in the cab of the truck while the rest of us sat on the truck's flat bed. Some of the best fried chicken I ever ate came to me sitting with my legs dangling off the flat bed and looking at God's Acre and Healing Springs.

Mama's potato salad tasted somewhat like regular potato salad, but she whipped the potatoes to a creamy texture. Even the slaw was good because we were on an adventure—we were seven miles from home.

PICKING COTTON

The first time I ever picked cotton, Big Lang, Nell, and Lang, Jr. and some other black people I don't remember gathered around waiting for my father's instructions. They talked about their techniques for picking cotton and several bragged about their cotton-picking abilities and past performances.

One of them walked about with nervous energy. "I want to get in the field," he said. "We hurry up, we can pick the dew."

That confused me until I found out what he meant. He wanted to pick the cotton still wet with dew because it would be heavier than dry cotton and they were paid by the weight of cotton they picked.

My father paid the top price of a penny per pound. Since he was getting nine cents a pound after all the expenses of land rent, seed, fertilizer, planting, plowing, hoeing, ginning, and baling, it was not only a fair price, it was all he could afford.

The men used several techniques and routines of picking. One didn't want to waste his time taking his cotton to his burlap sheet. My father provided each picker with a sheet to collect their pickings. This man had a bag about six feet long and it got heavy before he went to his sheet. Lang and his family used regular bags from fertilizer sacks because they didn't want to drag that much cotton down the row. That made sense to me so I used a smaller bag, too.

Cotton bolls ripened in late summer when they split open and exposed the white fiber. After drying for a few weeks, the cotton was ready for picking—usually at the end of August and the beginning of September. School started later in September to allow the children to pick cotton.

Our job was to pull the cotton from the boll. Most people called it picking cotton, but to some the process was pulling cotton. The pickers bragged about how much cotton they pulled. The dried boll had sharp points that tender hands had to avoid, but the black men had worked with their hands so much, their hands were callused. Joe, Nell, Lang, Jr. and I suffered from the points.

We walked between rows and picked the cotton on both rows. The black people talked, joked, and sometimes sang as we progressed down the rows. Lang, Jr. was a talker so he was the only black person Joe and I could keep up with. He talked to whoever was in hearing distance and when there was no one else, he talked to me. The more experienced men drew away from those of us who were new at it, but when they met us coming back, we joined in the talking and singing.

Cotton picking had its honor system. A picker's burlap sheet was inviolate—no one would dream of stealing cotton from another's pile. At the end of the day, the men tied the corners of those sheets and bound the cotton each picker pulled that day. Then they loaded the tied sheets on the wagon and brought them to my father for payment.

My father used a weighing tripod from which a cotton scale was suspended. The scale itself was a flat piece of iron painted black with printed notch divisions designating pounds when standard weights caused the suspended scale to be horizontal. My father had fifty, one hundred, and two hundred-pound weights. They didn't weigh that much, but with the leverage of the long scale beam, they gave accurate weights.

The tied burlap sheet of cotton to be weighed was lifted to the scale hook at the place where the four corners of each sheet were tied. The cotton's weight made the scale swing up until the standard weights were hung on the scale bar. When the weights on either side were the same and the scale bar was horizontal, my father read the weight. I picked one hundred and eleven pounds and got a dollar and eleven cents. Joe picked a little more but he had picked the year before. Some of the men picked more than three hundred pounds.

After weighing, my father got one of his regulars, Lang or Bub, to drive the wagon to the old house we used for storage. They spread the loose cotton so it could dry further. When the cotton was all in and dry, Lang or Bub would haul it to the gin in Elko for seed removal and baling.

GOING TO THE GRIST MILL

Tom Willis's pond was built to power the gristmill, but his neighbors found other uses for it. We fished the backwaters of the pond for perch, suckers, and catfish. It was a deep pond in places near the dam, but no one swam there. The huge alligator floated about a hundred yards from the dam and seemed to dare anyone to jump in. As far as I know, no one ever accepted the implied challenge, and not even Mr. Tom Willis challenged the resident reptilian about property rights.

My father set out traps for perch and brought many bream and warmouth perch home. We liked them better than the suckers, but we liked all fish. One night an alligator—maybe the large one we always saw—found the trap with some fish in it and tried to tear it open. Failing that, it crushed the trap flat in its efforts to get the fish. That was the end of my father's trapping in Tom Willis's pond. He still set out nets but the gator and/or his friends tore up several of those, too. Most people quit fishing and no one swam, but the pond performed its intended purpose of powering the gristmill and its unintended function—providing a home for the alligator.

The pond's millrace, a sluice about four feet wide and five feet high, was built on the east side of the dam so the mill could be near the road. The water entered the millrace and raced down the sluice to turn the waterwheel and provide the power needed for the various milling jobs. The miller adjusted the water flow by taking out restraining boards. He knew from experience how much water flow was needed to turn the waterwheel with the desired power.

The mill itself was constructed of wood and even some of the gears seemed to be of wood. The heavy grindstones turned and rumbled on each other, but we could see only through a narrow slot at the grain being ground. The distance between the stones determined the size of the product. Cracked corn for animal feed was the largest grain followed by grits followed by corn meal followed by wheat flour. Tom Willis's mill could do it all.

My father planted wheat and Lang cut it with the mule-powered mowing machine, raked it into bundles, and bound it up like oats. We had an old hand operated thresher and that's how we got the wheat grains. We made a lot of waste but the chickens enjoyed it and later we enjoyed the chickens. Mama still wanted white flour so we didn't have bread or biscuits made from our wheat very often.

My father planted almost as much corn as cotton because he had to feed the mules and the hogs. We had to harvest or "break" corn and put the ears in the barn. He taught us the rule of thumb—a barrel of corn in the shuck is equivalent to a bushel of shelled corn. During late fall and winter when not much was going on, Lang and Bub would shuck the corn, put it aside for shelling, and feed the shucks to the mules and cows for roughage.

Mama said some of the poorer people put corn shucks in bags and used them for mattresses and pillows. She said other people bored holes in stout boards and shoved the corn shucks in tight and close. Next they bored a hole in the stout board at an angle, inserted a handle, and used the thing as a scrub brush. She had such a scrub brush and it seemed to work well.

Our father assigned Joe and me to operate our corn sheller. One would turn the crank that turned a large wheel to get the shelling machinery going. Then the other would feed the ears of shucked corn. Corn grains fell out of the bottom of the sheller into pails and corncobs jumped from the machinery to the floor.

When we had wheat and corn, we could go to the mill for Mama when she needed it. We put the grain in our small Radio Flyer wagon and pulled it down the Elko/Spur Branch Road, across Hardemore Creek, and turned left on Tom Willis's Pond Road. The whole trip was about a mile and a half and we did it many times. We brought home stone-ground flour, grits, and corn meal and Mama converted these into many scrumptious things.

The dam is still there and so is the pond, but the alligator is gone. The mill was torn down years ago when Barnwell County was attacked by waves of progress.

UNEQUAL JUSTICE

My father and Hugh Bert ran a grocery store in partnership. They took turns managing the store during weekdays, but both worked hard all day Saturday. Mama went to the store with my father just after breakfast and she helped all day. She kept the counters clean, wrapped vegetables and meat, and sliced cheese. They didn't run a supermarket—you asked or pointed to the items you wanted on the shelves.

Mama made sandwiches for sale, the most popular being her fried fish sandwich. She fried slabs of mullet and croaker and served it between the bread from the commercial bakery. We called such bread "light bread" because it was not nearly as dense as biscuits and cornbread. I think Mama got a nickel for each sandwich.

With Mama helping in the store, we were in Nell's hands and we dreaded what she was going to do to us—she was going to scrub us clean. You felt like a skinned rabbit when Nell got through with you. Then she made us dress because Daddy was coming for us after dinner and the baths.

Nell dressed in her drab dresses when she came to take care of us or to help Mama with cleaning or washing. The first time I saw her in town on a Saturday afternoon, I was shocked. She had on a colorful dress and lipstick and her hair was curled with a curling iron. Nell was a belle and Lang had to beat up a few men who got too friendly with her. Lang could do it, too.

The black people liked to buy from my father and Hugh because they were fair—not generous, but fair, and that was a better deal than they could get most places. They crowded into the store, many to buy Mama's fish sandwiches or a slab of cheese or bologna between two slices of johnnycake. They bought their groceries and left the bags in the store because they knew they would keep them safe. They didn't want to be encumbered with packages while they socialized.

I don't know what the black people did after the sun went down because I never saw them unless they needed something from the store. The white people congregated in the several grocery stores and the Elko social circles were largely determined by where the families bought their groceries.

One night a black man bleeding from the head was shoved through the door into the store. Right behind him was the constable. "Need to call Barnwell to get the sheriff."

Mama and we children looked on in horror as did the families who were visiting with us. Daddy nodded the constable to the telephone and went to the black man. "What you do, Angus?"

Angus muttered something and the constable was on him like a chicken on a worm slinging his club. Daddy stepped between them and looked at the constable. "I ain't going to tell you your bidness, but this store is my bidness and you ain't going to hit him in here. There's chiren and ladies here. Make you call and get out of here or I'll call the sheriff on you."

The constable left with Angus. I never heard whether the sheriff came or not. I didn't learn what Angus was supposed to have done or what punishment he got. He had already been punished plenty when I saw him.

SANDY CLAWS

We knew about Santa Claus. Mama had confided the truth to Joe and me with the strict admonitions not to tell our younger brother, Richard. Then Christmas came and Santa Claus was reborn in the midst of the Depression, poverty, segregation, and tragedy. It left us certain of only one thing—Santa has multiple identities and he can be almost anyone.

When it was time to put up a Christmas tree, Mama gave us her usual vague specifications about the tree she wanted. "Get me a cedar about this high and that big around. Got to be shaped like an upside-down ice cream cone."

Joe took the axe, I carried the saw, and we went searching in the woods for a cedar tree of the right size and shape for Mama to decorate for Christmas. Lang, Jr. lagged behind with Richard who pestered him with questions. "What you want for Chrismis, Lang, Jr.?" Richard asked.

"Need shoes and clothes, but what I really want is a knife like Bub's. It's got a pearl handle and two shiny blades. My daddy seen it and he wants one his own self."

"San Claws bring you one," Richard said.

"Ain't no such of a thing as Sandy Claws."

Joe turned and frowned to remind Lang, Jr. that Richard had not reached the age of enlightenment. But Richard wasn't daunted. "Sho' there is. Mama done sent San Claws a letter and told him bring me a cap pistol. Want Mama send a letter for you, too, Lang, Jr.?"

Now Lang, Jr. understood and humored Richard. "Be too much trouble for Miss Gladys, Richard. What color you reckon Sandy Claws is—black like me or white like you?"

Richard blinked and frowned. "I don't know, Lang, Jr."

We all laughed with Lang, Jr. and kept looking until we found a tree. Mama accepted it and decorated it with things she had inherited. She had ball ornaments and colored paper decorations that came packed flat but expanded into bells when opened and fastened. She added silver tinsel and roping and put a star on the top. The tree was beautiful at night when the shiny things reflected light from the kerosene lamps and the fireplace.

Then the day after we decorated the tree, Big Lang got hurt.

Lang Roland was a strong black man who was my father's right arm on the farm and in the woods when there was timber to cut. We liked the Rolands and depended on them. But Jim Crow was at its worst during those Great Depression years in South Carolina where it was empowered and encouraged by laws and rules and social behavior. My brothers and I knew little about the general inequity and wrongs the black people suffered because what we heard was remote to us. We saw none of the brutality, hatred, and shunning we heard about. My father was no Atticus Finch, but he was honest and fair with his black workers. He would defend and help them when and if he could and that was a better deal than they could get on most farms.

Winter was a slow time on the farm so that's when my father cut timber for his little sawmill that he built himself. The logging operations were primitive by industrial standards because my father couldn't afford the heavy equipment used by large operators. So he, Lang, and the others went into the woods with crosscut saws and axes.

They directed a tree's fall by cutting downward on the backside of the tree at an angle toward the way they wanted it to drop. When about two thirds of the way through, they removed the saw and drove an iron wedge into the cut. Then they went to the opposite side of the tree and cut straight into the wedged cut. When the cuts were almost joined, they went back to the wedge and drove it with a sledgehammer. The tree usually fell toward the second cut, but if the tree's weight was not uniform or if a wind came up, the tree could fall in almost any direction.

Lang's tree was leaning the right way as he drove the wedge into the cut, but a wind gust twisted the tree just as it broke off the stump. Lang jumped away from the falling tree but it rolled on his leg and trapped him.

My father was about a hundred yards away cutting on another tree, but he heard Lang's saw partner calling. "Mr. Seese, come here quick. Big Lang's hurt."

My father and his saw partner ran to the scene and saw Lang lying with his leg under the log. My father grabbed an axe and hacked down a small tree, chopping at an angle all around to give the end a point. The two sawyers then cut the small tree into a short log and my father shoved the pointed end under the large log and drove it with the sledgehammer. The blows hurt Lang a little, but the small log raised the large one high enough to get Lang's leg out. Then my father took him to Dr. Lewis in the old truck. The leg wasn't broken, but it was bruised and badly skinned. He had to stay off of it and keep it clean. Lang couldn't work for two months, Dr. Lewis said, and it was five days before Christmas.

My father paid Lang his same wages while he couldn't work and Nell still helped Mama and got paid for that so their incomes were not changed. They still lived in the old tenant house on our farm and shared in the milk and vegetable garden so everything was about the same—except that Lang was hurt. We went to see him several times and he was always glad for the company. But being laid up, he fretted and lost interest in everything—Lang had always been an active man.

Christmas was coming and we all felt sorry for him and his family so Richard asked Mama to write to Santa for a pocketknife for Lang, Jr. despite his request that Richard not bother Miss Gladys.

On Christmas morning, we were up at first light and ran to our stockings to see what the jolly old elf left us. It was still almost dark inside the house so we had to feel our way around. I found a bag of marbles and some candy in the middle stocking that I knew was mine. Then I felt under the tree and found a toy machine gun that generated sparks when I turned the crank. Joe got the same things and we took the toys to the window to see who got which gun. Then we had fun shooting each other in the near darkness.

Richard got his cap pistol and was so excited he left his stocking for later. He went "Pow! Pow!" with his cap pistol because it was still too dark to see to load it, but we ground out sparks from our machine guns. When it was light enough to see, Richard found his stocking and pulled out candy, a bag of marbles, and a pocketknife with a tag tied to the ring. He handed it to Joe. "What that say, Joe?" he asked.

Joe took it to a window and read: "For Lang, Jr. From Santa."

We played with the sparkling guns until we got tired of them and showed Richard how to load the cap pistol and shoot it. Then we gulped down our breakfast and ran to take Lang, Jr. his knife. Mama sent the Rolands some of her famous fruitcake.

When we got to the Roland house, Lang lay in bed with his hurt leg resting on a pillow. He and his wife Nell thanked us for the fruitcake and seemed glad to have company. Lang smiled but we knew he was still in pain and poor spirits. Then we went outside with Lang, Jr. and Richard handed him the pocketknife. "Sandy Claws left it in Richard's stocking by mistake, Lang, Jr.," Joe said.

Lang, Jr. took the knife, opened it, admired the blades, then closed it. He read the tag and grinned. "Sandy Claws done made another mistake. This knife supposed to be for Lang, Sr. Sandy Claws had so much to do Christmas time, he done got everthing mixed up."

We followed him into the house and saw him give the knife to his father. "Daddy," Lang, Jr. said, "Sandy Claws done give you this knife, but he left it in Richard's stocking."

Lang grinned at Richard, took the knife, and admired it. "Bring the oilstone, Junior. Let's get it sharp. Right now, it wouldn't cut a ripe peach."

Lang sharpened the knife and began to whittle things. He kept Lang, Jr. busy bringing him pieces of wood to carve. Lang, Jr. was glad his father was interested in something again. Nell was glad too, but pretended to complain about having to sweep up the cuttings and trimmings.

Then Joe took Richard outside to shoot the cap pistol. Lang, Jr. smiled. "Sandy Claws been good to everbody this year."

"Thought you didn't believe in Sandy Claws," I teased.

"What you talking 'bout? Course I believe."

Big Lang smiled. "Me, too. But is his real name Miss Gladys or Mr. Seece?"

We laughed and left Lang whittling. I looked at Lang, Jr. "I didn't want to tell Big Lang, but I know Sandy Claw's real name for this Christmas," I said.

He stared. "What?"

"Lang Roland, Jr."

THE BEE SWARM

Grandma's farm was equipped with about every tool you could imagine, but all of them were old and most were ruined or out of date. My brothers and I didn't know what many of the items had been used for. Most of it hadn't been used since Grandfather died in 1915. He was mechanically talented and left many strange tools and things in those shop buildings. There was an old single-cylinder gasoline engine that no one ever got to run although my father kept it for years. He moved it to Bee's Creek and then to Turkey Hill, but I think we finally sold it for scrap metal during the war.

The most unusual tools Grandma used herself were the bee keeping accouterments. We inherited these things when she died, but she left no bees. She did leave a black rubber-coated hood with a fine cloth screen and long rubber-coated gloves to protect the bee worker. She had a bee smoker that would contain a small smoky fire inside a bellows-like assembly. By squeezing the bellows handles, the operator could force smoky air from the bellow and direct it through a nozzle. The smoke evidently stunned the bees and they would fly away and not attack.

Grandma also left two beehives but no bees. In those days, you waited for bees to swarm and then tried to entice them into your hive where you hoped a new queen would start a colony.

One day I heard something buzzing outside and my father did, too. His eyes got big and he grinned. He sent Joe and me to the pantry to get some cane syrup and told us to pour some in the two hives. If the bee scouts could find the syrup, they might like the sugar and stay. But my father said we had to get the bees' attention. So he gave each of us one of Mama's metal pots and a big spoon and told us to bang away. The noise was supposed to draw the bees down where they might smell the cane syrup, but if I were a bee and heard that racket, I'd have flown the other way.

We must have enticed the queen to come down, but I didn't witness her majesty's arrival. I do remember my father later using the smoker and the protective shield and gloves to get some honey from the hives so something got them to stay and produce honey to go with Mama's biscuits.

LANG'S OLD CAR

Big Lang was a veteran of the First World War. Being a black man in the then-segregated army, he served in a special organization—a transportation unit with trucks. That's where Lang learned to drive. He had little money and no job until he took the one my father offered in 1933. In addition to his pay, he got to use the tenant house and a couple of acres for pigs and chickens and a garden. His duties were generally to take care of Grandma's place where we were living.

Lang never talked much about his military service except the time he spent in New Port News, Virginia. I don't remember if he told me what he did there, but he often talked about being there. He served in France but he never said much about that either.

Lang talked more about what people did and said back home. He told us about the first airplane Nell ever saw. It almost scared her to death, he said. It happened during the war and she thought it had to be a German plane. Lang said their relatives still teased Nell about her declaration. "Lang n' nem done let them Germans get loose and they done come over here."

I don't know if General Pershing would have frowned or chuckled at Nell's designation for the American Expeditionary Force to France: "Lang n' nem."

It was about 1935 or 1936 when the veterans of the war to end all wars finally got their promised bonuses. I don't know how much Lang got, but he spent most of it on an old model A Ford. My father said right away that Lang had been cheated. He should know—he was cheated himself with several old cars and trucks.

Lang's car ran for a while, but one day it broke down. Lang didn't have the money to get it fixed. He had a few friends who said they knew how to fix cars, but they didn't. Every time they tried, they cost Lang more money and the car still wouldn't run. It sat in front of their house for a long time. We didn't have a car, either. We went everywhere in my father's truck.

Lang, Jr. said one of Lang's friends got it started once by blowing in the gas tank to pressure the gas through the line. One day we tried to get it started. My job was to put my mouth tightly on the filling throat of the gas tank and blow into it to pressure the gasoline. Lang, Jr. turned the crank while Joe worked the spark lever. Joe was also to push the choke in when the engine caught. I took a deep breath, bent over, and blew into the gas tank with all my strength.

I could keep my breath pressure for only a few seconds and then I had to let it out and get another breath. Each time the gas fumes came up and I breathed them in as I caught my breath. After about four times with my mouth on the gas tank opening, I felt dizzy. Everything spun around. I thought I was in a helical tube just large enough for my body and I was being carried around that spiral at enormous speed. Then I don't remember anything until I woke to Nell's voice giving Lang, Jr. and Joe a piece of her mind for making me blow in the gas tank.

"That stuff put you to sleep, don't you know? Don't never do that no more."

Nell was right. I never experienced that feeling again until I was operated on for appendicitis. When they administered the ether, I got dizzy the same way, everything spun around, and I went back into that helical tube and got spun around again.

I don't know what ever happened to Lang's car, but he didn't take it to Bee's Creek when he moved there with us.

ENTRAPMENT

My father took a deep drag on his cigarette and blew out the smoke. Then he handed me the butt. "George, take this here cigarette butt and throw it in the yard."

My father smoked a lot. He rolled his own with a package of thin cigarette papers that came in a flat pack about the size and shape of business cards. He would finger one of the papers from the pack and take a bag of Bull Durham or Bull of the Woods or a can of Prince Albert tobacco. He had tried a cigarette-rolling machine, but the thing (or my father) spilled as much tobacco as it rolled, so he went back to hand rolling his smokes.

He was pretty good at it. He would squeeze the paper with his left forefinger against his thumb and index finger on the same hand until it formed a groove. Then he would shake tobacco into the groove, spread it out evenly, and then roll the paper around using both hands. When the cigarette was rolled, he licked the edge of the paper so it would stick to the rest of the rolled paper and tobacco.

Then he was ready to light up. A few grains of tobacco fell out the end, but once he applied a match to it, the ashes seemed to hold the tobacco in. He took long drags, inhaled, and blew out. The smoke smelled so good and he seemed to enjoy it so much, I wanted to try it, but that way lay madness and a whipping.

Joe, Lang, Jr., Richard, and I had all tried rabbit tobacco, but it smelled awful, nothing like Prince Albert or Bull Durham. Dried corn silk was not much better, so my father's cigarette smoke worked on my curiosity. How would it taste?

Uncle Clint smoked ready-made Avalon cigarettes and Uncle Norman smoked cigars. We had no ashtrays to put the things in so they flicked the ashes into the fireplace. When they were finished, they handed the butts to one of us boys to take to the yard and throw away.

So that day I thought nothing of it when my father sent me outside with that cigarette butt still smoking. I was faithful to my assignment to throw the butt away, but as I walked to the porch, the aromatic smell of the thing and my curiosity worked on my sin nature. It all proved too much. When I got to the porch to throw it into the sand, I took a drag. I choked and looked around. My father had followed me and I got a whipping.

GOING TO CHARLESTON

When Mama's own mother died, she spent some time in Charleston with her aunt on Rutledge Street. Since then Mama was always homesick for the old city because she found some comfort and security there after the traumatic times surrounding the death of her mother. So she pressured my father to take the whole family to Charleson as we pronounced the city's name.

My father bought a truck to get into the business of hauling fertilizer and cotton. One of his hauling destinations was Charleson where he took cotton and cottonseed and brought back fertilizer. He kept talking about Charleson and Mama kept pestering him until the thing happened—the family went by borrowed car to Charleson.

Somehow none of the historic sights interested us. We wanted to see three things—the Francis Marion Hotel, the tallest building in the state (twelve stories); the beach on the Isle of Palms; and the Cooper River Bridge.

Seeing the hotel was anticlimactic. Once we saw it, we didn't care. We weren't staying there. The beach was nice, but getting there was the exciting part—we had to go over the new Cooper River Bridge.

The state had a toll on the bridge in those days so we stopped to pay. Then we saw the first span that looked like it went straight up and in the distance we saw the larger span waiting for those foolish enough to try to cross the first. The old car hummed and climbed the tall steel hill. I looked out as we climbed and then wondered why we should have been impressed with the Francis Marion Hotel. We were much higher and still climbing.

We looked down at the Cooper River and the Wando River and on the opposite side of the city we could see the Ashley River. We got a good view of the place where these rivers met, shaped the Battery, and formed the Atlantic Ocean. None of us had ever been that high before and were glad when we coasted down with the breeze in our faces. Then we saw the other span. It was no taller but much longer.

The highway made a turn to the left on Drum Island and led to the second span. Having spent anxious minutes climbing the first, we were even more apprehensive now. What if the car stalled? Would we roll all the way down backwards? If we had a wreck, would the fences hold us on the bridge? The old car seemed to strain and even my father looked a little worried.

But we finally got to the top and again coasted down to everyone's delight. We smiled all the way through Sullivan's Island on to the Isle of Palms where we had a picnic and got our feet wet.

My father decided to take the ferry back to Charleson. I think he was as concerned as we were about the Cooper River Bridge.

THE BEST FRIEND

The green and black monster hissed and belched and Joe, Richard, and I stood off terrified but fascinated by the awesome thing. It crouched on its iron haunches a hundred feet away and Joe wanted to go closer but Richard and I held back. The thing's awful breath was so bitter we could taste its hellish power—it had to be from the unholy place. "How can something that big move?" Joe asked.

"I don't know but let's back off a ways," I said.

Resting before us on the tracks in Elko, South Carolina, the locomotive grumbled and snorted and gave off odors of coal and sulfur. It terrified us because we knew steam boilers could explode. So we stood back and watched the monster exhale black smoke while steam hissed out under its belly. "Reckon when it'll move, Joe?" Richard asked.

Joe waved his head. "When it's dern good and ready."

We knew about the engineer and conductor roles but the huge contraption didn't seem subject to any human will. It mesmerized and confused us—we wanted it gone, but we also wanted to look at it.

Then the bell rang, the whistle screamed, and the locomotive huffed and blew smoke out of the stack and steam shot out by the wheels. Drive rods shoved the wheels and the wheels spun, caught, and jerked the thing forward. The monster inched down the track, picked up speed, and rolled into its rhythms of sound and motion, pulling a string of colorful captives. It rumbled away and in a few minutes it was gone, leaving an empty place in the sky where it had rested.

Like the rest of the South, the area around Elko, South Carolina grew cotton but needed ways to haul the heavy bales to ships and mills. Barges and steamboats were used on the rivers, but water travel was not an option in Elko or in much of the south.

Then in 1804 Richard Trevithick invented the steam locomotive and the idea came to America. In 1830 the South Carolina Canal and Railroad Company completed the first commercial rail line in the United States. It carried people six miles out from Charleston on outings and back again. Only two years later the line connected Charleston and Hamburg, South Carolina, a town across the Savannah River from Augusta, Georgia. And the line ran through Elko.

A funny looking locomotive named The Best Friend of Charleston pulled the first train that carried city sightseers out on a lark, but it blew up after a few months of operation. Other locomotives followed and they pulled trains through Elko long before the village was named that. They called it Ninety-Six Station because it was ninety-six miles by rail from Charleston, but a district and town farther north already had that name because it was ninety-six miles from some place else and they were ready to fight over it.

The hamlet stood on land purchased from one Ellen Mims, our great-great-great-grandmother, so they called the village Mims Turnout because the train went off the line there to get water and wood, refresh the passengers in the local hotel, and serve the community. Then it became Mims village or just Mims.

But upstate in Darlington County, they already had a town named Mims, so it was back to the Early American Think Tank. This time they named it Elko for a plantation near the village and the name stuck—nobody else in South Carolina wanted it and precious few anywhere else.

The Best Friend pulled cars covered on top but open on the sides so passengers could see better—they could also see the smoke better and the soot and ashes that fell on their clothes. It was the pride of South Carolina but it lasted only a few months before it blew up. Then they collected the pieces and reassembled them into its successor, The Phoenix.

More and larger locomotives followed and the company improved the roadbed, the rolling stock, and the rails many times. The line became the Charleston Augusta Line of the South Carolina Canal and Railroad Company. It later became part of the Southern Railroad System, providing mail, passenger, and freight service for towns along the route, including Elko.

In early 1865 after laying a belt of destruction in Georgia, Sherman entered the Palmetto State with even greater ferocity. The blue army came to Blackville and destroyed the railroad toward Elko and beyond. The Sherman technique was to heat the rail sections in huge fires until the steel was soft enough to bend. Then they bent the rail around a tree or telegraph pole until the ends met and crossed, making an overlap design called the Sherman bow tie. They didn't have to bend all the rails because they couldn't be replaced. It put the railroad out of service for years.

After the War, the town rebuilt itself along the restored railroad line and the Augusta Road, now U.S. 78 that paralleled it. The people built houses facing the tracks on both sides—in the early days, it was fashionable for houses to face the railroad. My grandfather had such a house on the southeast corner of Railroad Avenue and Thompson Street.

Elko had several cotton gins over the years, but when we were growing up, a large one-cylinder gasoline engine provided its thumping power to gin the cotton. The gin produced a prodigious number of bales over the years, but it took the railroad to get them out. When farmers made their snail-like move to other crops, the railroad moved those products as well.

Elko was much larger when the railroad ran through it and it boasted a large covered depot shed to keep cotton dry. The depot also handled asparagus, beans, cantaloupes, watermelons, and cucumbers and other crops grown in the area. It was a busy place much of the year and to support the activity, six or eight trains a day came by.

We were captivated by the sounds of the steam locomotives—chug, chug; choo, choo; chug, chug; choo, choo, but in our young fantasies, they sang their destinations. When the train headed south, we would hear it chanting. "Gotta leave Elko. Gotta leave Elko. Going to Charleson, Blackville and Charleson. Going to Charleson, Blackville and Charleson, chug, chug, choo, choo."

Note: we didn't pronounce the "t" in Charleston because it sounded rough, foreign, and affected. We used similar word smoothings and syllable-saving articulations for Clumbia, the capital, and Barn'll for Barnwell, the county seat.

When the train headed north, it coughed out another boast. "Gotta leave Elko. Gotta leave Elko. Going to Augusta, Williston, Augusta. Going to Augusta, Williston, Augusta. Chug, chug, choo, choo."

We lived three miles from the station, but we heard most of the train whistles. With only one set of tracks, the railroad took care to schedule its use, and it was so busy they had to keep to the rigid timetable. The newspapers printed the schedule in the weekly editions and people set watches and clocks by the whistle screams. If a clock and the train indicated different times, the clock was changed.

We went to town during the week on the school bus and on Saturdays for shopping and to meet with friends. We went there for church but trains didn't run on Sunday in those days. If a train was at the station, we would watch it, but we usually saw none. When we were in town and had time, we would find out where the next train was coming from and walk down the track toward it. We wanted to know when it was coming so we could get in position to watch it from a safe distance from the tracks.

We could see the puffing smoke of the locomotive a mile down the track and we could hear the whistle even farther away. Then it was time to run to our observation spots and watch the trains come in. They didn't often stop because Elko was smaller than other towns along the line.

When a train stopped we stared and wondered how the locomotive worked and what all the parts did until its ear-piercing scream and clanging bell bid us goodbye. Then it lurched forward and began to move, taking our cotton or produce to Charleson or Augusta, picking up more in Williston or Blackville and other towns along the way.

The highway still runs through Elko and the railroad bed still divides the little town, but the depot and railroad station are gone, and the water tank, the hotel, and most of the stores have vanished. The wooden cross ties and steel rails lasted a few more years, but they have also been taken up. My grandfather's house is gone. Even the two gravestones of my two little aunts are gone, but the old store that my father operated with Hugh Bert is still standing. We had hoped the town could pick up its pieces and rise again like The Phoenix emerged from the Best Friend, but it didn't happen. Now you can drive along the railroad bed for miles if you want to, but most of it has grown up in weeds.

The big black engines with the green cabs and the colorful cars are gone and they left a big hole in my heart. Now the Best Friend and the other early locomotives can lumber their way only through history. Their successors of my youth can chug and whistle and clang their way only through my memory. Gotta leave Elko. Gotta leave Elko. Going to Charleson, Blackville, and Charleson. Gotta leave Elko. Gotta leave Elko. Going to Augusta, Williston, Augusta...

GETTING PUNCTURED

It was a hot May day in our classroom at Elko Grade School and we waited at our desks with churning stomachs and trembling fingers. We shivered and a freckled-face boy choked out his dread and spoke for all of us—at least for me. "I hope that county nurse don't never get here," he said.

We agonized, dreading the pain we would endure as we waited for the grim crew to arrive and begin the torture. When I saw the nurse's white dress and heard the moans from my friends, the taste of fear rose in my mouth. Thinking back on it now reminds me of the smell I associate with that awful morning.

I remember many smells from my young years like the intoxicating perfume of Grandma's roses, the equally potent fragrance of the sweet shrub, the subtle bouquet of cotton blossoms, the devastating aroma of a pig over the barbeque pit, and the universal odor of the barnyard. But the scent that stands out in my memory is the smell of rubbing alcohol that I will always associate with the county nurse's white dress and getting punctured.

Uncle Clint started the whole thing—he came down with typhoid fever. We didn't know what that was, but my father and mother worried about him so we knew it was serious. They worried about us, too, because we could get it. Dr. Lewis isolated Uncle Clint at home and only Aunt Carrie could attend him. No one else could visit him.

Then we heard about others in the county getting sick with typhoid fever. County officials issued warnings for the schools and called for enhanced sanitation, but most rural homes and even our schools and churches used outdoor toilets. We didn't even have running water to wash our hands at school. I do remember the concerns and efforts being made, but I only remember one measure being imposed—the typhoid fever shot.

The county health department sent teams of nurses out to give injections against the salmonella typhi, but only the nurses knew the germ on such a formal basis. We all knew but one thing—the county nurse was coming and she was going to stick every one of us.

The teams gave injections in stores, churches, and schools, and eventually our turn came at Elko Grade School. The principal came to our room and announced that the county nurse would be there Friday. We talked and agonized and trembled all week dreading our coming fate on Black Friday. I went to Mama, my ever-present defender against all hurt and evil, but even she agreed with the heartless authorities—I was going to be punctured for typhoid fever.

Friday came and we all felt a little sick. The sun didn't seem as bright and everybody wore an unhappy frown. The teachers tried to conduct classes but who could listen? Then the principal came to the class room door and our hearts stopped. She ordered the students of the third grade to get ready for the shots or punctures as we called them. I didn't want to be punctured, but the county, the principal, the teacher, and my father and mother said I was going to get punctured for typhoid fever.

So I waited in terror. I don't remember how long we waited and cringed about the shots, but a lot of time passed. I heard the boys and girls complaining and dreading the puncture.

"I can't stand this waiting. Can't they hurry up and get it over with?"

"How does it feel? It hurt real bad?"

"I heard it's like a dull ten-penny nail drove in your arm with a ball peen hammer."

"Naww, it's more like somebody stuck you with a rusty pitch fork."

"It's more like a brace and bit. They don't drill down some, it don't do no good."

"Reckon we'll really die if we don't get punctured?"

"County nurse, don't never get here."

But she was already there and set up for punctures. We went in an unorganized mass to the table where the nurse sat staring at some papers. Then the teacher arranged us in line in alphabetical order of our last names and a poor girl named Adcock was leadoff victim. She went forward and the nurse began to administer punctures. I remember being glad my name was Youngblood.

But that soon became a disadvantage. I had to watch all the boys and girls go up and get punctured. I saw them all when they left and I was still at the end of the line. I suffered with every victim. No one screamed or yelled, although some had tears in their eyes. That didn't give me much comfort as I waited at the end of the shrinking line. Some boys squeezed their arms and bent over like it was really hurting and the line got shorter.

When near enough to hear what the nurse and the attendants said, I was no less terrified because they were known for understatement. "Roll up your sleeve and relax. It won't hurt much, but it's going to sting just a little bit."

When it was my turn, the nurse didn't even look at me. She stared at my arm and rubbed a strong smelling liquid on it that cooled the spot she had in mind. Then she punctured the top part of my left arm. I felt the painful stick and then the sting. It hurt but it was not too bad. It hurt a lot more later.

Uncle Clint recovered and we were all glad for his restored health and the disappearance of typhoid fever from our area. But to this day the smell of rubbing alcohol takes me back to the day in 1937 when I got punctured for typhoid fever.

THE CHAIN GANG

"Mama, lookee yonder," Richard said.

We stopped sweeping the front yard and looked at the cloud of dust on the road toward Elko. The dust seemed to be rolling our way. "Reckon what it is, Mama?" Joe asked.

"Must be the gang," she said.

I had heard about the chain gang all my life, but I didn't remember ever seeing one before. No one I knew, white or black, ever served time on a chain gang. "What you reckon they done, Mama?" I asked.

"Bad men get put on the gang," the strict Baptist said. "Them that run bootleg liquor and make moonshine. Some of 'em probably got caught hunting on somebody else's place or fishing with traps and nets. Sometimes men that go about drunk and scare people in public get to wear them stripes."

"How about stealing?" Joe asked.

"Some of 'em probably got caught taking something, but stealing is serious and most thieves wind up in the penitentiary in Clumbia."

"Why does everybody wants to steal something?" Richard asked.

Mama grinned. "Stealing started way back in Bible times, don't you know. Over the years some men in this county have got real good at it. Your daddy says some of 'em steal just for meanness. They'd steal the fuzz off a peach if they could."

"How 'bout fighting?" Richard asked.

Mama nodded. "But if they kill somebody or try to, they might go to the penitentiary and some of 'em get to sit in the electric chair up in Clumbia."

"All them men yonder bad, Mama?" I asked.

"Most of 'em. Some might be innocent because things ain't always fair or easy to know. But we need to punish the bad ones. The work and the shame of being on the gang is enough to make anybody want to change his ways and live a better life."

We learned that they suffered more than work and shame—they had a tough life while they served. "They get cathead biscuits and grits with fatback grease on it for breakfast," Mama said. "And black-eyed peas, cornbread, and rice for dinner and supper and all the water they can drink. They work all day on the county dirt roads with shovels and picks, digging out the ditches and building up the road."

"Why?" Richard asked.

"When the gang works a road, they leave it soft. They build up the crown and dig out the ditches. Your daddy don't like to drive on a freshly worked road because the loose dirt makes steering the truck hard work. But after a few days of traffic and a rain or two to pack it down, we'll forgot the chain gang ever come by."

Mama left to close the doors and windows to keep the dust out of the house. Joe, Richard, and I climbed onto our observation limb up in the large oak tree in our yard to watch the chain gang creep its way in our direction. They continued to work the road until they stopped about five hundred yards from the house for the noon meal. We scampered down the tree for our own dinner and we were surprised that it was black-eyed peas and rice and cornbread.

"Are we on the chain gang, Mama?" Joe asked.

"They get good food. Trouble is that's all they get. Everyday. Your daddy thinks some of them get caught on purpose so they can always have something to eat."

That afternoon Lang, Jr. came to see what was happening on the road. We did the feeding chores with Lang, Jr. and played with him almost every day. "Y'all been looking at the gang?" he asked.

We all nodded and got back to the tree in time to see one of the men with a shotgun follow some of the men out into the woods. "What they doing, Joe?" Richard asked.

"They go dig a toilet ditch," Lang, Jr. said. "Them's that got to go, that's where they go. Then they cover it up."

The gang kept working their way toward us and we could hear singing. "I wouldn't be singing if I was on the gang," I said.

"You'd better not. You sing like you do in church, one them mean rascals would bend a shovel cross your head," Joe said.

When they came closer, we could hear picks hitting the surface and shovels clanging against each other. They raised so much dust we couldn't make out their faces, but we saw men walking on the edges of the road with shotguns. When they came nearer, we could hear their chains rattle as they moved and worked.

When the gang was opposite our house, we looked at the dusty faces and shuddered. The column about four men wide worked the road surface. Men with picks broke up the dirt in the ditches and those with shovels threw the loosened dirt on the roadbed. The next rows smoothed out the dirt piles and broke up the clods with shovels. Others shaped the ditches so they would drain.

The chain gang stretched about seventy-five yards toward Elko. We could see only black men and we had heard things about a few of them. "Whicha one tried to kill his wife, you reckon?" I asked.

"I don't know but they all look mad enough to kill somebody," Joe said.

"Reckon them men with the guns can make 'em all behave?" I asked.

They ignored me. Lang, Jr. pointed. "He that one over yonder swinging the pick. He told the law he wasn't trying to kill her—just beat her up 'cause she wanted to leave him."

"You know anybody else out there, Lang, Jr.?" Joe asked.

Lang, Jr. nodded with his chin. "Yonder's a man named Shine. My daddy says his face shines when he gets drunk and Shine gets drunk a lot. He gets hot when he drinking. This time he beat up a man that said something about his face. Shine's bad. He's always on the gang. Something bad happens, the sheriff go looking for Shine first thing."

"You know anybody else out there?" Joe asked.

Lang, Jr. looked over the men. "Hard to see good with all the dust and dirt on their faces. Wait a minute. That no-account man standing yonder talking and dragging the shovel—he got caught stealing a hen from Mr. Norman's place. And that one toting the water bucket? Talk is he didn't do nothing wrong, but the sheriff said he pushed him when he tried to arrest him. Now he on the gang for six months."

Soon the chain gang passed our house and we could see them from behind. Another man with a shotgun brought up the rear. Joe said he counted more than a hundred men and they all wore the black and dirty white stripes of disgrace. About ten were white men. They worked toward the rear, separated from the black prisoners. "What you reckon them white men done?" I asked.

"One of 'em got caught making liquor in the woods other side Tom Willis's pond," Joe said. "But I don't know whicha one it was."

"I heard about another one," Lang, Jr. said, "but I don't know whicha one he is neither. He got caught with a colored gal and she got locked up, too. She's on the county farm."

"What them women do on the county farm?" I asked.

"Wash all them dirty clothes the men wear when they on the gang," Joe said. "Lookee yonder. Them men ain't wearing no shackles."

Joe pointed out a few of the prisoners who weren't shackled.

"My daddy told me them men is "trusties" on account of they can be trusted not to run off," Lang, Jr. said. "They behave their selves so they get to tote tools and water from the wagons to the men."

The gang maintained its snail's pace down the hill and across the creek. They had started up the hill on the other side when the workday ended. Then the gang came back by our house walking back to the county jail. Soon they disappeared from our sight and I was glad they were gone.

THE FOURTH OF JULY

Mr. Alex Weimortz looked up from the barbecue pit. "Clint, get you and Seese to turn the pig?"

Uncle Clint rose to help his father-in-law and my father got up to help Uncle Clint. Mr. Weimortz was Aunt Carrie's father and the acknowledged barbecue master of Barnwell County when we were growing up. So my father and Uncle Clint grabbed the ends of the cue sticks and rotated the pig over the barbeque pit. The scrumptious smell already had our mouths watering and now we could see the underside of the almost-done pig. Mr. Weimortz soaked his basting swab in his own special cooking sauce and mopped the meat while we drooled. "Turn it back over," he said, "be ready in half an hour."

Some people in the county probably had dinner parties and we all had Christmas and Thanksgiving feasts, but for most of us, social events meant barbecue. Family reunions, special occasions, and holidays might be reasons to have a barbecue, but the Fourth of July demanded it. As Thanksgiving is hard on turkeys today, pigs the right size and weight had little chance of getting past the Fourth in those days. I didn't know why the fourth was so important. I never heard it called Independence Day then. I'm not sure all the people who celebrated knew why, either, but celebrate we did—with food.

The barbecue took a lot of work. The morning before the event, the host—this time it was Uncle Clint—selected a place and had a pit dug. Uncle Clint's son, Clinton, Jr., nicknamed Bo, dug the hole. The hole was nominally three feet wide, six feet long, and two feet deep. Bo had already cut and hauled several wagonloads of Black Jack oak and hickory limbs to the site because barbecue cooking needed a lot of coals.

About a month before, Uncle Clint had selected the pig for the occasion. The pigs had to be young, about 200 pounds in weight and as perfect as a Levitical sacrifice, except no pig ever qualified for that because he never learned to chew the cud. He had the right kind of feet, though.

In the middle of the afternoon of July 3, Uncle Clint's workers had killed and bled the pig. The pig killing crew had water boiling in wash pots and a steel drum lying in a slanted hole. They poured hot water into the slanted drum and dipped the carcass into the hot water that was supposed to be 160 degrees or as close to it as they could get. They plunged the head in first and soaked it a few seconds, withdrew it and rubbed wet fire ashes into the hair and on the skin. Then the whole crew snatched at the pig's steaming hair that came off in patches and burned their hands. Then they repeated the process for the rear end of the pig.

When the pig hair snatching was over, they hung the pig head down on braces nailed to a tree. First Uncle Clint scraped the pig's skin clean of hair with a long-bladed knife. Then he washed the hair and ashes from the carcass, cut off the head, and sent it to the kitchen. Then he opened the body to get at the internal organs for the barbeque hash. He removed the liver, lungs, heart, kidneys, and sweet breads and sent them to the kitchen.

As time progressed, the skill of Mr. Weimortz, the cue master, had become increasingly important and his authority grew in proportion. The helpers laid the gutted pig out on a table where using a sharp hatchet, Mr. Weimortz split the backbone from the inside so the pig would lie flat on the table. He examined the carcass and cut holes on the butt of each ham and between several ribs. Then he called for the cue sticks, half-inch steel rods about eight feet long. Each cue rod was bent on one end at a right angle to provide a two-inch arm for control. The other end was machined down and sharpened to a point.

Mr. Weimortz pushed the cue rods through the hams, out of the carcass at the ribs, back into the body after four ribs, and thrust them all the way through the shoulders. Then he placed hickory sticks perpendicular to the cue rods to keep the carcass spread open and flat. Then he swabbed the inside with his secret cooking sauce and let it soak.

Meanwhile in the kitchen, Aunt Carrie and her helpers cleaned the head of hair, removed the eyes and the brain, washed the head thoroughly, and boiled it for about three hours. Then they pulled the flesh from the head, removing the skin, teeth, and the skull bones. Next they put the head meat through a meat grinder and did the same with the boiled organ meats.

Barbeque hash was as individual as the hostess, but most ground onions and added them and vinegar to the ground meat. Some women disdained the use of the grinder and hand chopped the meats, but Aunt Carrie used the grinder. After adding spices and flavors, many of them secret, she simmered the hash for hours.

The men started the barbecue fire about sundown and made a fire in the pit itself to get the surrounding earth hot. They laid two-by-four boards flat side down at the ends of the pit to support the cue sticks. When the fire had produced coals and the pit was hot, Mr. Weimortz placed more glowing coals around the perimeter of the pit bottom. "Bring the pig," he said.

Two men carried the pig to the pit by holding the cue rods, lowered the pig over the pit skin side up, and rested the cue rods on the two-by-four boards at the ends of the pit. That began the long watch and the men sat around the pit and settled down as Mr. Weimortz did his slow magic. Cigarettes, cigars, and pipes appeared and the men smoked and talked as Mr. Weimortz called periodically for the pig to be turned so he could swab the underside with his cooking sauce.

Pig turning followed a ritual procedure. Two men approached the pit from opposite ends, bent down, crossed their arms, and grasped the cue rod ends. Then they slowly pulled their arms apart and the pig rotated with the cue rods. Then they set the pig back over the coals, skin side down.

Most cue masters swabbed with vinegar-based sauces laced with salt, pepper, and God knows what. The pig spent a few minutes cooking with the skin side down during the swabbing exercises, but most of the time, the meat cooked with the skin up to capture the juices and keep the meat moist. When the pig was rotated back, they followed the same crossed arm rotation.

Some cue masters took the pig from the pit when they added coals lest the ash dust rise and get on the meat. Others like Mr. Weimortz used great care in adding more glowing coals so they didn't have to take up the pig. It was a tricky operation requiring skill and Mr. Weimortz had it.

During the long hours of cooking that started in late afternoon of the third of July and ended on the Fourth at noon, the men smoked, joked, lied, shared a few bottles, and listened to the fat and juices drip and sputter as they fell on the coals. The aroma made us all hungry but we wouldn't get barbeque until the next day.

The children had to go in after supper, but most of the men stayed until about ten p.m., when Mr. Weimortz asked men to volunteer. He organized teams to keep the pig cooking slowly and safely through the night. Mr. Weimortz returned early the next morning to see whether he would have a good barbeque or one dried out by too much heat. Although few could be considered real cue masters, most men knew how, and the meat usually came through the night in good order.

Next morning, the women were busy in the kitchen making several large pots of rice to go with the hash. Pies and cakes and ambrosia began to multiply as ladies arrived with their families. Pickles, breads, tea, and vegetables crowded the tables as the noon hour approached. All this time, the meat sent its devastating aroma across the yard. We all licked our lips.

Back at the pit, the subject of sauce came up. Some cue masters swabbed their own mixture on the meat and cooked it a few minutes longer. Others let the guests pick a sauce from several offerings. Some men brought sauces made by secret recipes, but all acknowledged that Uncle Clint's was the best. It was a mustard-based formula containing Worcestershire sauce and other things known only to Uncle Clint. When Uncle Clint died, the secret of his barbeque sauce died with him.

When Mr. Weimortz proclaimed the pig done, Uncle Clint and my father took it to a table and sliced the hams and shoulder. They pulled the ribs apart with care that some meat remained on each. Some people liked the barbecued skin and some of it was put on the platters. They chopped meat that didn't slice easily like that near the bones. Then they carried the platters of meat to the serving table followed by a train of hungry kids. Then we ate and ate and ate.

"I'm full as a tick," someone would say. After eating far too much, the men resumed smoking, lying, bragging, and drinking. The women kept nibbling on the cakes and hee-hawing then giggling about certain things. After letting the food settle, the kids played until the grown-ups called their families and the exodus began.

No one even thought of fireworks on those occasions. The historical and political aspects of the Fourth were never discussed in my memory. Maybe no one knew, but I later concluded it was because General Robert E. Lee began his retreat from Gettysburg and General John C. Pemberton surrendered Vicksburg, Mississippi, on the same day—July 4, 1863. Southerners have long memories.

HAIRCUTS

We had a few services in Elko in the 1930's, but a barbershop wasn't one of them. Our hair grew as fast as any boy's, but our father took care of that himself. He had a pair of clippers powered by hand—the same hand that was supposed to be guiding the clippers through our hair. If our father pulled too hard, the clippers might go astray or cut too much or do some other terrible thing.

Our father was almost competent at cutting hair, but one of the Richardson lads, Oliver by name and Skabo by nickname, who lived with Math Bolen, gave excellent haircuts. Mama tried to get our father to take us to Math's for haircuts and he did about half the time.

When our father cut our hair, he did it on the back porch. He placed a chair over spread newspapers and we sat for the trimming. He spread more newspapers over us so the hair wouldn't get in our clothes. Because of the hard times, he did many things he didn't like because he had to. Cutting hair was one of those things.

But when Skabo cut our hair, he did it in the back yard so he wouldn't have to clean up the clippings. He seemed to have a natural touch and the whole thing went smoothly, but I think he hated to see us coming. It would take him about an hour to cut the hair of three growing boys.

I was interested in the technique of cutting hair and liked to watch the clipper go clip, clip, clip and the scissors go snip, snip, snip. The severed hair fell to the newspaper that covered the one being groomed. It was one of the exciting events of the month and we liked to watch each other get haircuts.

On rare occasions, we went to Williston to get our haircuts. Those were memorable, exciting times. I can still smell the lotions and the soap and the lathers. The wide mirrors mounted on opposite walls seemed like magic—you could see yourself a dozen times with each image a little smaller than the one before it. The barber pole also charmed us. "How they get it colored that way, Joe," I asked.

"Man told me they had to use red and white striped paint," he said.

The pump-up chairs further fascinated us. The barbers viewed our sitting heights and pumped us up or down for the right elevation. The pump-up seats didn't go high enough for Richard's head; they had to put an insert seat on the arms then pick him up and set him on it. These magical chairs would also spin when the barber wanted to do the other side of your head. When the customer wanted a shave, the barber made the magic chair tilt back to the shaving position. Sometimes the barber tilted the chair all the way back so he could wash the customer's hair.

When they had us seated in the magic chair, they threw large striped cotton sheets over us to keep the hair from falling on our clothes. Then they pinned the cloth that smelled of other people's sweat about our necks. Sometimes the part they tightened about my neck was still wet with the previous customer's sweat.

Men who didn't need haircuts also came to the barbershop. They gathered there every Saturday to gossip and watch them give haircuts and shaves. Each weekend had two great social events for the men in Williston—on Sunday almost everyone went to church and on Saturday they watched them give haircuts.

The shaves were even more interesting. The barber would pour hot water in his mug and work up a lather with his brush. Then he tilted the chair back so the customer was almost lying and applied the lather none too gently or evenly to the man's face. While the lather softened the man's beard, the barber reached for the long razor strop (I never learned why it was called a strop rather than a strap) that hung from the chair. He stretched it tight and slapped the blade against it. That made a staccato sound as the blade beat the leather.

When the razor was sharp enough, the barber started on the sideburns and worked his way down the man's face. He scraped the lather-cut beard mess onto the towel wrapped around the customer's neck and attacked a new surface of the face.

The Williston barbers—there were three of them—used loud buzzing electric machines for cutting hair and I hated the sound. The smell, too. I could smell the electricity when they cut my hair. It felt like the vibrating thing was trimming me down to size. It was interesting to see other men and boys get their hair cut with it, though. The thing went through hair like a mowing machine through oats.

Some men didn't get their hair cut with the machine. The barbers went snip, snip, snipping through their hair with scissors and a comb. Sometimes the barbers used hand-powered clippers like our father had and went clip, clip, clip to trim or get a missed spot trimmed right.

I was always amazed by the accumulation of hair on the floor and how often they had to sweep. One barber kept track of whose turn it was, but I don't know how he did it. They didn't take numbers or sit us in any particular place, but when one of the barbers was ready for his next customer, the schedule-keeping barber would point his mowing machine—his electric clippers—at the man or boy who was next. Nobody ever argued with that barber. He was the last word and the master of his domain—the Williston barber shop.

MAKING SYRUP

Sugarcane "serp" or syrup was a staple in colonial South Carolina and it was still an important part of the diet when we were growing up. It differs from molasses, the residue from sugar crystallization, in that the full sugar content of the cane is retained in the syrup as the juice is concentrated by cooking to the desired thickness or viscosity.

We enjoyed our father's cane syrup on Mama's battercakes (some people called them pancakes), flapjacks, and biscuits. In the latter, we punched a hole in a biscuit, filled the hole with syrup, and carefully ate our way down. I tried to be careful but I never ate a syrup biscuit without getting syrup on me.

Mama and most cooks in the area used syrup in a variety of ways. It could be used simply as a sweetener, but most cooks used granulated sugar. Depending upon how well the flavors blended, syrup could be used to cook things like sweet potatoes and make fruit preserves and candies like taffy and peanut brittle.

My father planted about a half-acre of cane every year mostly for use as syrup, but chewing peeled cane sections was itself a treat. It was especially good around a blazing fire so that the cane peelings and the chewed wads could be thrown into the hot coals. Removing the chewed material from one's mouth was a social challenge that most girls and women did not care to take—most of them declined to chew sugarcane even though they would come to events featuring cane chewing.

Conversion of cane into syrup took specialized equipment, skill, and patience, and like many farms, Grandma's place had its cane mill/syrup kettle complex. The mill was out in the open, but the kettle was under a wide shed. The mill was a rotating two-cylinder device connected through gears to a long wooden beam pulled by a mule.

Lang connected the mule to the beam with a singletree. When it was time to squeeze the cane, the animal pulled on the long balanced beam made from a slender log. The mule walked around in a circle as Lang fed cane stalks into the cylinders. The cylinders squeezed out the juice and pushed the pressed cane stalks out the other side. In Louisiana, they call the pressed cane stalks bagasse, but we called them pressed cane stalks.

Cane juice ran down from the squeeze cylinders, dripped into a small reservoir, and flowed down a channel that emptied onto a burlap cover fitted loosely over a wooden barrel. The burlap sagged and formed a pocket. The burlap filter removed any husk or other solid matter from the juice, but it also kept the swarming bees from the juice. Cane squeezing and syrup cooking put bees in a frenzy. They buzzed the area during the whole operation. Nothing drew bees like making syrup.

Our syrup kettle was an iron bowl about six feet in diameter and about three feet deep at the center. It was mounted over a brick firebox that was connected to a brick chimney on the edge of the shed. When they had squeezed the juice from the cane, my father and Lang dipped ten-quart buckets into the barrel, carried the juice to the kettle, and poured it in. Then they made a slow fire under the kettle to cook the water out and condense the juice to syrup. Too much heat could give the syrup a strong flavor and that made patience the kettle master's most necessary qualification. My father knew what he wanted, but he was not as patient as Lang who usually finished it up.

Equipped with skimmers of porous cloth held by a ring attached to a long wooden handle, Lang removed debris like leaves, trash, and bees that might blow or fall into the syrup. He also skimmed off a foamy chaff that formed during the cooking. To prevent local overheating, he used long wooden paddles to scrape the bottom and stir the syrup until it was done.

Then Lang pulled the fire and used a large ladle to dip and pour the syrup into gallon cans. The last syrup was thicker and stronger than earlier poured product, but some people liked the stronger taste.

My father produced forty-five to fifty gallons of syrup a year and gave about half of it to the school to pay for our school lunches. Lang got five gallons. Lang also collected the skimmings and what he could scrape from the kettle and used it to ferment corn mash into moonshine. I don't know where Lang got the stuff fermented and distilled, but there were many woods in the area, and the black people had connections and secrets known only to themselves.

THE ELKO SCHOOL BELL

Elko had a school building as far back as I can remember, but we didn't go to school there until 1937. Until then, they bused us to Williston. Then some kind of renaissance came to Elko and my father was involved. He became chairman of the school trustee board as if he didn't already have enough trouble.

He had to help hire teachers, get the old building ready for classes, and purchase a bus.

Leaving the store and sawmill in other hands, he and one of his cousins went to Winston Salem, North Carolina, to get the cab and chassis. Then they had to take it to some other place for the body and we finally had a new bus to take us to the old building. I don't remember why that school had not operated during my first two years, but it opened again in September 1937 when Joe and I entered the fourth and third grades, respectively.

We had often seen the old red brick school building standing on a hill on the north end of town and sporting its bell tower. Now we saw what it looked like inside. As we entered under the alcove beneath the bell tower, we saw the bell rope hanging down, tied to a bracket on the side about five feet from the floor. Then we entered the hall that divided four large rooms on the first floor.

The first door on the right was home to the first grade and to the second grade half the time.

The first door on the left opened to the third grade room that also housed the second grade half the time. The two rooms down the hall served the fourth and sixth grades with the fifth grade sharing the space and the teacher half the time. We had six grades but only four rooms and four teachers.

Each room had a large pot-bellied stove for warmth and huge, high windows for air when it was hot. Even then the desks were ancient and large—large enough for me to sit beside Joe when the teacher was working with the fifth grade and my fourth grade class was in study or reading periods.

The bell tyrannized the school. It rang ten minutes before eight and then again at eight when we should already be in our seats. Fifty-five minutes later, it rang again to tell the teachers the period was up. It rang again at nine and the teachers taught second period. At 9:55, the bell signaled start of little recess. We could go to the outdoor privies, play, or get a drink of water. At 10:05, the bell rang for third period. At 11:00, it declared the start of fourth period, and at 12:00 it announced big recess.

Everyone went to the lunchroom for soup and sandwiches. We almost always had vegetable soup and sandwiches made from a peanut butter/cane syrup blend. My father paid for our lunches by donating the syrup for these delicacies.

Lunch took only about ten minutes and then we had time to play before the insistent clang ordered us back to class. After two more periods that seemed longer than those before lunch, the bell tolled dismissal and we went to the bus for the ride home.

One of the teachers doubled as school principal with various responsibilities and authorities, among which was maintenance of order and discipline. She used boys to ring the bell. Fourth, fifth, and sixth grade boys were put on the bell crew. When a boy's time came up, he reported to the principal who made the first two rings to show the ringer of the day how to do it.

We untied the bell rope and pulled it down to swing the bell. We let the bell swing back to pull the rope up. Repeating this several times made the bell swing far enough to make the clacker strike the inside of the bell and produce the ring. Then the ringer was to pull gently against the rope when it clanged and make it clang on the other side. After ten gongs, the ringer was to pull on the rope to help the bell resume its rest position and tie the rope again to the bracket.

The boys learned how to ride the bell rope up when the bell's weight pulled on it. It was fun, but it ruined the rhythm and the bell sometimes missed a ring or rang when it shouldn't. That made the principal furious so we didn't dare do it when she was about. But we always listened for the bell between the periods because that's when somebody was likely to ride the rope. More boys were punished because of bell antics than for any other school transgression.

I entered the fourth grade just before we moved away from Elko. I was on the bell roster but I already knew much about it from Joe and the other older boys. I let the rope lift me several times and I never got caught until one day the rope broke about half way through the bell ceremony. Then I had no way to make the bell ring. The principal left her class and came quickly to see me with the broken rope at my feet. I was pronounced guilty with no opportunity to lie and say the rope just broke when I was pulling it.

The school handyman who lived nearby came and replaced the rope. I don't remember whether the principal sent for the man before or after she gave me three swats with her paddle.

FROGS IN THE WELL

Almost everyone we knew had open water wells like ours, and they drew water the same way—in galvanized ten-quart buckets using a chain and pulley. Some used ropes, but they rotted pretty fast, broke, and dropped the bucket in the well.

The well at Grandma's house was about thirty feet deep and it was a scary thing for us. Our father and mother never allowed any foolishness around the well—it was too dangerous for children. One reason for this fear of wells was that Melvin Youngblood, my great uncle, was a well digger and he was killed by a well cave-in. The tragedy was evidence and a constant reminder that wells were dangerous.

Sometime during the Depression, the Bank of Williston failed, and everyone lost whatever money they had in it. After that Grandma went on a strict cash basis. She insisted on cash for her products and paid in cash for her purchases. According to her sons, she kept money buried in Mason jars in the yard, but she kept some in a Mason jar that hung from a cord down below the water. My Uncle Money (Alvin Roscoe Youngblood) swore it was true. He lost money in the Bank of Williston failure, too, so he remembered the thing well.

One day, Mama noticed strangeness in that well water. At first she couldn't tell what it was, but she was fussy about what she ate, drank, and cooked with. This water had to be investigated. It tasted all right, but Mama knew something was wrong. She quit using it for food and drink and made my father bring cooking and drinking water from Elko.

We still used the water for the mules and cows and Lang drew water every morning and night for them. It was Lang who found the problem—he hauled up a bucket of water with a frog in it. The frog jumped out and got away, but Lang reported it to Mama and she had a fit.

When my father got home she lit into him. "Get this well cleaned out, Cecil!"

My father called in well "experts" who condemned the well and started to clean it up. They tried to draw the water out of the well, but it was a deep well and a good one. The frogs thought so, too. Anyway the well experts couldn't empty it.

The well workers had to fill the well with dirt until there was no water, wait until the frogs were dead, and dig it out again. That took weeks. I remember the men going down into the well. Already terrified of wells, I trembled for them. They used a large wooden cylinder with a crank handle that served as a windlass to lower the men into the well and bring up the dug clay. They made a real mess of the yard near the well when they brought up all that dirt.

Even after the well was cleaned out Mama didn't trust the water. She boiled it and strained it and worried about it until we moved to Bee's Creek.

GRANDFATHER WOODWARD

We used to dread visits to Robert Edward Woodward, our great-grandfather. He was the consummate southern gentleman. His own father, John Ardis Woodward, served during most of the Civil War in the Army of Northern Virginia. John Ardis named his sons for Confederate generals like Maxey Gregg Woodward and Wade Hampton Woodward, but our great-grandfather was named for the greatest and he wouldn't let you forget that.

Robert Edward Woodward was a pretentious man because of his family. His grandfather William Henry Woodward owned a plantation and about sixty slaves when the Civil War started. Robert Edward Woodward inherited some of that land and bought more. He had about two hundred acres when in 1949 the government decided to make a thermonuclear bomb. The authorities determined that they needed to build the bomb in South Carolina on the Savannah River that had a high natural content of tritium, the fuel for the nuclear fusion bomb. Then they decided on the site and it included Robert Edward Woodward's farm, house, and barns. They condemned his land and that of his neighbors and ordered them to move off so they could produce the needed tritium.

He died a few months before The Removal and was buried in the Woodward Cemetery that still lies inside the Savannah River Plant Site. His father, John Ardis Woodward, and his grandfather, William Henry Woodward, are also buried there with their wives. Two of Robert Edward Woodward's uncles, also Confederate soldiers, are buried there

Robert Edward Woodward boasted about his father. He always seemed to trap me for history lessons when the others ran off. He claimed that his father volunteered with his brother and a cousin before First Manassas and that his father fought all the battles the Army of Northern Virginia was involved in. That's not true. John Ardis Woodward was indeed in service for the entire war, but he was wounded at least twice (The Wilderness and Newmarket) and probably another time in the final fighting around Five Forks and the desperate retreat that ended at Appomattox. So John Ardis missed some of the battles due to wounded furloughs.

But Robert Edward Woodward didn't major in facts but in generalities. Striving to be the ultimate southern gentleman, he called every man "sire" and every woman "ma'am." He was a member of the strict Fairmont Baptist Church that tolerated no backsliding. Members with sharp eyes for records reported him several times for failing to attend as regularly as deemed necessary. Robert Edward

Woodward repented and the good folks reinstated him. He didn't tell us this historical tidbit; I found out later from the church records.

I also learned from those records that he was attending Fairmont Baptist Church when a young lady named Helen Blanche Weathersbee began to worship there with her family. Robert Edward Woodward and Helen Blanche Weathersbee began to see each other at church functions and were attracted to each other, but...

Helen Blanche Weathersbee and her sister and brother learned about a dance hall trying to get started and their curiosity got control of them. They went to see first hand this den of iniquity. That was bad enough, but then they danced and were spotted leaving the hall by the eagle eyes of a church matron. She reported this fall from grace to the deacons of the church who called the young people to task, examined their testimony, and revoked their membership.

This disturbed and disappointed Robert Edward Woodward. He was trying to walk the narrow line of the spiritual life demanded by the church because he had his heart set on becoming a deacon. Should he continue to see this disgraced young woman or look for a more spiritual life partner?

Helen Blanche Weathersbee and her brother and sister repented of their sins and the forgiving church reinstated them. So Robert Edward Woodward continued to see her. Then some members of the church left and organized the Pleasant Hill Baptist Church. Robert Edward Woodward became a deacon in the new church and married Helen Blanche Weathersbee. They had six children, including my grandmother.

Helen Blanche (Weathersbee) Woodward died in childbirth with her sixth child and was buried in Pleasant Hill Baptist Church Cemetery. Her mother, Elizabeth (Hankinson) [Weathersbee] McNab, is buried in another cemetery inside the bomb plant reserve. Robert Edward Woodward's house, the Pleasant Hill Baptist Church Building, and the Fairmont Church Building were all moved from the Savannah River Site, but none of these cemeteries were. All of the people are still resting in their original graves practically in the shadows of buildings and equipment used to produce tritium for the nation's hydrogen bombs.

TWO ELIZABETHS—DIXIE HEROINES GRANDMA MCNAB AND GRANDMA WOODWARD

When William Tecumseh Sherman's raiders came through our county, they visited homes of many of my ancestors. Great-grandmother Julia Youngblood, nee Herbert, was in labor with my grandfather, James Thomas Youngblood, so they spared her house. Samuel M. Youngblood, her husband and my great-grandfather, was in service at the Augusta, Georgia Arsenal.

Delilah Weathersbee, nee Green, my great-great-great-grandmother was still living on her farm. So were others, like Eleanor Mims, nee Brown; Sofie Hutson, nee Etheridge; Louisa Jowers, nee McDonald; Cynthia Bell, nee Jowers; Sarah Woodward, nee Folk; and Sarah Hankinson, nee Blewer, but I have no information on their experiences with the Blue Horde.

When we were children, we hated William Tecumseh Sherman, but we didn't know why. We never did hate him as much as Mama did because we never met anyone who saw what the red-bearded general did to our people. Mama had first hand information on what he did because she had visited and talked to both Grandma McNab and Grandma Woodward. These two heroines faced Sherman's blue-garbed thieves when they came to Barnwell County. The conclusion was that they had run out of Confederate men to kill and mistreat so they took it out on the women.

Grandma McNab was born Elizabeth Hankinson and when she was about seventeen she married Dr. Wyatt Weathersbee who caught some disease from a patient and was too weak to go to the army as a surgeon. They had eight children, one of whom was Helen Blanche Weathersbee, my great-grandmother.

One of Elizabeth's brothers, Glen Hankinson, went to the war and came back alive. Dr. Wyatt died soon after the war, and his widow married Reverend James McNab and that's why she was called Grandma McNab. She died in 1916.

Sherman came up from Savannah in several columns of blue-clad troops. The one that came to Barnwell County crossed the Savannah River and assembled at Robertville, South Carolina. Confederate General Hardee evidently thought this wing would have a difficult time crossing the Salkehatchie River Swamp so he tried to stop the other wings. But the corps out of Robertville moved rapidly through the swamp and came to Barnwell Courthouse in two weeks' time.

After bullying the Barnwell women, forcing them to meetings and dances, Sherman's heroes split, one group moving on Blackville and the other in a feint toward Augusta. The latter force went into Rosemary Township where both Grandma McNab and Grandma Woodward lived.

Grandma McNab was the sole defense of her invalid husband and young children, but she was unsuccessful. The blue coats stole all the food they could carry and destroyed the rest. Grandma McNab had grits and flour stored but the Yankee soldiers delighted in mixing it with dirt and barnyard filth. They poured the cane syrup on the ground and stirred it with sticks. Subsequent writings (to mitigate these war crimes) indicate that the blue bellies left enough food for the families to live on. Grandma McNab and Grandma Woodward both said that was just a Yankee lie.

The raiders drove off Grandma McNab's cow and caught the few pigs and chickens the small subsistence farm depended upon. General Wheeler of the Confederate Cavalry had already taken the horse and mule, but at least he left a receipt. He was not engaged in war crimes.

Grandma McNab said the Yankees threatened to burn the house, but they didn't because her husband at the time, Dr. Wyatt, was inside confined to a bed. The Yankee patrol moved on but others followed. They became angry when Grandma McNab told them everything was gone or already destroyed. They didn't believe her but nine or ten waves of blue uniforms belonging to the Grand Army searched the house and did further damage. They all finally marched off.

Grandma McNab told these stories and instilled in Mama an uncharacteristic hatred. Mama had a warm heart, liked people, and loved most of them, but Helen Gladys Jowers Youngblood died thinking the worst swear word or nastiest adjective or most vulgar comment possible was spelled

S-H-E-R-M-A-N.

Mama also told us stories about the Yankees that visited Grandma Elizabeth Woodward a few miles away. She faced the same blue raiders that came stealing, destroying, and ruining things. Grandma Woodward couldn't even save her house. The Yankees learned her husband, Private John Ardis Woodward, served in Company E, 1st(Hagood's) Regiment, South Carolina Infantry. So the house was torched as were the barns and stables.

This great-great-grandmother managed to support herself during the war by operating Woodward's Mill, a small water powered gristmill. The Yankee officers ordered the dam blown up so the mill could not be used and they could pick up the fish when the pond emptied. Grandma Woodward stood on the dam and told them to go ahead and blow it up. She would die, but she would starve anyway without the dam and the mill. The gallant marauders backed down.

Grandma Woodward died in 1927 at the age of 89. Mama visited her often and piled high her hatred for William Tecumseh Sherman. Like I said, I don't care for him either.

PART TWO

JASPER COUNTY MEMORIES OF BEE'S CREEK (1) THE WALL PLACE ON BEE'S CREEK
1938–1940

GUIDE TO THE MEMORIES

THE MEMOIRS	PAGE NUMBER
THE SOUTH CAROLINA LOW COUNTRY: THE PEOPLE AND THE SETTING	123
THE FLOWING WELLS	125
RIDGELAND SCHOOLS	126
THE JOE LOUIS FIGHT	127
THE HURRICANE	129
FISHING ON SUNDAY	131
RIDING THE MULES	133
AUNT ESSIE AND THE REPUBLICANS	136
THE WAMPUS CAT	137
CORA AND THE WHITE DOG	138
MY CORN AND HOG PROJECTS	139

THE SOUTH CAROLINA LOW COUNTRY: THE PEOPLE AND THE SETTING

My father's many attempts to start businesses in Elko had all failed by mid-1938. Then he got a chance to try again in the Low Country, but we had to move. It was sad for us all. My father and mother left Barnwell County, the only place they ever knew as home. Joe was in the fifth grade, I was in the fourth, Richard had just begun the first grade, and Helen was four years old. We left friends and relatives, but Big Lang, Nell, and Lang, Jr. Roland moved with us.

We moved seventy-five miles south to a farm on Bee's Creek in Jasper County between Ridgeland and Coosawhatchie, South Carolina. The place encompassed about 375 acres and more than half was wooded. My father was to manage the farm for Raymond Pender for a small salary and twenty percent of the profits.

We experienced culture shock especially in the way people talked. This was "Geechee" country where the water smelled like rotten eggs and the speech, strongly influenced by the Gullah Negroes of the sea islands and the tidewater, was almost unintelligible. Even when we understood the words, the local idioms and expressions were foreign to us. At first we felt like outsiders because we didn't talk "Geechee," but that dialect is easy to fall into and we were soon as comfortable with it as the natives.

We missed our friends and kin and always looked forward to trips back "up home" to Elko where we visited Uncles Norman and Clint and their families as well as old friends. But we soon enjoyed the new and different things in Jasper County. We took the bus to Ridgeland for school. We went there in the Model A Ford pickup truck on Saturdays for shopping and the picture show. We could fish in salt water and play on Civil War artillery embankments on Bee's Creek. The land we lived on and worked was near three Civil War battlefields: the Battle of Ocean Spring, the Battle of Honey Hill, and the skirmish at Bee's Creek Hill to delay Sherman after he entered South Carolina.

We had moved but it was still a time of poverty and apprehension. The Great Depression had dragged on during Hoover's and Roosevelt's term and neither the Republicans nor the Democrats had any idea what to do about it. We were then immersed in Roosevelt's alphabet soup of more than twenty organizations of his

New Deal known to most only by acronyms as he tried to implement the NRA (National Recovery Act).

Jobs were scarce and some men went to work for the Works Projects Administration (WPA) and some younger ones enlisted in the Civilian Conservation Corps (CCC). Even my father got into the soup with a job with the Rural Electrification Administration (REA), and the farm Mama inherited in Barnwell County was affected by the Agricultural Assistance Administration (AAA).

Scarier than the Depression were sounds of war from Europe as Hitler and Mussolini continued to gain power. Nobody wanted to talk about the vague but frightening revelations of Japan's naval buildup in the Pacific. But Roosevelt promised there would be no war because his dog and wife hated war and promised that things would get better. That was plausible—they couldn't get any worse.

THE FLOWING WELLS

When we arrived in Jasper County, the greatest obstacle to happiness on the Bee's Creek place was the strong smell of the water. We walked around holding our breaths and our noses. The artesian water contained sulfur compounds and perhaps a little hydrogen sulfide or something. Anyway it stank. We could smell it a hundred feet away. It was bad enough at a distance, but we had to drink and bathe in the stuff. Joe said it was punishment for leaving Elko.

I didn't know what I had done worthy of such chastisement, but it made me look at what I was doing. Was I obedient to my parents? Was I honest? What was I doing wrong? Whatever it was, I was ready to denounce it and lead a better life.

But after a while, we got used to the water and drank it as readily as water "up home" as we called Grandma's place near Elko. Mama was the first champion of the water—it came from hundreds of feet underground so frogs couldn't contaminate it like they did the well on Grandma's place.

The hand pump for household water for the old colonial house was originally on the walkway to the detached kitchen, but my father installed a new one in the new kitchen when he built it. One of the things I never got straight in my mind was why the water at the house didn't flow like so many artesian wells in the area. The flowing well at the creek produced a strong flow and the one on Oakhampton Road trickled a steady stream as did neighboring flowing wells.

Visitors from "up home" didn't like our water. Mama boiled the smell out of it and made tea for them, but Math Bolen liked it. He could never get enough of it. He carried some back home as people did at Healing Springs in Barnwell County and Math lived only four miles from Healing Springs.

RIDGELAND SCHOOLS

When we moved to Jasper County, we were six miles from Ridgeland, the county seat. The county had three schools, the largest being in Ridgeland. We were on Mr. Russell Cooler's school bus route that took us to Ridgeland. Joe and I entered the Ridgeland Grammar School and Richard went to the Ridgeland Elementary School.

Mr. Russell Cooler was a one legged man who had a wooden limb to walk on and he did well on it. He was a conscientious bus driver and at least twice that I know about, he went back in his car for children left because they didn't show up on time at the bus loading spot.

When we moved to Ridgeland, Joe entered the fifth grade, I enrolled in the fourth, and Richard was in the first grade.

THE JOE LOUIS FIGHT

We lived six miles from Ridgeland but many black people on Bee's Creek lived several miles farther. They had local rural stores where they did most of their shopping. They didn't buy much—if they had rice, they could subsist with fish, oysters, and shrimp. They were skilled at wrestling a living from nature on the tidewater. They were as mistreated as the people in Barnwell County but better able to cope because of the saltwater food treasures. Their standard of living was far below that of the white population, but they had each other, plenty to eat, and a racial champion—Joe Lewis.

Joe Louis was the heavyweight champion of the world when we were growing up and he was the hero of most black people. People today have other boxing heroes, but many believe that Joe Louis was better than any of them. Some of his fights went less than a minute before he had knocked out his opponent.

"Joe Louis hits like a mule kicks," Lang said.

Sometime in 1939, Louis had a major fight that was to be broadcast by radio. The black people got word and on the night of the fight they flocked to Buckner's store.

Buckner's store stood at the fork of the Coosawhatchie, Old House, and Ridgeland Roads, an out of the way branch of unimportant roads. In early days, however, it was a junction of such importance that it was the scene of several Revolutionary and Civil War battles.

Mr. Buckner and his wife Bea ran a grocery store and sold gasoline to the few people who owned cars. He had a good trade among the black people who had no way to get to Ridgeland or Coosawhatchie to shop. It was usual for them to crowd around the store on Saturday, but the Joe Louis fight was on a weeknight.

The black people flocked to the store anyway because they were all excited about the fight. For weeks before the fight, it was the prime subject of discussion among black people. I listened to Lang and the other black workers make jokes and share anecdotes about Louis. One of them involved the German boxer Max Schmeling who had beaten Louis earlier, but in a return match Louis defeated him soundly in 1938. The story said Schmeling was on a train approaching town and the conductor went through the cars announcing the train's arrival in St. Louis. Schmeling, the story goes, sprang from his seat and ran to jump off the train. "Why did you jump off the train?" a man asked. "Why didn't you wait until it got to St. Louis?"

Schmeling was still breathing hard. "I thought the conductor said Joe Louis."

Louis had been the champion since he won the title from Jimmy Braddock in 1937. I don't remember the boxer who fought him that night in 1939, but most white people wanted him to win and the black folks wanted Louis to remain champion. The black people came to hear the contest because none of them had a radio and Mr. Buckner would turn up the volume so everybody in the store and a few outside could hear.

In due time, the fight started and the black people listened with interest and enthusiasm. I don't believe my father or mother cared anything about boxing, but they were doubtless pulling for the white man. That was not to be. With a minute still remaining in the first round Joe Louis knocked out that contender. The blacks were delighted but then felt cheated. Some of them had walked six miles to hear a fight that didn't go a single round. They looked confused, happy, but sorry the fight didn't last longer. They slowly drifted away and walked home.

THE HURRICANE

In September of 1939, a vicious hurricane blew through the Bee's Creek area. The government had poor forecasting equipment and methods in those days, and even if they knew it was coming, we would still have been unaware of it because we didn't have a radio.

My father went casting with a friend for shrimp the night the storm came in. The shrimp evidently moved ahead of the blow because the shrimpers filled their tubs quickly. Then they came home in the heavy rain that preceded the hurricane.

Joe, Richard, and I were asleep upstairs when we heard a crack. It must have been lightning. It woke us and we heard the wind howling and rain pounding on the windows. The old house creaked and groaned. We shivered and tried to sleep through it.

In the morning, the furious wind was still blowing. We went to the windows to see the damage. None of the buildings were down, but a large tree had been blown down on the rear of the house over the dining room area where we kept the kerosene powered Servel refrigerator. We were fortunate—the roof didn't leak. We had plenty of stove wood in the house so Mama could cook my father's great catch of shrimp.

We ventured outside in the rain and wind to see if the livestock and farm implements survived. We were thankful they had. Joe ran under a shed to check on something for my father and stayed there only a few minutes. Just as he left that shed collapsed under a gust. The mules were terrified but they were unhurt. They were standing in a foot of water but the roof of their shed had not been removed.

Then a lull came. We thought the storm was over, but we were in the eye of that hurricane. When the winds blew again, Mama fried shrimp and I thought I would founder on them because they were so good. We had only graham crackers for dessert because my father had bought a box of them at Crosby's store in Coosawhatchie for some reason.

The hurricane seemed stronger when it blew from the opposite direction. We watched the wind snap trees like matchsticks. Limbs broke off and sailed across the yard away from the house, thank Goodness. We had several pine trees in the front yard and they were all lost. The live oaks withstood the winds better, and the old house came through with minimal damage—only that caused by the falling tree.

We stayed inside waiting for the winds to stop. We were totally ignorant of the welfare of even our nearest neighbors, the Buckners, who operated a store about half a mile down the road.

Late that afternoon, the winds diminished and we went out again to see the damage. The front yard was full of tree debris. My father wanted to let the mules and cows out, but we had to help him repair the broken wooden fences before the animals could be let out.

We had an old tractor with which my father pulled the trees off our road to the county road in front of the house, but it did no good. The quarter mile stretch to Buckner's store was blocked with more than twenty huge oak trees. We were isolated. Thank goodness we had a lot of shrimp.

In a few days county workers pulled the trees from the road and we were able to go to Ridgeland. But the hurricane had changed the area. The old timers said the hurricane ruined the fishing in the area. They said it was never as good again, but I didn't hear of any serious injuries or deaths.

FISHING ON SUNDAY

When we lived at Bee's Creek, one of my father's friends, Jack Roberts and his wife Mary, came to stay with us for a while. Jack was working with a stump turpentine company that was digging up stumps from trees harvested many years before. The stumps had become resinous with time and they were collected for the contained pine spirits.

My parents gave the Roberts the two upstairs rooms in our old house on Bee's Creek. For that period, Joe, Richard, and I found places to sleep downstairs.

Mary was a thorn in Mama's side. She was from the Columbia area and was always wanting to go home to her people. She moaned all the time. Once in a while she would help cook. It was always disastrous and Mama didn't like disasters in her kitchen.

That winter when we killed hogs, Mama went about making her sausage and liver pudding the way she had been taught and the way we knew would give us many delicious meals. Mary made one of her rare offers to help and Mama let her mix the sausage. Somehow Mary mistook turmeric for sage and mixed the pickle ingredient into the sausage. Mama was ready to make sausage out of her, but she kept her composure.

Jack and Mary liked Joe and me, but not Richard. I never learned why they didn't like him. He was only seven or eight at the time and he was a busy but not a bad boy. Jack and Mary took Joe and me to the picture show once to see the Cisco Kid, but Richard couldn't come. That added to Mama's reason to dislike the Roberts.

Mary was quite religious but I don't know what church she was associated with. In her catechism or rulebook or twisted persuasion, fishing on Sunday was a mortal sin. Work seemed to be all right because her husband got money for that, but fishing on Sunday was a sure ticket to hell.

Jack's job involved blowing up old stumps for the contained turpentine and that gave him access to dynamite. He had heard about shocking fish with dynamite and he had decided to try it. He asked my father to help him, but he always found a reason not to do that. My father was not above bending the law, but dynamiting fish was too much for him.

One Sunday afternoon Jack and Mary asked Joe and me to ride down to the creek in their Model A Ford sedan. Mary was good-natured that day and she was friendly to us. She gave each of us a Dope—that's what everyone called the Coca-

Cola beverage so popular in those times. She talked and joked with us, and I began to feel that maybe Mama was wrong about Mary.

But Jack was not taking part in these pleasantries. He was working on something behind the car. We had seen him put a croker sack in the back seat with us, but we didn't know the sack contained dynamite. He had stolen some of the explosive with detonation caps and a length of fuse. When Mary called him to come for his Dope, he said he would in a few minutes. Then we saw him walking to the bank with a stick of dynamite armed with a detonation cap and a length of fuse.

Then Mary began bawling. "Don't do that on Sunday, Jack. It's a sin to fish on Sunday."

Jack stood on the bank and told her and us to stay back. Mary was yelling her sadness by this time begging him not to fish on Sunday. "Let's go back to the house, Jack. Don't do this, Hon."

He ignored her. Joe and I were uncomfortable and afraid. "What if it blows up when he's still holding it?" Joe asked me in a whisper.

I didn't know but Jack knew what he was doing. He lit the fuse, held the stick in his hand for a few moments, and tossed it out into the creek as far as he could. We stood there with our mouths open and Mary was choking on her sobs.

A tremendous explosion blew water up from the creek and we got sprinkled with it even on the bank. When the water settled, Jack looked about for the fish and we did, too. We didn't see a single one. Jack stood there looking disappointed. "Well, all right. Let's go."

He drove us back home and Mary cried all the way. When we got home, she rushed through the house to the stairs and went upstairs still weeping for her hellbound husband who had fished on Sunday.

RIDING THE MULES

In addition to an old truck, an old tractor, and a pickup truck, Raymond Pender provided four mules for my father's use for the truck farming operations. Truck farming referred to agriculture devoted to growing things for human consumption like vegetables and melons rather than things like oats and corn for the animals and cotton. The 4-H Club distinguished farm products as food, fodder, and fiber. Now we were involved in food production. Truck farming required precise plowing for things like asparagus, cabbage, and tomatoes, so my father had to have men who were skilled with plows.

Two black families had moved from Elko with us to Bee's Creek. One was the Roland family—Big lang, Nell, and Lang, Jr., but I don't remember the other family's name. The unremembered father and two sons also worked on Pender's truck farm. All were good plowmen and good workers. They could handle a single mule or a pair for jobs needing extra power like breaking the soil.

Joe and I watched the younger men ride the mules to and from the fields and we wanted to ride, too. One day, Joe looked at me with his look that meant he was determined to do something. "Let's go to the field and ride back with them."

We did and it became a regular thing. We sat behind the young plowmen on the mules, held them about their waists to hang on, and rode bareback to the stable. When we got there, Richard was begging to ride. "You too little," Joe said.

After a while, riding double was no longer thrilling—we wanted to ride by ourselves, but Mama would not hear of that. We would have to sneak it.

One Saturday afternoon when my father, mother, and Helen went to Ridgeland to buy groceries, Joe got that look. "Let's go ride one them mules."

I agreed and Richard wanted to ride also, but again Joe told him he was too small. We picked the mule that Lang had always said was the gentlest and least likely to bite. We wanted to avoid that because a mule bite could be serious and impossible to hide from Mama. Deciding which mule to ride was the easy part. The next thing we had to do—and we had never done it before—was to bridle the mule. We soon saw that other things had to be done first. We had to get the mule into the stable because there was no way to put a bridle on a mule in the pasture where it was grazing with its companions. It was their time off, too. But it was Saturday afternoon and we three boys were the sole humans on the place. The black people had also gone to Ridgeland for groceries and socializing.

We tried to drive the one we wanted into the lot in order to entice it into the stable with some corn, but we had not yet learned that mules without a bridle are almost wild things. They like their freedom and they don't like to be driven. Neither do they like to be separated from their own kind. Each time we tried to get it through the gate into the lot, it bolted away from us.

"We got to wait for feeding time," Joe said. "Daddy told us to feed the mules, the hogs, the dogs, and the cow. When that mule's in the stable, we can put the bridle on."

But feeding the cow meant we would also have to milk the cow while she ate. Feeding time was at sundown so by the time we did all the chores, it would be too dark to ride. We saw no way to ride that day so we decided to go to Bee's Creek and fish from the dock and the bank. We gathered the poles and the hooks, lines, and sinkers. Then all we needed was bait and the stable floor was a good place for worms because they loved the manure.

We went to the stable with a hoe and a tin can for worms, but as we entered the open gate, we saw that the mules had come back and each was in its own stall eating hay. Joe shut the doors and sent me for a bridle. "Get that small bridle. This mule has the smallest head so it must be the one."

I found the bridle and brought it to Joe. He stepped inside and the mule shied away. "Hand me some shelled corn," he said.

The mule ate the corn from the feed trough and Joe got the bridle in its mouth as it was licking up the last grains. We left the other mules in their stalls to keep them from exciting or disturbing the one we were trying to ride. "Pull the mule up to the fence so I can get on," Joe said.

"Let me ride first," Richard said.

We ignored Richard again and I held the mule while Joe got on. "Now give me the reins."

Joe clucked the mule out into the pasture and it went at a slow walk. It didn't want to leave the stall and its friends. I followed while Joe walked it around the pasture for a few minutes.

"I can ride better'n that," Richard said.

Then Joe decided to run. He clucked again and kicked the mule's sides and it broke into a slow trot. After a few minutes, Joe walked her back to us. "Here," Joe said. "You can have this dern mule. It's shaking the dern life out of me."

"Can I ride now?" Richard asked.

We didn't even acknowledge his question, but led the mule back to the fence where Joe held it while I got on its back. I was scared but I had to act like I wasn't. "Give me the reins, Joe," I said.

I walked the mule out into the pasture and walked it around like Joe did. Then it was time for me to run so I clucked and kicked its sides like Joe had with one exception—the mule's head was pointed to the stables not away as it had been for Joe.

The mule leapt forward and almost ran from under me, but I managed to hang on. The mule gave me the run Joe wanted. I was scared so I pulled back on the reins, but it made no difference to the mule. It was going to the stable and to its friends. It was running fast but the ride was smooth so I began to enjoy the thrill. I was already thinking of bragging words to throw at Joe when I got back.

Then the mule made a sharp turn around a corner. I leaned away from the turn—the wrong thing to do. I went flying through the air and hit the ground hard. Joe and Richard came running up. "You all right?" Joe asked.

"I don't know," I said, "but it hurts."

"If its my turn," Richard said, "I'll skip it. Y'all just go ahead."

I was bruised and hurting but nothing was broken. That ended our riding until we moved to Turkey Hill.

AUNT ESSIE AND THE REPUBLICANS

Our Great Aunt Essie Messervey, daughter of Robert Edward Woodward, married, left Barnwell County, and went to live on Rutledge Street in Charleston. She inherited a large portion of her father's fantasies and pretense. When her husband died she also inherited the house and a lot of property and money. Despite her riches, she was the black sheep and shame of the family—she joined the Republican Party. To us, that was the party that nominated and elected Abraham Lincoln and started the War of Northern Aggression. To remind us, we had only to walk a few blocks from her house and look across the bay at Fort Sumter in Charleston Harbor. But Aunt Essie was a Republican and because of her husband, she was richer than the rest of us put together.

Aunt Essie drove her lemon yellow Packard all over the state campaigning for Wendel Wilkie in 1940. She visited us at Bee's Creek in the summer of that year only to be assaulted with jokes about her party like this one: the Democratic Donkey has turned traitor; he wears a Wilkie Button. You can see it every time he wags his tail.

Another joke was a boast Wilkie was supposed to have made to his wife on election day. "Darling," he said, "tonight you're going to sleep with the president of the United States."

"Oh, my," she said, "is infantile paralysis contagious?"

We didn't agree with her politics, but we all acknowledged her as a free spirit. She went all over the country sight seeing and saying she was a Republican from South Carolina. When the state finally went Republican she had the last laugh.

THE WAMPUS CAT

Several men in our county became so used to exaggerating hunting stories they couldn't tell the truth without lying. There were traditional stories like the snipe hunt for the witless newcomers, but in the Low Country there was a game bird called the snipe. That story could never fool anyone. But all neophyte hunters trembled at the stories of the dreaded Waumpus Cat that prowled the woods and swamp. The Waumpus Cat was reported to kill panthers for practice and it loved bear and alligator meat. The tales of the Waumpus Cat petrified beginners and made the bravest men tremble.

My father warned us about lying—it was still lying even if it was for fun—even if it was about hunting. My brothers and I heard the hunting stories and laughed, but we didn't laugh at the Waumpus Cat stories. My father said it was just a made-up prank to play on the unsuspected, but we weren't convinced. Then one night I decided to try to scare Joe and Richard.

We had been playing cowboys and Indians by gathering up broom sage or dog fennel, bundling the stalks into a "horse," straddling the bundle, and racing like the wind for each other. We were still outside playing when darkness came. I saw my chance, slipped away from them, and let out a howl like I thought the Waumpus Cat would make. WEEOWW. WEEOWW. Then I ran to another part of the field and did it again. I ran to do it a third time, but I didn't make it.

I ran into a single strand of barbed wire. It caught me in the mouth and threw me down on my back. At first I thought the Waumpus Cat had attacked me, but then I got up and found the wire and my cut mouth. Now I had something to support my prank.

I ran home and found Joe and Richard telling Mama and our father about the Waumpus Cat they heard. Then I came in bleeding at the mouth with a torn shirt and overalls. "It jumped on me," I said.

For a few moments I think even my father thought the monster had attacked me. Mama cleaned my mouth and put something on it. I still have a scar where the barbed wire ripped my lip. A few days later, my father gave me a whipping for claiming the Waumpus Cat attacked me because a lie was a lie.

CORA AND THE WHITE DOG

We took Cora, my father's bird dog, with us to Bee's Creek, but found few quail. Somewhere we picked up another bird dog, a white pointer. Cora was a setter, but my father said the dogs hunted well together. We never saw them hunt, but we had fun with these gentle dogs. They went with us all over the place on Bee's Creek.

They did the things expected of dogs like barking when strangers arrived until they were commanded to stop. They were good watchdogs, but they were on their own most of the time. They ranged throughout the place and perhaps beyond.

Cora was a smart dog and the leader of the two. One day we watched her sniff at a log almost submerged across a creek. She crossed tentatively and from our perspective we couldn't see the log so it looked like she was walking on water. She crossed and the white dog followed. Joe, Richard, and I bragged about our dogs walking on water until someone had enough. "Them sorry dogs don't know how to swim so they had to walk to get over the creek."

One day Cora ran to us in the backyard. She looked at us and whined, then took off running to indicate we should follow. We didn't understand until she had done the thing three times. We followed her for about a mile through the woods until she brought us to the white dog. It was trapped. One of its back legs was caught between two strands of barbed wire.

When the dog jumped over the wires, its back leg somehow went between the top two strands. When she went over, the strands closed on her leg. We released the white dog and she ran off together with Cora.

MY CORN AND HOG PROJECTS

When I was in the fifth grade, I joined the 4-H club and remained a member throughout my school years. Joe used to make fun of me about a song they sang about the club:

"Who dida, who dida join the 4-H? Who dida, who dida join the 4-H?"

He taught Richard the song and the two were always taunting me.

When I was in the fifth grade, I was supposed to have a 4-H project. In my ignorance and audacity, I selected corn—I would grow an acre patch of corn. I determined to keep the project a secret from my father and surprise him with my daring and hard work.

An unused field lay fallow about half a mile from our house on the Wall place. The field was too small for the tractor and my father never used it. I decided that was the place to plant my corn.

The farm was becoming mechanized and I couldn't find farming equipment that I could use. There was an old horse drawn plow on wheels and I decided to use it. It had been out in the weather a long time, so I tried to oil and grease it so it would move more easily or at least not make as much noise. My father saw me trying to get the thing ready. "What you doing?"

I had to tell him. "Getting ready to break land for corn for my 4-H project."

"Well, son, it's too late to plant corn this year. Our corn at the Frampton Place is already high as your head. You might make some corn stalks, but you won't make a grain of corn. Besides, you could work yourself to death and might get hurt with that old thing."

My father saw how disappointed I was and decided to let me choose the best looking acre of corn on the Frampton Place for my project. I would have to hoe it and put some nitrate of soda on it for a side dressing, but he would have it harvested with the rest of the field.

That presented another problem. I had already changed projects and selected four pigs to raise instead. My father was pleased with my interest in farming and let me do both. I had to feed the pigs twice a day and take care of the corn as noted. I kept records of how much feed I gave the pigs and how much fertilizer I put on the corn. Mr. Joe Graham was the county agent and volunteered to help the 4-H kids keep records. He came out to check on my projects from time to time.

I never saw corn I could call my own, but the pigs were a constant reminder of the projects. They had to be fed every day and Joe and Richard did as much as I did. They were never really my hogs, but my father let me have them for the project and for whatever money they would sell for.

The acre of corn I selected made eighty bushels. That was a good yield but nowhere near the winning levels. Several boys topped that. But the four pigs grew into large animals and each was given the top rating. My father sold the hogs for me with all of the others hogs and harvested my acre of corn with the rest in that huge field. We got $27.00 for the hogs and nothing but my records from the corn because it was never really my own.

We didn't get the money until we left Bee's Creek and moved to Turkey Hill.

PART THREE

MEMORIES OF BLACK MINGO CREEK TURKEY HILL PLANTATION
1940–1944

GUIDE TO THE MEMORIES

THE MEMOIRS	PAGE NUMBER
THE PEOPLE AND THE SETTING	145
THE ACCIDENTAL PADDLING	146
OUR FIRST CHRISTMAS ON TURKEY HILL	148
THE LONG STICK	149
FOLLOWING JESSE'S PLOW	151
PEARL HARBOR	152
COON HUNTING WITH MY FATHER	153
WASH DAY	155
MALARIA	157
MY FATHER AND THE RATTLESNAKES	158
DON'T GET ANY OF IT ON YOU	159
THE BELT LINE	161
THE FIRE ESCAPE	162
WASHING FERTILIZER SACKS	163
THE HOME FRONT	164
BANDOLIER'S PASSION	166
SAM FORD	169
THE BLACK MINGO FISHING HOLE	171
THE HEADLESS GHOST AT BLACK MINGO BRIDGE	174
MY FATHER AND THE CATFISH POND	176
JOHN NEWTON AND THE STALLION	178
HELEN AND THE TICK	180
THE AIRPLANE CRASH	182

COLLAPSE OF THE OLD BARN'S SECOND FLOOR 184
THE WAR COMES HOME 185
RETALIATION 186
TALE OF TWO HONEYMOONS 187
THE FBI INVESTIGATES ME 189
THE CLUB-FOOTED GUARD 192
THE DOUBLE-DOG DARE 195

THE PEOPLE AND THE SETTING

After my father left the employ of Raymond Pender, he worked about a year with the REA, the Rural Electrification Administration, one of the ingredients in Roosevelt's alphabet soup. It's one of the few that survived. But my father was essentially a farmer, so when county agent Joe Graham became superintendent of Turkey Hill Plantation and Cypress Woods Corporation, he asked my father to join him as foreman or manager and we moved to Turkey Hill. Guess what? Big Lang, Nell, and Lang, Jr. moved to Turkey Hill with us. Our only disappointment was that Lang, Jr. soon left home and went to Savannah to seek his fortune.

Turkey Hill/Cypress Woods Corporation was a huge place of about forty-five thousand acres. It stretched east to west from U.S. Highway 17 to U.S. Highway 278 and beyond and from a line somewhere south of Black Mingo Creek north to the Gillisonville Road. It was mostly second growth forest, the place having been clear-cut by the Savannah River Lumber Company before Jeremiah Milbank, Sr., a New York capitalist, bought it.

It was a fascinating place. Many cotton and rice plantations must have flourished on the place at one time or another because we found several home sites where only brick and broken glass remained. Several tram roads used by the loggers to haul logs ran through the forests and across swamps and creeks. Except for some obvious home sites under groves of live oak giants, the place had become a jungle. It was a great place for us boys to grow up.

THE ACCIDENTAL PADDLING

When we moved to Turkey Hill, Joe was in the seventh grade, I was in the sixth, Richard was in the third, and Helen had just started to school. We moved in the winter, and everything was the same in school as they had been when we lived on Bee's Creek except for the buses. We had to come and go home on a different bus that parked at a different place. School continued despite the upheaval of moving.

The principals of Ridgeland Consolidated Schools held assembly of all the pupils once a week. They brought in a visiting pastor from one of the churches to give us a short devotional. When we had sung a few traditional songs, we would watch a film.

Shortly after we moved to Turkey Hill, the principals arranged for showings of the American Chronicles of History films every week in the assembly.

One assembly day, I had a cold or something. It annoyed me and I wasn't interested in what the pastor said. I felt bad and had a bad cough so I couldn't sing. I was still looking forward to the film because I had an interest in history. I was just beginning to understand how the country was discovered, settled, and organized. High points were the Revolution and the Civil War because so much of each war had occurred in our state and county. But I had interest in other states as well, so when they announced that the film would be on the Jamestown, Virginia, settlement, I was excited. This was the first permanent English settlement in what became the United States. I waited through the singing for the film.

The movie began normally. The colonists came ashore, built the stockade and some log cabins inside. They planted corn and had a few skirmishes with the Indians. All went well to that point, but then the film slowed and the actors only talked. Although the dialogs were interesting to those of us who knew a little history, most of the pupils were of the IHHP (I Hate History Persuasion).

Interest in the film dropped and whispering began. Whispering grew into murmuring, and murmuring became shouts. It was dark for the movie and the boys thought they couldn't be seen. Soon they were calling hogs and shooing chickens and mooing like cows. Some used their hands to focus their yells and calls. So when I raised my hand to cover my cough several times, witnesses, probably teachers, thought I was yelling, too.

The principal stopped the film and turned on the lights. He announced that we had ruined the program. He would not show these films again.

We marched back to our homeroom classes where the boys who were spotted yelling and calling were brought before the class. My name was called and I protested my innocence. The boy who sat beside me in assembly supported my story, but his word was insufficient to stop the wheels of injustice.

I understand how it happened and I hold no bitterness, but I was not guilty. The boy admitted his guilt but testified to my innocence. "I hollered but George didn't."

I got a paddling anyway. Mrs. Miller, my sixth grade homeroom teacher, hit me across my bottom with two hefty swats and I felt them. Then it was over. She felt she had done her duty, and I knew I was caught up in something I could neither explain nor deny. I reasoned that things had balanced out. I had escaped detection on many things for which I was guilty and now my luck had run out.

OUR FIRST CHRISTMAS ON TURKEY HILL

We moved to Turkey Hill in 1940 when Joe was in the seventh grade, I was in the sixth, Richard was in the third, Helen was in the first grade, and Bob was a month old. It was about Christmas time, so my father took the check for the hogs I raised at Bee's Creek and applied it toward three bicycles for us boys. We got the bikes for Christmas and we were delighted. None of us knew how to ride and both Joe and Richard learned before I did. I remember getting so mad when the bicycle threw me down, I threw a brick at it and knocked off some paint. That paint scar always reminded me about my bad temper.

We used our bicycles to ride to the horse barn every morning in the wee dark hours to feed the horses. We had to use flashlights. I can still remember the animals. Daisy was in the first stall, then came Maggie, Annie, Nancy, Sonny Boy, Dan, Maud, Nellie, and a mean gelding whose name I don't remember.

When my father went by the barn during the day, he let the horses out so they could use the run down to the branch for water. Then in the evenings we had to feed them again. We liked doing this and we got paid fifty cents a week each, but one week's pay from each of us had to go toward paying off the bicycles Santa brought. Even so, we felt rich.

THE LONG STICK

Theodore Roosevelt's motto was: "Speak softly and carry a big stick."

If I were asked to write a motto for Big Lang, it would be similar. "Be careful and use a long stick."

Big Lang, Nell, and Lang, Jr. moved with us from Elko to Bee's Creek and then to Turkey Hill. They lived next door to Jesse and his wife. Jesse moved away after two years, but the Rolands were still on Turkey Hill when we left. Big Lang's chores kept him near the cattle barn and that was a good thing because we often needed him.

One day Joe spotted a large alligator walking the edge of the pasture just below our house. We knew alligators lived in the pools of the small streams in the swampy region about three hundred yards east of our house, but we never saw one on dry land before. He must have been migrating from one pool to another.

We called Big Lang who came armed with only an axe. That was enough because he killed that nine-foot gator with a few head blows. He took the gator home in a Jersey wagon, skinned it, and divided the meat with his friends. We had always respected Big Lang's strength, but now we admired his courage. It was hard to believe but I saw the dead alligator.

Big Lang was not only strong and brave, he was smart. He didn't take unnecessary chances and that became evident only a few days after he killed the alligator. Joe, Richard, and I were playing some kind of cowboy and Indian game, running all over the cow pasture in front of our house at Turkey Hill. Some large pine stumps from logged timber lay between the pasture and the woods. We came out of the woods running and chasing each other. I leaped up on a pine stump and then jumped off and sailed through the air. While I was still in the air, I saw a huge rattlesnake coiled beside the stump. Richard followed me but before I could warn him to avoid the stump, he was already on it and jumping off. He ran to where I was standing. "You see that snake?" he asked.

I nodded and we caught up with Joe and went to the barn for Big Lang.

"Rattlesnake, eh?" Big Lang asked.

Richard nodded. "He's all coiled up. We jumped right over him, but we didn't see him crawl off."

"Let me find me something to kill him with," Big Lang said.

I expected him to get a hoe, shovel, or rake to attack the snake, but that was evidently not what he wanted. Big Lang just brought his trusted axe. I was a little nervous, wondering if he was going to try to get close enough to chop the snake.

Big Lang had no such thing in mind. He went into the woods and cut down a small sapling and trimmed it into a pole about eight feet long. Now Big Lang had his long stick, so we went back to the spot where we saw the snake. It was still there, coiled. Big Lang brought down the pole on the snake with great force and probably fatally wounded it. The thing tried to strike, so Big Lang let him have another blow. It twisted and tried to strike again, but Big Lang stepped closer with the axe and chopped off its head. "Now y'all be careful. Plenty snakes out here and I might not be here next time."

In the years we were at Turkey Hill, we often got into trouble and often found ourselves in danger, but Big Lang was always somewhere close at hand.

FOLLOWING JESSE'S PLOW

Turkey Hill Plantation had several large-tired Farmall tractors and an Allis-Chalmers crawler tractor for soil preparation and cultivation. But for some crops, the tractors packed the soil too hard, so my father used the old fashion methods on those fields. The plowmen had to first break ground with a sodbuster, then come back later when the uprooted grass was dead and rake it up. Then it was time for the harrow to level the field. Then with another plow point, the plowmen formed the beds and furrows.

Several of the hands on Turkey Hill were skilled with the plow, but none so skilled as Jesse was. He made it look easy but I knew it wasn't. I tried several times and I couldn't concentrate on the plow's orientation and the direction of the mules. These things were effortless for Jesse. He plowed a straight row as if he were taking a stroll and he never seemed to tire.

We did a little fishing in those days so I liked to follow Jesse with a can to get upturned worms. He also turned up many stones, glass fragments from previous occupants, and sometimes an arrowhead. Everyone teased me for walking behind the plow, but I got good worms that way and found a few arrowheads. The other things were probably interesting objects, too, but not to me.

Jesse and I became a team. When he went to plow, I went to his field to follow if I could. We talked and he told me things. I always brought him cool water on my bicycle. One thing he mentioned was how much he liked turtle meat. He called it "Gopher meat." After that, whenever I saw a large turtle, I picked it up and carried it to Jesse in my bicycle basket.

PEARL HARBOR

Sundays in our house on Turkey Hill were lazy, peaceful times, interrupted only by going to feed the horses. Mama always had a great meal on Sunday and we ate too much and waited for time to "feed up." December 7, 1941, was such a Sunday. We had a radio, but we didn't turn it on until after supper to conserve the battery. Then my father would listen to the war news from Europe with Edward R. Murrow and we could listen to Lux Theater, Mr. District Attorney, and finally to Walter Winchell's commentary.

That delay caused us to learn the Japanese attacked Pearl Harbor about six hours after it happened. My father said nothing. He just kept staring at the radio and listening, so we knew it was serious. I don't think he said a thing before he went to bed, but his eyes radiated what we felt. What now? Are we ready for this? What will we do now? What will Japan do next?

We weren't ready and we didn't know what to do, but President Roosevelt asked for and got a declaration of war against the Empire of Japan. The Japanese kept their lightning assaults going, striking in China, Singapore, Malaysia, and the Philippines. Within days they were sweeping through the island chains of the Pacific like locusts until they reached New Guinea and threatened Australia.

A few days after we declared war on Japan, Hitler and Mussolini declared war on us. So now we were in it up to our necks. We were unprepared, and our enemies looked so strong. We were scared.

COON HUNTING WITH MY FATHER

The war made everything scarce, and rationing became a way of life. The federal Office of Price Administration (OPA) instituted and regulated rationing of food, rubber, gasoline, and fuel oil. Some items like cocoa and sugar were almost impossible to find even when you had ration stamps. Red food stamps enabled us to buy meat, cheese, and butter. Blue stamps permitted purchases of canned vegetables, fruit, and things like catsup and mustard.

We raised our vegetables and hogs so meat was not a problem for us. We canned a lot of fruit, so Mama got extra sugar. Gasoline was not so much of a problem because farming was considered an essential occupation. Things not rationed, like flashlight batteries, were sometimes the hardest things to find. Shotgun shells and .22 caliber bullets were usually available, but not .30 or .303 cartridges.

The price of animal skins went sky high for some reason, and my father wanted to go coon hunting. Joe begged off every time he asked, but I was always in trouble with my father so I agreed to go to make up for my sins. He was a forgiving man and this made us pals again.

With no flashlight, we had to do it the way he learned as a boy. We would use "fat lightard" or fat lightwood from resinous pine stumps. He carried his rifle and the dog leash and I carried a bag of fat lightard over my shoulder. We both wore mud boots because we were going into the swampy woods off Black Mingo Creek about a mile downstream from the bridge.

Once in the woods, he released the dogs and they dashed away sniffing for a coon scent. After a few minutes, we heard barking and the chase was on. The dogs followed the trail through the swampy woods making a "ruff" with every step. Finally the dogs' barking became slower paced and more earnest. "They got him treed," my father said.

We arrived at the tree a few minutes later and my father took one of the lightard splinters from the bag and lit it. "Hold it high as you can," he said.

He backed off looking for the coon's eyes and the dogs kept barking. My arm was getting heavy and still he walked around trying to get a glimpse. Then he stopped, aimed, and fired, and we heard the coon crash through the tree limbs and hit the ground with a thud.

My father picked up the coon and carried him by the hind legs. "Why don't you carry him by the tail, Daddy?" I asked.

"Tail might break off. Buyers don't want the hide without the tail."

We followed the dogs trying to get another coon, but they didn't tree another one. We walked out of the woods with our prize.

My father skinned the coon and tacked the hide on the side of the smokehouse to dry and took the meat in to Mama. She squinted and turned up her nose. "You want me to cook that thing, Cecil?"

He nodded, Mama sighed, and she roasted it like a turkey with dressing. I ate some and it was not bad, but there were many other things I would rather eat. My father enjoyed it and made a pig of himself.

He later sold the skin for five dollars.

WASH DAY

The school bus driver let us out at a point just west of the barn complex and we had to walk across two cattle guards past the barn then a hundred yards to the house. Our cattle guards were bridge-like coverings over a dug trench with two-inch thick boards spaced on edge two inches apart. Cattle wouldn't go near it because their feet would slip between the boards, but tires and shoes bridged the gaps and made it easy to cross.

We always approached the house with apprehension because once a week Mama met us with the news that it was wash day. While we ate our snacks, she gave us the assignments. "Joe, fill up the wash pot and get a fire started under it. George, you pump them tubs full of water."

Living with Mama made wash day an afternoon of hard labor. Living out in the country was hard, but Mama insisted on clean people and clean things. So Joe carried water from the pump to the wash pot while I placed and filled three No. 3 galvanized tubs on a stout bench my father had built between two pine trees. That bench was used for many activities like hog killings, watermelon cuttings, or just playing or sitting. But today there was no hog to kill, no watermelon to cut, and no time to play or sit. It was wash day.

When I had the water pumped, Mama came out with the scrubbing boards, soap, and that strong determination on her face to get the job done. First she soaked the colored and white clothes in different tubs lest the colors run. She added a little bleach to the white things. Then using some of Joe's hot water to temper the cold water and lye soap she made from hog fat the previous winter, we scrubbed the clothes with our knuckles and the balls of our fists against the scrubbing boards.

After the first wash, we had to wring the water from the clothes by hand and repeat the process. Then the colored clothes would be "wrenched" (rinsed) twice, wrung dry, shaken out, and hung on the lines. The white clothes got another soaking in hot water before being "wrenched" and hung out to dry.

Things became a little better when my father erected a water tank near an artesian well and used a hydraulic ram to fill it. Then we had running water, at least. Later Mama used Oxidol Soap or Super Suds washing powder and they seemed to clean better than the lye soap.

When we started to high school and played football, Joe and I were on the practice field when we would otherwise have been washing clothes. Then my father took the dirty clothes to a nearby woman who washed, dried, and ironed them for several dollars. One day when there was no other way, I took the dirty clothes in a bundle on horseback and two days later went the same way and brought back the clean clothes.

Wash day was unpleasant in many ways, not the least of which was the food. Mama was so busy she couldn't work her usual magic in the kitchen and we ate easily prepared things like grits and cheese or salmon balls.

I didn't like wash days.

MALARIA

I got my first malaria attack at Bee's Creek in the summer of 1939. It was a series of fever spells followed by chills, then more fever as my body tried to kill the parasite that was causing it. We knew mosquitoes caused malaria and tried to keep them out of the house, but some mosquito probably bit me when I was outside working, playing, or fishing.

My father drove to Ridgeland and bought some syrup of quinine because they didn't think I could swallow the capsule. The stuff worked and in a few days my nausea, chills, and fever were gone.

My next malaria attack came in 1942 when the U.S. Army, Navy, and Marines were striking back at the Japanese forces at Guadalcanal. Many thousands of American servicemen were serving in the jungles of the islands overrun by the Nippon onslaught. The Marines were fighting furious battles on Guadalcanal against a fierce enemy with deadly allies—malaria-carrying mosquitoes. The war effort took all the available quinine and sent it to these fighting men. No one could question that, but I had a serious attack.

It started one day about dusk when I went to the pasture to bring home the cows for the evening milking. That day they had gone to the far end of the pasture, and I had trouble finding them. On the way back the fever hit. This time I was older and I knew it was malaria. It came on me all at once. I became disoriented with the chills because I had no jacket or sweater. It had been hot when I left the house.

I couldn't see well and had trouble determining where I was. I remembered a story of a man who had to go through a rattlesnake-infested field. He, too, had been driving cows so he grabbed the tail of a cow and walked behind her to the barnyard. I tried the same thing and the cow brought me home.

It was too late to go to the drug store, so my father went to the hospital and asked for some quinine. They told him it was not available but they had some Atabrine, a substitute. He brought it home to me and it worked, but not as well as the quinine had. I had to take it for more than a week. By the end of the treatment my skin was orange, and we learned that was an undesirable side effect of Atabrine.

The armed services did not have enough quinine, either, so they also used Atabrine not only as a treatment but also to prevent the disease. I learned later they called the daily administration of the drug "the Atabrine cocktail hour."

I had malaria for four summers in succession. It ended in 1943 but I couldn't donate blood for many years when they learned that I had malaria as a child.

MY FATHER AND THE RATTLESNAKES

My father hated rattlesnakes but rattlesnakes loved Turkey Hill. That presented my father with many opportunities to express his hatred. If he saw a rattler, he would hunt it down and kill it. He took chances only a driven man would take, but he was driven. I don't believe his own efforts reduced the rattler population, but he had other weapons, the most effective being the hogs.

Mature swine are almost invulnerable to rattlesnake poison for several reasons, but I believe the slow absorption of the venom through the thick fatty layers beneath the skin is the principal reason. On the other hand, the rattlesnake has no defense against the hogs; swine love to eat them and any other snake, worm, or fish they can get. They can root up the snakes from their holes, so one of the first things my father did on Turkey hill was to get several hogs for his own use. He let them roam in a hog pasture near our house.

At the time, the patriotic Milbanks were considering ways to use the plantation for the war effort. My father suggested hogs. "They reproduce fast, they're ready for market at six months, and they are more efficient meat producers than cattle."

My father partially won the argument; Milbanks decreed that Turkey Hill would become a significant producer of both pork and beef. These ambitions were never realized because of tragic herd circumstances, but for a while we had plenty of hogs and no rattlesnakes.

Rattlesnakes were still abundant in the areas beyond the reach of the hogs, and Turkey Hill as an entity was still loaded with rattlers. When we went to town, we often saw rattlesnakes sunning themselves on the black macadam at the top on Black Mingo Hill, and if my father was along, we saw a snake die. One time he had only tire tools to use and we saw him kill a six-foot rattler with the foot-long jack handle.

When we went through the woods to Bee's Creek to visit Lonnie and Midget Givens who succeeded my father as Raymond Pender's manager, we would cross a section that my father said reeked of rattlesnakes. He stopped the car and told me to get a good smell of the thing. It smelled something like a wet goat, but I thought the smell was even worse. "That's probably a rattlesnake pilot. He crawls ahead of the rattler, but they both stink that way. I've killed three rattlers at this crossing."

Shortly after the hog project was terminated, my father left Turkey Hill. The rattlesnake was once again king over the whole domain.

DON'T GET ANY OF IT ON YOU

Farm work involved many unpleasant and dangerous materials that irritated the skin and offended the nose. There were no handbooks on worker safety in those days except age old common sense that said: "DON'T GET ANY OF IT ON YOU."

That advice was picked up and popularized in later years by Jimmy Dean, but this was years before Jimmy made music, movies, and sausage.

But the advice was and is sound. Neither Jimmy nor the ones before him specified what "it" was—over the years the warning was applied to many substances. This episode adds gasoline to the materials covered by the precautionary statement. DON'T GET ANY OF IT ON YOU.

This is about me. I didn't want to talk about it at first. Privacy is a right of everyone, but the first thing I learned from this experience was that we sometimes have to give up privacy for our own good. I sure didn't like it when the veil of privacy was lifted on me, but it had to be.

During World War II, gasoline was scarce, but we had enough on Turkey Hill to carry on the farm operations. I don't remember who I was with, why I was pouring gasoline, or what I was pouring it onto or into, but I spilled the stuff and got my whole front soaked with it. "Aw, it'll dry off in no time," someone said.

So I went about doing what I was doing. The wetted areas burned a little, but I paid no further attention to the spilled area until about two hours later when I had to urinate. I went behind the trees to keep from being seen and got the shock of my life. My member was swollen to about twice its size.

When this happened to me, we didn't have a bathroom at home, but we did have an enclosure where you could soap down and pour water over your body. I washed the area well, but it felt even more irritated after I washed it.

What a predicament. I was hurting and seemed to have a serious problem, but I was too embarrassed to say anything about it. I let it go hoping it would be normal the next day. It wasn't. It was more swollen the next morning. I had to tell someone and Mama was more sympathetic about foolish accidents than my father so I went to her.

"Mama, I got gasoline on me yesterday and it swelled up on me."
"What swelled up?"
"Where I spilled it."
"Where did you spill it?"

"On my stomach and it ran down."
"And it made your diddle swell up?"
"Yessum."
"Well, go get Cecil to look at it. He's working at the barn."

I had not avoided telling my father after all. He looked sheepish when I told him what happened. He was uncomfortable but he was a good father so he had to look. He told me to take down my pants so he could see. He took one look and shook his head. "Unh, unh, unh," he said.

He looked at me with a look I couldn't distinguish. I saw compassion for me, disappointment I had done such a stupid thing, and humor at the whole thing. But all he said was: "Unh, unh, unh."

We stood there looking at the ground and the things around us, but not at each other for a few moments. "Keep checking it during the day," he said. "If it ain't gone down by tomorrow morning, we got to take you to Dr. Ryan."

Next morning it was less swollen and the next day back to normal. I didn't have to let anyone see it again. It was quite an experience but I learned an important lesson—DON'T GET ANY OF IT ON YOU.

THE BELT LINE

A leather belt folded and doubled will separate into a loop when the two ends are held in one hand and pushed toward the middle held in the other hand. Then if the two hands are jerked apart, the belt will snap shut and pop.

That was the dreadful popping sounds we heard one day in September 1942. It signaled the freshmen boys to gather to run the gauntlet. The sophomore, junior, and senior boys had come together and formed parallel lines between which we had to run. Each of the older boys would take a swipe at our bottoms with his belt as we raced through. This was the terrifying Belt Line—the right of passage—our introduction into high school.

I didn't know if they were taking names to make sure every freshman boy went through, but I was tempted to hide. Some did hide but they were found and dragged to the dual lines of popping belts. I decided I had to brave the Belt Line, but I waited in the rear to see what factors might minimize the pain.

Some boys wore two pairs of pants for days because they knew someday the older boys would form the Belt Line. Others padded their backsides with towels and thick cloth to absorb the stinging blows, but there I stood with only my underwear and my thin trousers between my bottom and more than a hundred belts.

I watched my fellow victims run and observed that the rat-a-tat of the pops indicated their speed. The faster ones made the pops sound like woodpeckers, but the slower ones more like an old horse plodding along. The best response on my part was speed, so I ran as fast as I could. I was pretty fast but I don't know what my whacks sounded like when I ran—I was totally concentrated on the last boy in the line. I didn't feel many individual slaps. I think a few missed me, but I experienced pain for the few seconds I was in the Belt Line.

When I ran past the last belt, the thing was over for me. I had finished grade school and run the Belt Line. I was in high school and next year about this time I would be popping my belt to terrify the next class of freshmen.

THE FIRE ESCAPE

Ridgeland High School was housed in two buildings. The older high school building was joined by a second story corridor to the newer vocational building where they taught typing, home economics, woodworking, machine shop, and welding.

The fire escapes from the second floor were unique if not strange. If possible, we were to use the wide stairs to the first floor. If that was not possible, those in the old building had to go through the library, upstairs through a reference section, and out the backdoor to steel steps leading to the ground. The escape route presented several good opportunities for tripping and falling.

The fire escape on the opposite end of the vocational building was a slanted steel tube about three feet in diameter. Entrance to the escape tube was through a hole in the wall where they had installed a hand bar above the entrance. The escapee was to swing into the tube and slide down the chute to safety.

At recess we sometimes ran upstairs and slid down the fire escape tube. It was the best play equipment in the school, but it had its hazards. When the principal caught a boy, it usually meant two or three swats with the paddle. Perhaps worse was a prank devised and practiced by Henry Fickling and others. If Henry knew someone was coming down the chute, he would throw raw eggs up the chute and the person would slide though the broken egg mess. I got egged at least twice and had to wash the stuff off with cold water. I still spent the rest of the day in wet, stiff trousers.

Henry once egged the principal who was coming down to catch a boy for playing in the fire escape chute. Henry had already run away when he threw the egg so he was never found out. Henry was lucky that way.

WASHING FERTILIZER SACKS

Turkey Hill had large fields—one was one hundred and sixty acres and several were over fifty acres. When my father began the corn silage project, he knew he would need a lot of corn and planted many of these fields in corn. That crop takes a lot of fertilizer as did the sweet potatoes, green beans, and oats.

The fertilizer was delivered by rail on the plantation's Jericho Siding off the Atlantic Coast Line Railroad. Hundreds of bags containing two hundred pounds each came to Jericho. Transferring those heavy, clumsy bags on the rough floors of the boxcars and trucks without getting a tear was tricky business. The first bags on the boxcar had to be lifted, carried, and laid down gently on the truck bed. Once they had a layer of bags, the men didn't have to be as careful until they removed the last layer from the boxcar. Then when they unloaded the bags under the shed, they had to exercise care again.

My father had an outstanding offer to treat the crew to a cold beer each if they could unload a boxcar, take it to the shed, unload, and stack all the bags without a tear. He had to pay off several times.

The tractor drivers worked the fields into rows, distributing fertilizer along each row and covering it with soil. After a mellowing time, the corn or other crop was planted in the enriched row. These operations produced hundreds of fertilizer bags. Joe, Richard, and I were too young to handle the fertilizer bags and far too young to drive the tractors, but we had our job—washing the fertilizer bags.

We had several small creeks with enough flow to float the fertilizer away as we washed the sacks, but it was not easy to do in only three or four inches of running water. So when they drilled the large flowing wells, we were delighted. Two of these were ten-inch pipes that came out of the ground about four feet high and flowed about a hundred gallons a minute. They were ideal for washing fertilizer sacks.

All we had to do was turn the sacks inside out, hold the sack over the discharge pipe, and watch it to be sure the fertilizer was washed from the folds. Then we hung the wet sack on fences to dry. We got a penny for each bag we washed.

My father used the bags for shelled corn, threshed oats, and for wheat that came to Jericho Siding in bulk. He also used the sacks for hammer mill-ground corn and wheat. I don't know how many hundreds of sacks we washed while we were at Turkey Hill.

THE HOME FRONT

World War II was raging in Europe and the Pacific, but it was being felt at home. Every few weeks we heard of another Ridgeland man being involved in a major engagement. Rationing had become a way of life, but nobody complained. "There's a war on, don't you know?"

We had sailors at Pearl Harbor when the Japanese attacked. Some of our men served in North Africa and everyone knew the invasion of Hitler's Europe was just a matter of time. Many of our men served in the 8th Air Force that bombed the manufacturers of the German war machine. We had men who served on submarines and one who lost his aircraft carrier in the Battle of Midway. Another lost his carrier in the Battle of the Coral Sea.

Miss Mixon, our sixth grade teacher had a brother who was a belly gunner on a B-17 Flying Fortress in the 8th Air Force. She told her classes about it and the thing she was looking for—his twenty-fifth mission. When the men had flown twenty-five combat missions, they didn't have to fly anymore. They might even come home. To keep her class aware of the war and to remember her brother, Miss Mixon kept the class up to date on her brother's missions. She put up a chart with twenty-five lines, each representing a mission. When her mother got a letter from her brother telling them that he had completed another mission, she moved the marker to that point. The chart was the talk of the school from first grade to seniors and among teachers and coaches as well. We were all praying and pulling for Sergeant Mixon.

Meat, sugar, lard, and butter became so scarce we couldn't find these items to use our ration stamps. People learned to do without sugar and became acquainted with saccharin. Coffee was extended with chicory and more people than ever used Postum, a roasted grain that made a beverage similar to coffee. We collected aluminum, rubber, and copper junk items and sold them to dealers for the war effort. Steel and iron were even more critical. From our roving through the woods, my brothers and I knew where several old trucks, some large steel water tanks, and a boiler lay rusting. We sold them where they lay and they were recovered for reprocessing into war machines.

Our subsistence farming mode of the Depression years was again a way of life. We kept two cows, half a dozen pigs, several hundred hens, and planted gardens and patches for vegetables. As a consequence, we fared better than most. We even got extra sugar to preserve fruit.

On a social event in which the students had to bring sandwiches to be shared with each other, Mama boiled a ham and made about a dozen ham sandwiches. It was our own meat so I felt embarrassed because it was not purchased in the store, but the other boys and girls learned what it was and ate them all. I had to eat a peanut butter and jelly sandwich.

Gasoline was the most serious problem, but farming was considered essential and we got all we needed. Black markets sprang up. Gasoline stamps were available from several men in Ridgeland. Stamp prices were about the same as the price of the gasoline. The tractors on Turkey Hill were converted to use a fuel like kerosene that was colored green to distinguish it from red gasoline. Rubber was scarce and tires hard to get, but farmers were favored for those items as well.

We were learning to cope.

BANDOLIER'S PASSION

I have lots of memories of Black Mingo Bridge, but the most memorable event involved John Newton, a black man I must now introduce.

My father was manager of the livestock operations on Turkey Hill Plantation until 1943 when he went to the turkey operation. When my father first managed the livestock, Lang Roland was still his right hand, but he was made caretaker of the Milbanks' clubhouse and grounds. My father and all of us missed Big Lang, but John Newton replaced him and looked after my father's interest with the livestock with the same zeal Lang had shown.

John was a deacon in his church, but gossip said that when he was younger, John was a hellion. He got in many fights. In one, he got smashed in the mouth and suffered some permanent damage to his mouth and lips. As a consequence of the damage, when John smiled, his lips curled up and exposed his gums in the widest grin you ever saw. When John smiled, everyone felt better because no one could ignore that display of enthusiasm.

I often went with John to check cows in the remote pastures. I believed John wanted me along for someone to talk to. I was too young and inexperienced to be of much help, but he acted like he needed me. He taught me as we rode and I learned more about life from John than anyone else—even my father and mother because there were some things they wouldn't tell me.

One day we rode our horses along one of the old tram roads from the plantation's logging days. It crossed the swamp and gave us access to the distant pasture. It had rained recently and several puddles of water remained on the roadbed. All at once my horse, a mare John had named Annie, went down into one of the puddles. It was not a hot day so Annie must have been trying to stop a horsefly or something from biting her belly. At any rate, Annie went down, lay on her side, and trapped my leg. I looked back to John for help and saw that huge grin. Then I felt good and laughed, too.

John was good to me so I liked to please him. But when he came to me one day leading a young mare he had named Maud already saddled, I knew John wasn't in the joking or the teaching mood. He was dead set on some immediate project. "Little bull done busted the gate, broke out, and he headed for the wrong cows. Come on."

By little bull, John meant Bandolier, a prize Aberdeen Angus weighing about thirteen hundred pounds. He was little only when compared to the other bull, Black Cap, who weighed almost a ton.

My father had scheduled both bulls' romances, but Bandolier had his own agenda and John and I rode hard without speaking to make sure he didn't fulfill his intentions. We had to reach the bull before the herd's forward genealogy had to be rewritten.

When we closed on Black Mingo Bridge, John pointed to the bull in the creek cooling off. He laid out his strategy. "I go pop him on his rump with this here whip, and he go jump out the creek and head up the hill. You get ready to run up the hill and head him off."

John was expert with that whip. He practiced popping corncobs placed on fence posts and some of the other black men made bets on whether he could hit a particular cob. His admirers said John could pick horseflies on the horses without touching the horse. Maybe he could but I didn't believe it. I doubt if any of the horses would let him get that close with the whip. The noise as well as the pain made his whip feared among the animals.

When John popped Bandolier on the rump, he exploded out of the creek. I kicked Maud with both heels to go after him, but she balked at the bridge and reared up. While her front legs were still in the air, John cut her back legs with his whip. Transformed into Pegasus, Maud cleared the bridge in one leap. It was all I could do to hold on. I caught the bull, though, and turned him at the top of the hill. I looked back and knew everything was all right. I had turned the bull and my father wouldn't be upset. God was in His heaven and John Newton was smiling that huge smile.

I don't know if Bandolier felt thwarted, exhausted, or beaten. He walked slowly back to his pen where he was confined until the following week when my father had arranged a series of blind dates for him with another herd.

Bandolier was something to watch. I suppose he gained his awareness of cow receptivity by pheromones or something. If so, transmission and detection of the signal had to be sensitive. When I was around cattle, I got only one smell and everybody knows what that was. But I have seen Bandolier look up from grazing and stare across five hundred yards of pasture at the distant cows. By some means, he knew hours before the cow bellowed her mating call that she was coming into season. Then with his eyes fixed on his love target, he would speed across the space as fast as a horse to the poor cow who would run trying to avoid him. His weight slowed her and made her sag and that's all Bandolier needed.

But Bandolier's romances that autumn were tragic—the cows all aborted. Black Cap's offspring were born prematurely dead, too. One of the cows or bulls came to us with Bang's Disease, a contagious venereal disease caused by brucella abortis. It ended pregnancy in cattle, and it ended the lives of all our cattle because Black Cap and Bandolier had mated with one or more of the same cows, they had infected the whole herd. They were all sold for beef. That helped the meat shortage, but the cattle operation had to be started over.

Note: Joe remembered the event at Black Mingo Bridge as happening to him and he may be right, but the story is the same.

SAM FORD

The war was still going on and Miss Mixon's brother had completed thirteen missions. The cattle operation on Turkey Hill was growing again. The superintendent imported about a hundred cows from Colorado and bought two more prized registered bulls.

My father had planted plenty of corn for silage, but because of the war it was impossible to get metal or concrete silos built. He had to resort to hog wire and thick plastic cloth. That was his greatest asset to his employers—he could find a way to make things work and expected his workers—and his children to do the same thing.

He spread plastic cloth on the ground for a bottom and made a circular enclosure with the hog wire fencing. He arranged more plastic into walls for the silo by draping it over the fence and overlapping the bottom surface. Then a belt-driven machine chopped the stalks, ears, and leaves of the green corn into bits and blew them into the plastic lined fence.

When the level of silage reached the top of the section, a similar fence was wired to the one already filled, and also lined with plastic cloth. We went up five or six wire sections before we started another silo.

Tight packing was critical to silage curing and preservation so we needed heavy men to walk around and tramp the silage. My father knew an older black man, Sam Ford by name, who weighed about two hundred pounds. My father hired him that summer to pack the silage.

Sam Ford was eighty years old in 1942, so he was born a slave in 1862, in the middle of the Civil War. Of course Sam didn't remember the war, but he learned much about it afterwards.

Sam liked to talk and since I was a silage packer, too, we spent a lot of time together. He told me where all the plantations were on Turkey Hill and the surrounding area. Names like Jerico, Bashan, Roseland, Oakhampton, and others I can't remember came up. Sam said all the masters were good to the slaves except the largest plantation—Roseland. Good, I knew, was a relative term.

The Huguenin family owned Roseland Plantation as well as nearly three hundred slaves. Control of captive labor had been a difficult thing and the larger the operation, the harder it was. Consequently, slaves on the larger plantations faced more rigorous control measures than those on smaller plantations.

Roseland was about nine miles from Turkey Hill, but Sam Ford knew much about it. I wish I had talked more and asked more questions, but I was only thirteen when I saw him last.

THE BLACK MINGO FISHING HOLE

Black Mingo Creek is a small black water stream flowing through the southern part of Turkey Hill Plantation. An old wooden bridge, a deck of planks without rails, crossed the creek, and a sandy road approached the bridge down hills on both sides. Although the plantation lay on either side for miles, the road was even then public.

Fishing was pretty good from the creek bridge and even better on the banks. I never fished on the banks because of snakes and because alligators might be floating in the creek, but our black neighbors fished there all the time.

The local people, black and white, had many stories about the creek and the bridge—like the story about the depth of the creek. They said a deep, wide spot near the bridge had no bottom. They also said nothing would float in the water. I would never go swimming in that water because of the depth and the alligators. I didn't float or swim well even in regular water.

According to one legend the black people told about that part of the creek, a pirate ran there with all the gold he could carry. He was trying to escape from a treasure burying party on a saltwater river about six miles away. They caught him at the creek and began to strip him of the gold, but he tried to get away by jumping into the deep part still weighed down with gold. When the gold thief never came up, the story goes, the other pirates assumed the gold took him down.

The pirates found some slaves at a nearby cabin and ordered them to come and fish out the drowned man. The slaves told the pirates the creek had no bottom. "It go all the way down to hell and then some," an old black patriarch said.

One of the pirates got mad. "Look at this pistol, old man, and don't play with us. Now get what you need and come fish our friend out so we can bury him."

The old man picked up an old board and carried it with his rope and gator hook. When he got to the creek, he braided the rope end into the hook's eyelet. "Here," he said, "my arm weak with age, so one of y'all better try to hook him with this, but you ain't go find him."

They tried a few minutes, but hooked nothing. "Told you ain't got no bottom," the old man said. "Won't nothing float in it neither."

He threw the old board into the water and the pirates waited and waited, but it never came up. They gave up and walked away.

Some old folks claimed the Patriots and the Tories fought several bloody skirmishes at the bridge during the Revolution and others say the local militia had fights with the Yankees at the creek in the War of Northern Aggression. There's a legend about a black slave being decapitated there. Lynching a slave who became a ghost was a common legend in the South, but this one was supposed to be still walking around, looking for his head.

The bridge is also supposed to be haunted by Indians and some soldiers who were killed there. Another legend says a girl drowned herself in the black water when her lover rejected her. The story said that she could still be seen sometimes on moonlit nights.

We didn't know if these stories were lies or truth, but except for the tale about the bottomless water that wouldn't float wood, we could almost believe them. If they aren't true, I don't know who started them. We wondered about that, too. Joe thought moon-shiners started the stories to scare people away from their sour mash sheds and stills.

My father did find a still back in the swamp and turned over the fermenting barrels of mash. He let some of the hogs out near the barrels and had a herd of swine under the influence for a while. I don't know if contributing to the delinquency of swine was illegal then; it probably is now.

We lived about a mile and a half from the bridge in an old unpainted farmhouse. Several black families who worked for my father lived in even poorer quarters between the bridge and our house. So we often wondered if the black folks didn't make up the stories to keep us from their fishing holes. In fact, I learned about the headless slave from a black fisher lady who told me while we sat on the bridge with our cane poles.

But she had no need to scare me—she had a string of fish and I didn't get a bite. She had a decided advantage—she chewed tobacco and when she wasn't getting any bites, she pulled the worm in, spat tobacco juice on it, and threw her hook out again. It worked.

The slave, she said, was hanged up on the hill to the south. "But they hate him so bad they brought he body to the bridge, cut off he head, threw the head off one side the bridge, and rolled the body off the other."

She watched me shudder as she brought up her worm for another basting. "His head and body didn't sink?" I asked.

"Naw and that there ain't the worst of it," she said. "He still walking round this swamp looking for he head."

She let that sink in. "And he ain't the only haint who like the bridge and the creek. Whole mess of them. Sometimes they on the road and sometimes they out in the swamp crying like hungry cats."

I shivered so much my fishing pole shook. I don't remember going fishing in the Black Mingo Fishing Hole after that.

THE HEADLESS GHOST AT BLACK MINGO BRIDGE

I can't trust my memory about this thing and neither could Joe. It gets more blurred as the years go by. Sometimes I wonder if it really happened. I'm talking about that ghost we saw on Black Mingo Creek Bridge.

On Sunday afternoons, Joe and I met with the boys on our side of town to play baseball. Joe would put our glove and coverless ball in his bicycle basket and I taped our bat to my handle bar. Then we started pumping. We had to go several miles beyond Black Mingo Creek and play ball in Mr. Bedell's cow pasture where the local boys gathered.

Black Mingo Creek runs through a vale between two modest hills. The hill toward town was steeper and its upper section was covered with macadam to slow erosion, but sand still washed down the slope during rainstorms and deposited sand in the lower sections. It was hard pedaling through that sand with a bicycle.

By the time we got to the bridge, we were already pretty tired. Then we had to pedal up the steep side and most of that was sandy road. We were always glad to get to the macadam part of the road, but that part was only about thirty feet long. Then we were back into the sand again. It was hard pedaling but we did it—meeting for the games was one of the few social things we could do.

When we got to Mr. Bedell's pasture, I was "wore out," but being tired lasted only a few minutes. We talked a while and I learned that Sergeant Mixon had completed his fifteenth combat mission over Germany.

We had to share the bats, balls, and gloves because none of us had a complete set. Only seven boys showed up so we played three against three with the oldest boy pitching for both sides and the side at bat providing the catcher. I don't remember the scores, but they were pretty high. It's hard to play defense with three players.

We played a couple of hours before Joe and I had to leave. It was late and we had the longest ride home. Already tired, we started pumping our bikes back home trying to stay in the ruts of the sandy roads. When we got to the macadam patch, we built up a little speed to race down the hill.

Pedaling down the hill, I enjoyed the wind on my hot face and I'm sure Joe did, too. At the bottom of the hill, the shade was more intense and the dry heat of the pine forest gave way to heavier air of the hardwoods in the swamp. The denser shade made it seem that dusk had already fallen.

Near the bridge, I could smell the dank fragrance of the swamp and the tales of horror came to me. The air was deadly still and nothing moved. I thought about the ghosts and every bush took on a demon shape. I tried to keep my eyes on the sandy ruts and fought the handlebars. When we got to the bridge, it happened.

I never found out who the black man was that stepped up from the creek bank to the road beside the Black Mingo Creek Bridge. I don't remember what he looked like. I don't even remember if he had a head or not. I don't remember being tired any more or worrying about sandy ruts. I only remember pumping the bike for all I was worth.

Joe saw him, too, and was as scared as I was. I'm not going to tell you he was the Headless Ghost of Black Mingo Creek. I'm certainly not going to say he wasn't. The thing is too fuzzy in my mind. But to this day, I shudder when I cross the new bridge over the creek—even if I'm in a car.

MY FATHER AND THE CATFISH POND

Black Mingo Creek flows east through the southern part of Turkey Hill Plantation and in the region where it crosses Log Hall Road, it flows through two modest hills. During the war years, the management of the plantation got the idea of damming the creek between these hills to make a pond to water the cattle. We thought it was a good idea. We wanted a place to swim and fish.

Work began in the spring of 1942 and they soon had an earthen dam across the creek and for about two hundred yards on each side of the stream. They built a spillway on the eastern end of the dam to control the pond's depth. It took several heavy rains and all winter to fill the pond, but when it was finished, we had a twenty-acre pond between the hills. Then water flooded the tree roots in the backwater and killed the trees. The pond doubled in size.

The sport fishermen in the management team wanted to poison the water to remove all fish and then restock it with several species of perch and their predator, the large mouth bass. My father pointed out the possibility of cattle or deer drinking the treated water, but the project went forward. The trash fish were poisoned and the pond "cleaned." My father didn't really think the treatment would hurt animals, but no fish tasted as good to him as catfish. He knew catfish preferred the areas around trees and stumps. Since much of the pond's backwater on the northern part of the pond had live trees standing when the pond was treated, the poison brigade did not penetrate very far. My father reasoned that most of the catfish would survive the chemical warfare attack.

We saw them pour fish poison in the open spots of the pond and soon saw suckers, perch, and a few bass with their white bellies up in the water. The pond was becoming polluted with the dead fish and my father had to send men in the pond to net them out. They were unfit for food but my father fed some of them to the hogs. "You can't hardly poison no hog," he said.

My father's hope was evidently well placed—few catfish bellies were seen during this "fishicide," but he didn't like to be thwarted. He wanted to make sure the pond had a good population of catfish. So he kept his eyes on several other small plantation streams with deep holes or runs. In late summer, these deep holes became isolated when the stream stopped flowing due to lack of rainfall. My father visited the holes on Saturday afternoons when the plantation was almost deserted and, using his shrimp cast net, caught hundreds of catfish fingerlings trapped in the isolated pools. He gave these little orphans a ride to the new pond and dumped them in. As a consequence, catfish abounded in that pond, at least until we left.

My father said the catfish didn't really bother the bass fishing, but it wouldn't have mattered if it did. We had many meals of catfish in our house, and my father made several catfish stews on the bank of the pond for his fellow managers and workers. My father was the most popular of the managers, and it was not all due to the catfish—my father's character drew people to him, but he did make a fine catfish stew.

JOHN NEWTON AND THE STALLION

John Newton was working with the livestock when the superintendent decided we needed more horses. He bought two large unbroken gray mares from some place. As far as I know they were never named and never ridden. Another unknown gray mare, a small horse, showed up one day. I don't know who bought that horse, but it brought the total to twelve.

The superintendent wanted even more horses so he arranged for the use of another plantation's stallion for a month to breed our mares. My father had never bred horses before, but John had, so he left the whole thing with John.

On the scheduled day, John went for the stallion and brought him to Turkey Hill in the back of a truck. The stallion—a large dark red Tennessee Walking Horse with a long thick mane—seemed calm until he saw our horses grazing in the pasture. Then he went berserk. John had the driver back the truck up to the cattle unloading dock, but he couldn't get the stallion calm enough to get him out.

Then John had the truck backed against a bank inside the horse pasture with only a short leap for the stallion. When John released him, the stud leaped from the truck bed and galloped to the herd. Most of the horses ran from him, but one mare, I believe it was Nancy, stayed for him. She seemed to be ready for him and they reared up on their hind legs and playfully pawed at each other. The she ran off and he followed. He smelled her nose and tried to work his way back, but she ran away again. She finally waited for him and he bred her. John let them stay together all day. "Got to cool that stud down. He come here ready for love."

My father told John to keep records and make sure each mare was bred during the month we kept the stallion. So John left the stallion with the others and watched for mating. He asked me to watch, too. "You see him with one them mares, tell me which one."

So when I was around the horses, I watched, but I never saw the stallion and the mares do anything like they did the first day. Maybe they did at night. John must have seen them because he had records that all the mares had been bred except two, a young mare named Maud and older one named Annie. I knew these mares well. Annie was the one who went down in the mud puddle and lay on my leg. When Bandolier broke out of his stall, John brought me Maud to ride and help him bring the bull back.

John put these mares in large stalls where we kept the bulls. The stalls were empty because the bulls were with the cows. They were also working hard to increase the animal population of Turkey Hill. Every morning, John put the stallion in the stall with Maud and then with Annie. Both fought and kicked him so hard, John was afraid they were going to hurt him. He didn't keep them together long.

With only three days left, John was desperate. He racked his brain trying to figure out how to get the mares to accept the stud. He knew some tricks, but none seemed to work. He had tried to give them things to eat that were supposed to be horse aphrodisiacs, but Maud and Annie still rebuffed the stallion every time.

One day, I found John examining the joists and rafters of the barn. He looked at me and nodded. "Them joists will hold them mares," he said.

I didn't know what he meant until he put Maud's head in a halter and threw the rope over the joist. Then he looked at me. "Go bring the stallion here. Just let him in the stall but you stay out. It's about to get busy as hogs eating slop in this stall."

I did as instructed and put a halter on the eager stallion and brought him to the stall. Then I opened the gate, let him in, and shut the gate behind him. The stallion tried to smell Maud and she lifted her front feet to get momentum to let him have both back hooves. Then John pulled the rope and left her front feet dangling in the air and the stallion made an easy conquest. "You and me done help that stallion with that mare. She won't fight him no more."

It was like John said. Maud was receptive to the stallion the rest of the day. On the last day we had on the stud's monthly rental, John repeated the procedure for Annie. Then he loaded the stallion in the truck and took him back to the owner.

During the gestation period, one of the large unnamed gray mares died, but the other had a foal. We got five foals altogether. Nancy had one as did Maud and Annie, the two we had to force. Maud's foal was a beautiful little thing and we named him Flicker. Everybody was happy—even Maud, but she had put up a real strong fight to keep from being happy.

HELEN AND THE TICK

The year 1943 was not a good one for our family. It was the year my father lost control of the things he knew and liked best—cattle, hogs, and crops, and was put in charge of the thing he hated most. My father couldn't stand turkeys and now he had to supervise hatching, brooding, maturing, slaughtering, dressing, and packing about twenty-five thousand turkeys. Then the new Black Angus herd the corporation acquired brought disaster for our little sister Helen.

Helen was an active child. She had to be to run and play with her brothers. She was a little daredevil and would try to do anything we did. Our house was surrounded by a picket fence and we liked to walk the top studs to which the pickets were nailed. The never-defined object of the game seemed to be to walk as far as you could walk on the fence without falling off. It could be a challenge because our fence connected to the pasture fence that led about a hundred yards to the cattle barn. There a network of fences for cattle handling procedures greeted us little walkers. And if that were not enough, the cattle barn fences connected to a long fence that went all the way to the horse barn six hundred yards away. None of us ever walked all the way without falling off.

One day Helen tried to get on the fence and couldn't. Mama found her crying and almost panicked. The child could not move her legs, and it was late summer, the prime time for polio.

My father and mother hurried her to the hospital in Ridgeland, where after observation and discussion, the doctors pronounced it polio. The hospital called all around to locate an iron lung, but they were all in use saving or prolonging other lives. My father decided to tell Helen what the doctor said. She cried a little, then seemed to accept it.

Mama stayed with Helen every night and we took turns with her during the day. My father was back and forth several times a day as Helen's limbs quit functioning. Every time someone came home from the hospital, he brought news that she was worse.

But a young intern, Dr. Canning, had just come to Ridgeland Hospital and he questioned the diagnosis. "Polio doesn't develop that fast." He was aware of spinal injuries and infections that cause such symptoms so he thoroughly examined her back but found nothing.

I was on duty with Helen one day after the thing got worse. She couldn't even talk. She could move her lips and eyes, but nothing else that we could see. I left her that night expecting never to see her alive again.

Sometime during the night, Mama said, Dr. Canning rushed into the room with a nurse and ordered the nurse to cut Helen's hair that covered her neck. Then he looked, and gouged, and found a tick imbedded deep in the back of her neck. He cut out the bloated thing and put it in a jar of alcohol. He said it was a female tick that secrets a toxin that causes paralysis, especially in young children. It was not an indigenous tick so it must have come with the cattle. Dr. Canning was a brilliant student of medicine and a damned good doctor. He saved Helen's life.

By morning, Helen could talk again and move her hands. Her improvement was so dramatic she was home after three more days to begin the long journey to recovery. She never got there, but she developed a spirit of can do that whatever limitations the tick left her with, she would master.

She missed a year of school, but started back in the fall of 1944. During her year of recovery she went with us everywhere with my father carrying her in his arms like a huge doll. She went to the movies, shopping, and church, but she couldn't walk. I remember Mama looking out the kitchen window and weeping. "I wish I could see her walking that fence again."

I remember Helen's first steps because I'm the one who urged her to take them. Her balance was back and she could stand, but she hadn't taken a step since the tick struck her down. So one day when she was standing on the back porch, I held out my hands and told her to walk to me. She hesitated, but she realized she was in an undeclared but definite dare situation. She took a stumbling step, looking scared and surprised. I backed off and she took another step. Then another. She was smiling now so I took her hands and sat her down in a chair.

I told Mama and she got upset with me. "Don't make her do what she can't do. It'll kill her spirit."

I didn't have the words or the sense to tell Mama you couldn't kill that spirit. When my father heard, he was delighted and we all took turns helping Helen walk again. By the time she went back to school in the second grade, she could walk well and carry her own books. She could even write using her crumpled hand rather than her fingers. She never regained control of her fingers, but she took control of her life and enriched all of ours.

THE AIRPLANE CRASH

Ridgeland had a small airport out on the Gillisonville Road where planes could set down and visit. No planes were hangered there, but stunt men would come and put on air shows for a price. Some of these pilots would give airplane rides. One Sunday afternoon, James Exley and I decided to do it. His sister was a teacher so he had some information before the rest of us. He told me that Miss Mixon's brother had come back from his eighteenth bombing mission over Germany.

We paid five dollars each for our first rides in an airplane over that field and surrounding Jasper County. It was like a roller coaster ride—thrilling but terrifying. The pilot banked sharply, dove at the ground, and made some rolls. I was glad when he set the plane down. I was about to throw up.

Later that year, an experienced pilot came and starting giving lessons, but only a few took him up on it because of fear and the expense. Donald Garbade was a free spirit and the banker's son. He had the guts and the money so he signed on and began to take flying lessons.

One Saturday morning, Donald was supposed to do his first take-off and the instructor took the front seat where passengers usually sat. Donald lifted off, but when he reached about one hundred feet, the plane's engine caught fire and didn't produce enough power to land. The instructor seized the controls but the plane crashed nose down on the runway and burned.

The airport had no employees, but people rushed to the scene and pulled the instructor and Donald from the plane. The instructor was already dead and Donald would have been but he was wearing a heavy leather jacket that protected his chest and arms from direct flames. The aviation helmet helped protect his head, but his legs, thighs, and hands suffered third degree burns.

They rushed Donald to the hospital and stabilized him, but he remained critical. His life was still in jeopardy—he needed blood, and my father and others with his type of blood rushed to give it. The doctors saved his life but they were afraid his lower limbs would have to come off.

But Donald was a fighter. And my father was convenient for his initial blood needs because my sister Helen was in the hospital at the same time. He gave Donald a direct blood transfusion—from one person to another. After a few weeks, they began grafting skin from his stomach and back to his legs and thighs. His legs remained a horrible sight, but he proudly showed them off to visitors.

Joe and I visited Donald whenever either of us was in the hospital with Helen or otherwise. My father gave him blood every six weeks and Donald said he felt more kin to my father than Joe or I because he had more of his blood than we did. He never forgot the visits or my father giving him blood. Donald was in Joe's class, but the accident knocked him out of school for a year. Then he was in my class and he was an inspiration to us all. He became one of my best friends.

COLLAPSE OF THE OLD BARN'S SECOND FLOOR

My father no longer had responsibility for the cattle and the feeding operation, but we still felt close to it. We were literally in the middle of it. The picket fence around our house and huge yard was there because the cattle had free reign over that part of the plantation. We had to walk past the old barn twice a day to go to and come from the school bus. We still played in the old barn because we knew John Newton.

Joe, Richard, and I no longer rode horses because of a growing dispute between my father and the superintendent, but we still went to the cattle barn to talk to John Newton. Bob was four years old and he liked to roam around the old barn, too. Except for her tick attack, Helen would have been right there with us.

Cynthia was only six or seven months old and still nursing. Mama was also busy with Helen's needs, so Bob often wandered off looking for us and he usually found us at the old barn.

One afternoon in the late summer of 1943, we heard a loud rumble that sounded like it came from the old barn. Then we saw a cloud of dust pouring out of the doors. We didn't know where Bob was so we ran to the barn, but we found nobody at the scene. Bob didn't answer our calls.

Panic-stricken, we searched the old barn and saw that the second floor holding ground wheat for the cattle had collapsed. The loss was not too great because the ground grain could still be used. But where was John Newton? Was he under all that feed and rubble? And where was our four-year old brother?

In a few minutes John Newton came up on his horse and looked around. "Everbody here? Anybody missing?"

"We can't find Bob, but we don't know if he was playing in there."

John went around the feed hall and up the stairs. He called and we called, but no answer came. We were getting worried and John started digging away the ground grain to see if anything was beneath it. We helped him dig until we were exhausted. Then we heard a sound behind us. "Whatcha doing?"

It was Bob. We quit digging. We no longer cared about the barn's collapse because Bob and John Newton were safe.

THE WAR COMES HOME

When Richard entered Miss Mixon's class in the fall of 1943, Sergeant Mixon had flown nineteen missions over Germany. Every week or two, Richard would come home with the report that Sergeant Mixon had flown another successful mission. The whole school was getting excited about him and praying for safe completion of his twenty-fifth mission so he could come home. We talked about it at recess and the other teachers mentioned it sometimes during their classes. The coach kept us up to date on Sergeant Mixon's missions at each practice. We had prayer for the young man at each assembly on Wednesdays. Many other men from our town and county were in service, but none more in harm's way than a belly-gunner on a B-17 Flying Fortress.

Helen was still at home with the effects of the tick bite. Joe and I were on the football team in 1943 and we had lost all ours games through October. My father had been moved to manage the turkey operation and he detested it. The only good news was that Sergeant Mixon had completed twenty-two missions.

Then the first week in November, we won the last football game of the season. We didn't have much to brag about, but we had learned teamwork and how to compete. Football was over and we could turn our attention back to studies and homework, and the war was beginning to go well for the Allies.

We had taken Sicily and invaded mainland Italy. Mussolini had been overthrown and killed. The tedious, bloody advance through the Pacific Islands was on schedule. Bombing runs had severely damaged Hitler's war machine. But for a month we heard nothing from Sergeant Mixon. Then we found out. His plane did not come home from the twenty-third mission. It had been hit by enemy fire and it exploded in midair over Germany.

There were other deaths and even more Purple Hearts. Men from Ridgeland fought in the Battle of the Bulge, the Battle of Midway, the Battle of the Coral Sea. They fought all across France and Germany and several fought in the naval Battle of Okinawa. Two other men died in the air war over Europe and two infantrymen died in Germany. The little town of about a thousand people had seen its share of sacrifice.

RETALIATION

Black Mingo Creek flowed through the southern part of Turkey Hill where they dammed it and made a pond. Then it flowed in it original path to the haunted bridge and on for three miles until it left the plantation and ran under at the Atlantic Coast Line railroad and U.S. Highway 17. Between the railroad and highway it formed a wide, deep stream, much like a small pond. Fishing there was pretty good and when the large new pond was treated to remove the native fish, we had to look for other fishing holes. My father set out lines for catfish there once or twice. He caught some of the largest mudfish I ever saw but not many catfish. He fed the mudfish to the hogs.

We had to watch for trains as we walked the railroad bed to get to the creek. One day while we were going there to fish with some friends, the crack liner, the Champion, blazed by so we had to get off the tracks. Somebody evidently flushed and unloaded some raw sewage on the track. This was common practice in those days, but when you think you have been sprayed in such a manner with such material, other perspectives and traditional procedures don't merit much forgiveness. We had been insulted, disgraced, and dirtied. We swore revenge.

We planned our revenge with care because we would be on the outside of the law whereas they had legally insulted us and soiled us and our dignity. We planned it well. Each of us filled several liquor bottles (empty liquor bottles were easy to find around Ridgeland) with our urine and waited on Ridgeland's overhead bridge that spanned the railroad until the Champion made its return trip. Then we dropped the urine bottles and had the pleasure of seeing the glass bottles break on top of the express passenger train.

Those people were not the ones who soiled our dignity and they probably never heard, saw, or smelled our revenge liquid, but we had struck back and felt good about it.

TALE OF TWO HONEYMOONS

Silas Brown was one of the tractor drivers for Turkey Hill Plantation and he worked under my father. Silas worked hard and seemed to like his job, but when my father had to take over the turkey operation, Silas took a job with a Mr. McDonald in Ridgeland.

Mr. McDonald had a son, Jack, who was a dashing young man around the town—he had money, a new car, and plenty of girls. By contrast, Silas was quiet and some said a bit slow. We knew him well when he worked for my father, but now he worked for Jack's father and still had little money. He did have an old truck, but he was just not a ladies man. Jack and Silas had only one thing in common—they got married the same weekend.

Jack and his wife Betty took a week's honeymoon in New York, but Silas went to work the Monday after he was married. When Jack returned from his honeymoon a week later, he came to work the following Monday and he set out to tease Silas.

"How was everything at your wedding, Silas? We had a church full and almost two hundred at the reception. Great food and dancing and lots of presents. How about you?"

"Didn't go to no church. Just went to the justice of the peace and he done it for us."

"Lot of people there?"

"Yeah. There was Jimmy and Mary and my mama and daddy and her mama and daddy."

Jack laughed and kept at it. "What you eat afterwards?"

"We went down to Craig's Cafe and had a hamburger and a dope apiece."

"Get many presents?"

"I didn't see none, but Laura mighta got some."

"Where did you go after that? You go dancing, too?"

"We don't dance. We just went to my place."

"We went to New York on the Champion to celebrate our wedding. Went to shows, great restaurants, and nightclubs. Where you spend your honeymoon, Silas?"

"My place. Laura come over the week before and fixed it up real nice."

"How was your first night with Laura?"

"Real good."

"How many times did you and Laura do it? Betty and I did it five times."

"Just once. Laura wasn't used to it."

People laughed at the story, but I didn't understand it for a long time, and it happened so long ago, it's not even funny in this permissive, promiscuous society.

THE FBI INVESTIGATES ME

I made fair grades in school, but I was not a good student because I didn't like to study. I did have strong interests in some subjects like history and chemistry. Bill Highsmith shared my enthusiasm for history, but nobody liked or would admit they liked chemistry.

Bill and I both lived on Turkey Hill and we spent many days on horseback riding the pastures and woods of that huge Yankee-owned plantation. We would take turns directing the invincible and invisible Confederate Army, because we took turns being General Lee. At the time neither of us had the slightest idea what General Lee actually did during the war. All we knew was he was a great general.

Sometimes we would range far from Turkey Hill to places like Coosawhatchie and Bee's Creek. Neither knew that General Lee had actually commanded the Department of South Carolina, Georgia, and Florida, and had spent the late summer and fall of 1861 in Coosawhatchie. When the federal navy took Hilton Head and other sea islands, the Confederates responded by building defenses along the rivers and creeks. Thus it happened that Lee was in Coosawhatchie at that time directing the construction of earthen ramparts to protect the tidewater from Yankee gunboats. But nonetheless, Bill and I had fun in our ignorance.

As for chemistry, I knew a little about the power of chemicals. I knew certain chemicals reacted with others, sometimes violently, but I never envisioned chemicals outside of lab glassware.

I was fascinated by the reactivity of acids on metals and bases, of the precipitates that formed when soluble materials reacted to form insoluble ones, of the reactions producing color or gases. So I began my mad scientist pursuit and collected some of these materials, but I needed a place to carry out my diabolical reactions.

At the time, Mr. Eustace Pinckney was building a huge new barn near the place where I wanted my lab. Mr. Pinckney not only gave me scrap lumber, but tons of advice and so I built a large hut of mostly gum wood, tar paper and shingles. It had a door and two windows, but no running water or electricity because we didn't even have these things in our house.

I found laboratory catalogs and ordered some equipment like alcohol lamps, flasks, test tubes, a ring stand, and a pneumatic trough to collect gases by displacement of water from inverted containers. I had everything but chemicals.

I ordered hydrochloric, sulfuric, and nitric acids, sodium metal, silver nitrate, and cupric, ferrous and ferric salts, potassium permanganate, manganese dioxide, and other chemicals I don't remember. I bought sodium hydroxide and bicarbonate in the grocery stores, and denatured alcohol from Dr. Tanner, the pharmacist. I was all set.

Then I got a notice from the railway express office that my shipment had arrived. I went down to get it, and the agent was hopping mad. Some of the acid had leaked out and ruined several cartons of clothes consigned to Mr. Ulman. When I saw my box of chemicals, I was appalled. My fuming nitric acid had stained the wooden case it was shipped in, and Mr. Ingrahm, the agent, was also fuming. I took the offensive and asked him why my valuable chemicals had arrived in such terrible condition. He backed off and I thought I was through with the problems surrounding that shipment.

A few days later I found I was still being blamed for the problems, but I claimed that the shippers or the railway express people had not delivered my chemicals in a satisfactory manner. I argued that I had worked all summer for these chemicals and felt I should be reimbursed.

That stopped the railway express's complaints, but another factor entered the picture. One Saturday morning a man came to our house and asked for George Youngblood. My father talked to the man and called me out. My father was a swarthy man because he was always outside, but that day he was as pale as skim milk. The man looked at me and said, "I'm Jack Payton, FBI."

My father turned several shades of purple and I froze. "I'm George Youngblood," I said.

"I know," Mr. Payton said. "I know quite a bit about you. Did you order these chemicals?"

He handed me the invoice and I couldn't deny it. "Yes, sir."

"Why?"

"For my laboratory."

"Laboratory?"

We walked back into the woods to my laboratory. This was the first time my father was ever in the hut with me, and he was afraid I was in real trouble.

"He's only a boy, Mr. Payton," my father said.

Mr. Payton nodded. "He was born on February 9, 1929, in Elko, South Carolina. He works at night as a watchman for turkey brood houses and he gets twenty-two dollars a week."

That cured my father of offering information. Then Payton turned to me. "The authorities are worried about chemicals being used in sabotage against the home front. So we check some chemical shipments. You know some of these thing can make explosives and some are poisonous?"

"Yes, sir."

And I told him what I knew about those chemicals. He nodded, smiled, and rose to leave. "This is a routine search to see where those chemicals went. Every shipment of nitric acid in this country is checked. I see you still have most of it. Good luck with your research."

"Th-th-thank you, sir."

Mr. Payton left, my father blew out, and I breathed again.

THE CLUB-FOOTED GUARD

Ridgeland had a good football team in 1944. Our center and right end went on to play for the University of South Carolina and Clemson, respectively. Neither were starters, but just being on those college teams put some glory in our 1944 class B team. We didn't win our district; that honor almost always went to Beaufort.

I was a junior and right guard on that team. Ed Hughes, a senior, played left guard and Bailey Preacher, a sophomore, was substitute for both positions. Bailey was fast and brave to be playing with such large boys, but he was always ready when he was needed. Coach Younce let him and the other subs play if we got far enough ahead. But Bailey had to play most of the second game.

Here's what happened. We kept two cows for the family milk, and Joe and I alternated the milking duties. He was a senior and I was a junior so we didn't want our friends, especially the girls, to know we had to milk cows. That was too country-like and the people in Ridgeland were trying hard not to be considered country. Buying milk and eggs was the refined way those things were obtained. Our milking duties were not well known in the school—until Thursday night before the Walterboro game.

I went barefoot down the path swinging the pail that contained clean water and a cloth to clean the cow before I milked her. Before I reached the shed, I stepped on a rusty eight-penny nail in a board that should have been discarded. I should have been wearing shoes. But all the should have dones in the world didn't alter the awful tragedy. I had knocked myself out of playing in the Walterboro game. The injury was also painful and I had to pull the nail out myself, finish milking, and limp back to the house. Mama soaked my injured foot in Lysol or something phenolic to kill the tetanus germs until I could get to the doctor the next day.

I rode the bus the next morning with my brothers and Helen and we went to school. The foot was painful by the time I got to school so the principal sent me to Dr. Canning at the hospital. I asked the principal to tell Coach Younce what happened. There was no one to take me so I limped seven or eight blocks to the small hospital in Ridgeland where Dr. Canning was on duty. He was an intern at the time and a fervent football fan.

Dr. Canning examined my foot, gave me a tetanus shot, wrapped the foot and sent me back to school. I don't remember if I limped back or someone took me. I limped from class to class for the rest of the day and stayed after school for the game. About six o'clock I limped to Coach Younce and told him I was sorry I stepped on the dumb nail. He said that was all right, just go ahead and suit up. "What for?" I asked.

"It'll help the other boys see you in uniform."

So I dressed and waited with the usual anxiety that preceded our games. Were we going to win this one? Walterboro was pretty good, so we needed to be at full strength and I had already let the team down by stepping on a nail and the whole world would soon know I did it milking the cows.

About twenty minutes before kick-off, we started out on the field to do warm-ups, but Coach Younce led me to a car. I saw Dr. Canning get out. Coach Younce went on out on the field with the team and left me with the good doctor.

Dr. Canning told me to sit down on the back seat and take off the shoe and sock from the injured foot. Then he took out a needle and gave me a shot near the hole. It hurt. He waited about a minute and stuck me again. It didn't hurt. "What's that stuff, Dr. Canning?" I asked.

"Something to take care of your foot. It feel better?"

"Yes, sir. I don't feel no pain."

"Can you stand on it?"

"Yes, sir."

"Put your shoe on and run over to that tree and tell me how it feels."

I ran and it felt fine. "You want to play, you can. Go tell Coach Younce."

I ran to the coach but he told me to wait until we got the ball. If I played at all, he wanted me to play offense and block. I was a pulling guard and ran interference for Ted Malphrus and my brother Joe, our running backs.

Our defense held and I went in on offense. Henry Fickling, blocking back and signal caller, whispered in the huddle. "Thirty on one"

That meant the number three back, Joe, would on the count of one take the ball snap and run through the zero hole, the space between the opposing defensive guards. After he snapped the ball, Warren Spivey was to charge ahead for the linebacker. My job was to knock their left guard to the right out of the play, and Ed Hughes was to knock their right guard over Blake Crosby to the left. Bobby Tuten was the tackle on my right, and we had worked our high-low block on opposing guards down to a science, so I knocked their left guard over Bobby Tuten who had gone low behind him. Joe got a nice run. "All right!" somebody said. "George can block."

"Forty-six on two," Henry said.

Now I would pull out of the line on the count of two, take a quick step back, run right, and block the defensive left end knifing in to tackle our number four ball carrier, Ted Malphrus, who would be trying to sweep the right end—the sixth position. I got to the defensive end in good time, planted my right foot to throw a body block, but I couldn't feel my numbed right foot. I didn't know where it was. I tumbled and got tangled up with the defensive man and Ted and we all went down.

Coach Younce called me out of the game and I told him the problem. I could run straight ahead as usual, but pivoting on my right foot was out of the question. It was dead. He told me to undress and get in my street clothes and watch the game from the stands.

We scored and after a while scored again. By that time the half ended and the feeling was coming back into my abused foot. It throbbed and ached, but I had to endure the pain. Dr. Canning had gone back to the hospital. We won the game but all I got out of it was embarrassment for knocking down my own runner, a very painful foot, and the humiliation of everybody knowing I had to milk cows.

THE DOUBLE-DOG DARE

Doug stared at me and I was almost afraid to say anymore about it.

"You really see that Black Mingo Creek ghost?"

"I don't know, Doug," I said, "but I saw a colored man and he scared me and Joe to death when he stepped up on the road by the bridge."

"He was just a man fishing," Doug said. "How can you believe that old tale about the lynched slave?"

We had just finished football practice and were sitting with Tracy in Dr. Tanner's drug store drinking milkshakes and talking about mid-term exams, ghosts, girls, and other scary things.

"You ever see a ghost, Tracy?" Doug asked.

Tracy shook his head. "But I think I heard one once."

Doug laughed. "Where?"

"In the graveyard."

"What it look like?"

"I didn't stay around to look."

Doug laughed louder and Tracy was getting red-faced. "You so smart and you so brave, I double-dog dare you to go through that cemetery by yourself when it's dark."

Doug smirked. "Anytime you want to watch me, I'll do it."

"Don't you believe in ghosts, Doug?" I asked.

"Of course not," he said, "that's superstitious junk. They ain't real."

I tried to act brave. I wasn't about to tell them about the other times when I was scared to death that ghosts might be real. Ghost stories bothered me anyway because I didn't hear enough of some stories to discount them. I also had some experiences myself like the Black Mingo Ghost that I could never explain.

The night after that discussion in Dr. Tanner's drug store, an incident made me certain for a short time that ghosts were real and two other boys thought so, too. One of them was Doug.

Tracy had use of his family car that night so it was a good time for Doug to face Tracy's double-dog dare. Tracy and Doug had dates for the movie. They were juniors then but I was a sophomore and as scared of girls as I was of ghosts and that large tackle I would face Friday when we played Beaufort.

While they took the girls home, I waited at the theater. When they returned, Tracy was daring Doug again to walk through the cemetery. "I'll do it right now," Doug snapped. "Get in, George."

We drove toward the cemetery in silence, Doug with his jaw up and Tracy smirking.

"We gonna stop at my house," Tracy said.

"We not going to the graveyard?" I asked.

Tracy nodded. "But we ought to walk to it. Wouldn't be much of a dare if Doug had a car to run back to."

It was about eleven o'clock at night when we got to the rear of the brick fence around the cemetery. The challenge for Doug was to climb the fence, walk through the cemetery, and out the entrance to the parking area. Tracy and I would walk around the graveyard on the outside of the fence because we had nothing to prove—we admitted being afraid of ghosts and graveyards.

Doug hand vaulted over the brick fence and walked off through the graves while Tracy and I went along the brick fence. We were half way around when I heard a low moan. "Oooo. Ah. Oooo."

It scared my breath away. I couldn't breathe. I know Tracy heard it, too, because he stopped.

"Oooo. Oooo."

Tracy and I took off running back toward his house, but I stumbled and hit my head against the brick fence. It hurt and took my mind off being afraid. I shook my head and looked for Tracy, but I couldn't see him or hear him. All I heard was: "Oooo. Ah. Ah. Oooo."

It sounded like a female ghost, but gender was not a consideration at that point. I was too afraid to run. Then I heard grunting. Umm, umm, umm."

That had to come from a man ghost. Then I heard a sweet female voice. "Do we have to go, Honey?"

"I got to get back before my wife gets suspicious and finds out. I'll pick you up at the hospital parking lot after the game Friday night."

They didn't sound like ghosts now, but I had to stay out of sight. I hid behind a cedar bush until she got in her car and left. Then he left. I recognized both of them and that presented a fact as unbelievable as ghosts. Nobody would believe these people would do that. Nobody saw them but me and I was too bashful to tell anybody about things like that. I kept my mouth shut.

I walked back to Tracy's house and found them waiting for me. Doug ran up to me. "You hear that ghost, George?"

Before I could answer, Tracy did. "He heard it all right because we both shot away from there. What happened to you, George? Thought the ghosts got you or you died of a heart attack."

"I heard it and ran into the brick fence and almost knocked myself out."

The scandal broke about three months later, but not from me. I never told anyone I saw that man and that woman come out of the cemetery that night carrying a blanket. When some other boys saw them down an otherwise unused country lane, they couldn't keep the hot news to themselves. Their mothers got on the phone the next morning and everybody in the county knew before lunch.

Tracy and Doug were as shocked by the news as everybody else because I never told them what I saw that night. Doug was soon back denying that he believed in ghosts, but I remember a night when he did.

PART FOUR

LATER MEMORIES OF BEE'S CREEK
1944–1945

GUIDE TO THE MEMORIES

THE MEMOIRS	PAGE NUMBER
THE PEOPLE AND THE SETTING	201
BEE'S CREEK BRIDGE	202
BULL DOGGING THE HOGS	203
GETTING EVEN	204
ROSE ISLAND AND THE BULL	206
THE SHIPYARD	207
THE REDHEADED VAMP	210
FAMILY PROBLEMS	211
HUNTING ISLAND	213
THE DAY THE WAR ENDED	214
CATTLE JUDGING	215

THE PEOPLE AND THE SETTING

In the fall of 1944 my father quit his job at Turkey Hill and went to work in a shipyard in Savannah, Georgia. The pay was much better and he didn't have to raise turkeys anymore. We moved to a house at a fork in the road only half a mile from our first house on Bee's Creek.

Coosawhatchie Road crosses Bee's Creek about five miles from Coosawhatchie and after another third of a mile forks into Old House Road and Grahamville Road. When we moved back to Bee's Creek, the old Buckner store at that fork was still there, but it had not been used for years. We lived in the adjacent house on the Grahamville Road side of the Fork.

The house had large rooms but not many of them. There were three bedrooms on the south side of the house off a wide hall. The front porch was wide and deep and stretched across the front of the house. The front door opened into a living room/dining room combination that connected to a small kitchen.

The Buckners rented the property to Sam Byrd who sub-rented it to my father. My father used the store's gasoline tank and pump to store his gas. He had a job in the shipyard so he got extra gasoline to drive to work. We had no use for the rest of the store, but I used one back room for my laboratory.

Joe was then a senior and I was a junior. Richard was in the seventh and Helen was in the third grade. We rode on the bus with Mr. Russell Cooler, Sr., again. But our lives seemed disrupted. We had enjoyed Turkey Hill. The new house was all right, but we didn't seem to feel at home there. Our short time there was interesting but not happy.

BEE'S CREEK BRIDGE

Bee's Creek bridge was only about four hundred yards from our house, so we often went there to swim but only at high tide. There was only mud and the shallow channel at low water. The distance from the bridge rail to the surface at high tide was seven or eight feet, a good diving distance, but return was not easy. We had to swim out to a marshy inlet beside the creek and pull ourselves from the water by grabbing marsh grass and wading through mud. But diving and swimming were fun. We had several games like tossing things to the jumpers or divers who tried to catch them in the air.

When we returned from the bridge, we stopped by the flowing well near the old store and washed the mud from our legs and the salt from our bodies.

Down stream from the bridge was a small island surrounded more by marsh and mud than by water. I went to it once by boat but had to wade the last fifty feet or so through mud and marsh. It was so hard to get to, I think I'm the only person who ever set foot on it. Nobody else had any need to go to it. I didn't either but something made me violate its natural isolation.

The island had a few scrub oak trees and several kinds of shrubs. I saw shells and the bones of some small animal, but I didn't know what they were. I often saw birds go there and marveled at how easy it was for them to go there and how hard for me.

Many years later I returned and saw a moderate-sized alligator swimming from that island and it continued on to the place where we used to swim and dive into that creek. Did it have ancestors who did the same thing when we played in the creek?

BULL DOGGING THE HOGS

My father had to sell our milk cows when we moved back to Bee's Creek, but he tried to continue his garden, chickens, and hogs. He had access to several acres of land and several buildings but no tractor or mule to plow the garden. We chopped up some soil and planted tomatoes and squash, but my father's usual substantial garden was not possible.

We kept the hogs in an old shed. Except for the gate it was a strong enough structure. We chained the gate shut each time and kept them well confined for a while, but one day they broke out. The neighboring plantation manager told my father they were destroying his crops. My father was on his way to his shipyard job so he took Richard and me out of school to take care of the hogs.

My father was mad at the hogs, the neighbor, and us for not keeping them confined. He was also mad because he couldn't help us—he had to go to the shipyard.

I was fuming at the whole thing. Richard and I fussed at each other, the hogs, and the whole rotten mess as we tried to find the hogs. We didn't know what we would do when we found them, but we carried some kitchen waste in a bucket to entice them.

We found the two hogs deep in the woods of the neighboring plantation, well off our rented property. They ran from us a short distance, but we called to them and let them smell the kitchen waste. That did the trick. They came for that fragrant smell, and while Richard held the bucket, I was able to seize a hind leg of the largest animal. It kicked for all it was worth, but my temper and determination were up. I dragged that large hog more than half a mile through the swamp to our field, pulled it across, and put him back into the pen he had broken out of.

The smaller hog followed and we chained the door shut and gave the exhausted hogs some water and corn. My father had given us one of his impossible tasks and we got it done.

GETTING EVEN

The names and relationships in the following story have been changed to protect the guilty.

He who laughs first had better watch out, the old saying implies. I can testify to it. Buddy Dunbar and I were football teammates and friends, but we were always trying to get the other in trouble, especially with the teachers or the girls. We would tell lies, say nothing when only a word would make things better for the other, and try to mess up whatever the other tried to do.

One day Buddy said Barbara, one of the more sought-after beauties in the school, asked where I was. She had something to tell me. So I wasted little time and walked into the trap. Barbara told me she didn't want to know where I was that morning or any morning. Furthermore, she had nothing to tell me except to leave her alone. Score one for Buddy, but lookout. I was embarrassed and I was mad.

The chance came my way in an unexpected sequence of events. Judy was one of the more friendly girls with the boys. Then I found out Walter and Judy were making out on a regular basis and it was usually at some school activity. They sought privacy in a utility school bus that was parked inside the schoolyard.

One day after football practice, Walter wanted to talk about Judy and he told me about their relationship. I was the only person other than Walter and Judy who knew this and Walter knew I would tell no one. He was older, stronger, and meaner than I was and he said something about a busted mouth and losing teeth to ensure my silence.

My chance to get back at Buddy came one night at a basket ball game—I saw Judy and Walter go to the bus. Then I told Buddy that Judy had come to the game, but seemed lonely and had gone to the bus alone. Buddy swallowed the bait and went to the bus to comfort Judy in her loneliness. He tried to open the door but found it latched so he knocked on the door softly and called in a whisper: "Judy? It's Buddy Dunbar."

The door opened and Walter came out. He took one swing, hit Buddy in the mouth, and went back inside. Buddy got up, tried the door again, and found it locked. He didn't knock a second time.

I had more than evened the score, but I could tell by looking at Buddy for weeks after that he was plotting. He chose to make his move one day when the principal went to the bathroom.

Buddy had planned his revenge carefully. The scene would be the principal's office, a large room on the first floor with a coat closet near the door. Buddy got someone to forge the principal's signature on a note, then he or someone placed the note on my desk when I was looking the other way. It read: "George Youngblood. Report immediately to Principal Jones's office. Signed T.J. Jones."

Oh, Lord, I thought. What have I got into? Why does he wants to see me? I'm not innocent—there were some things. Was I going to get swats, expelled, or what?

I learned afterwards that Buddy had hurried to hide in the coat closet while the principal was in the bathroom. He wanted to be a witness to me making a fool of myself from start to finish. He had the door cracked such that he could watch me report to the principal. I walked in trembling, went past the closet, and cautiously approached the principal's desk. He looked up.

"You wanted to see me, sir?" I asked.

"I most certainly did not. Get back to your class."

"But, sir…"

I handed him the note. The principal waved me out, got up, followed me to the door, and threw the note into the trash. "Who wrote that nonsense?" he asked. "Well, now I'm up, might as well sharpen these pencils."

I saw an opportunity to try to ingratiate myself to the principal. "I'll sharpen them, sir. Where's the sharpener?"

"In the coat closet, but I'll do it. Get on back to class."

I got a good view of the principal opening the closet door and a good view of him studying Buddy scrunched down behind the principal's coat. The shocked principal figured it out and gave Buddy some swats.

We kept trying to get each other in trouble, but I still laugh about that one.

ROSE ISLAND AND THE BULL

Donald Garbade's father, Henry Garbade, seemed to accumulate camps on the rivers. He had places on both Little Chechessee and Big Chechessee Rivers as well as a place called Dawson's Landing on the Coosawhatchie River. He also owned several islands in or near Broad River. One of these was Rose Island. By the summer of 1945 Donald had recovered physically from the plane crash, and to make things interesting, he signed up for flying lessons again.

Donald and the flight instructor agreed to make a landing strip on Rose Island, but they needed help—shovel help. The instructor and Donald planned the short runway, but they needed some grunt help to chop up the rain-packed surface and level the old fields that still had rows from the time it was farmed. Donald asked Bill Highsmith and me and we agreed.

The pilot could take us in one at a time with our tools. Donald went first and Bill second. They were already working when I got there, but they were quick to give me a shovel. The work was backbreaking—the field was like concrete. We got about a hundred yards cleared the first day.

We ate pork and beans and had moon pies for dessert. It's a good thing we brought water because we couldn't get the pump at the old house to work. We slept in the old house because it was relatively clean. We had been to another island owned by Henry Garbade, but the resident goats there had taken over the house that was a foot deep in their droppings. The only domestic (?) animal on Rose Island had not made his presence known yet. He did next morning.

We went out to dig and sweat some more and extended the leveled area another hundred yards before a large red bull broke out of the woods and headed toward us. We ran to the house. He had us trapped in the house. He went away after a while, but we had to devise a way to get him away from the landing strip when the instructor came to pick us up.

We sneaked through the woods to a place near the landing strip and depended upon the plane to frighten the bull away. It did and Bill was the first taken off. I was second and Donald last.

We went back to Rose Island by water a few times, but I never saw the red bull again.

THE SHIPYARD

As soon as school was out in late May 1945 I applied for a job in the Savannah Machine and Foundry Company Shipyard where my father worked. I got on the night shift as a driller/grinder's helper at seventy-two cents per hour. The shipyard built minesweepers the navy needed to clear the waters of the Pacific. Some said Japan had deployed a million mines all strategically placed, but that may have been an exaggeration.

The shipyard ultimately launched about thirty minesweepers and when we worked there we were assigned more or less permanently to one of the small ships. I was put on hull No. 25, but my father was working on No. 24. We checked in every day and went directly to the ships.

My father and I were on the same evening shift and went to work five days a week and sometimes worked the weekend, too. Most of the time I did very little. My grinder knew how to avoid work and spent his time trying to embarrass me. The first night I was assigned to him, he sent me to the stock room for a quart of volts. "Not bolts, volts," he emphasized.

He grinned at his associates and they all thought they were going to have a laugh on me. "AC or DC volts," I asked.

My grinder glared at me. "Either one'll do."

So I went to the stock room and asked for a quart jar. I poured a handful of salt tablets I got from the dispenser at the water fountain, poured them into the jar, and filled the jar with water. By the time I got back, the salt had dissolved but the coating on the tablets made the mixture murky.

When I had come on the ship at the start of the shift, I had noticed a short piece of insulated wire lying on the deck. Everyone was ignoring it, waiting for some one else to pick it up. I made my plans around that wire.

I trimmed the ends to expose wire, put one end in the salt water, and kept the other end in my hand. Then I took the quart jar to my grinder. He stared at it. "What's this?"

"The volts you sent me for. They're out of the AC volts so I got the DC kind."

He blinked and grinned. "You can't put volts in a jar, boy."

"That jar is full of volts ready to jump out."

He grinned. "How you gone get them to jump out?'

The men all laughed again. I knew the total ship was grounded so the welder had only to touch any metal on the ship to get power in his welding rod. A welder was working nearby so I dropped the other end of the wire to the deck and stepped on it. I called to the welder and he came. "What you want, boy?"

"Mr. Welder, would you just touch that rod to the liquid in the jar. We want to see some volts."

They all laughed and the welder wrinkled his forehead. He probably thought I was some kind of dumb kid, but he stuck his rod into the liquid. Sparks and water flew until I pulled the wire out of the liquid. Then I took the jar and dropped the wire to the deck.

"What the hell was that?" the welder asked.

"Some of the volts got away. I'd better get rid of the rest. Y'all don't know how to handle them."

So I threw the jar with salt water into the Savannah River. When I turned around the men were staring but they weren't laughing.

A few days later the grinder tried to pester me again and sent me for a left-handed monkey wrench. I dutifully went to the stock room and told the attendant about the trick they were trying to pull on me. "The older men keep me busy sending you chaps over here for some kind of foolish thing."

The men were all on the deck looking and laughing at me talk to the attendant. "I wish I knew how to turn this back on them," he said.

"I think I know how," I said and left.

When I got back the grinder asked me for the left-handed monkey wrench. "The shop man said you should know they're years out of date. Left handed monkeys went extinct about twenty years ago and they quit making wrenches for them."

The leaderman caught on to my grinder's ploys to keep out of sight and began to give him extra assignments on other vessels. In addition to minesweeper construction, the shipyard had a dry dock for ship repairing. Liberty and Victory ships were sometimes towed in to be repaired, some having taken torpedoes or shells. When those ships came in with huge holes blown in the side, my father and I worried because Joe had joined the Merchant Marine about the time I started working in the shipyard.

These hulls and bulkheads were thicker and more difficult to drill so I had to bear down on my lever to push the drill into the metal. My driller still tried to avoid work, but one day he got a big job. A torpedoed Victory ship's hull had been repaired and the internal structures were being welded into place. One bulkhead was re-engineered and they decided to close a door temporarily by bolting a huge plate over the opening. The leaderman gave my driller the job of making the holes.

The work order called for ten one-inch holes along each edge of the plate for bolting it to the bulkhead. The day shift had already made the bulkhead holes for the one-inch bolts. We went to the site where the driller moaned about having to drill forty holes through one-inch steel in one shift.

The first order of business was to mark with a small drill the places where we would make the larger holes and that took about an hour. Then the driller looked at me. "You better be strong tonight. You gonna have to push long and hard."

I wasn't looking forward to the night either. We had to push against the handles of the large drills by finding a fulcrum for the long wooden rods we used as levers. So we began to drill and after a few holes, I counted how many holes we had left and saw that we would drill only thirty-six holes because of the corners. When my driller complained at break to our leaderman about having to drill forty holes, I said we wouldn't drill that many.

He looked at me like a child who spoke out of turn. "Ten plus ten plus ten plus ten is forty. Bet you five dollars it's forty."

I accepted and the leaderman wanted a similar bet. Soon several men working in the area took the same bet. Somehow the quarterman and the foreman heard and they came looking for me to bet. I took all the bets and the foreman conducted the ceremony. He counted the holes plus the marks for those still undrilled. "…thirty-four, thirty-five, thirty-six. Must have miscounted."

He counted twice more and all the losers joined in the count. They shook their heads and reached for their wallets. I collected thirty-five dollars but the foreman never paid me.

Men from all over Georgia and South Carolina came to work there. The pay was better than anything they had ever had received at home. Some men drove as far as a hundred miles each way to get the work. Farmers, laborers, and bums all came to help build minesweepers.

Then in August the atomic bomb ended the war, the need for naval ships, and our jobs.

THE REDHEADED VAMP

Most of the time I didn't have a car and Donald Garbade would take me with him and his steady if I could get a date. One night I had the use of our old Ford and I had my own transportation. Nevertheless, we decided to meet after we saw our girls home and talk a while.

I got there first and waited for Donald on top of the overhead bridge over the railroad. Only one train came by and it was a long freight. I almost fell asleep while it rumbled under me. Then something hit the car from the rear and I was almost afraid to look. When I did look, I was afraid to keep looking.

There she was. The woman of reputation. She hit me to get my attention or because she was too drunk to drive or both. She had turned on the overhead light to get a cigarette or something. When I looked back I saw the scarlet woman in her red hair with fire in her mouth. I was certain I was looking at the devil and I might have been.

I started the old Ford and headed back for Bee's Creek. I would tell Donald I waited until I could wait no longer. I didn't want him or any one to know I had any kind of contact, even contact through steel bumpers, with the woman ladies talked about and men joked about.

FAMILY PROBLEMS

During the summer of 1945 we lived in the Buckner house at Bee's Creek. My father and I both worked in the Savannah Machine and Foundry Company Shipyard in Savannah. We had to travel the thirty-six miles everyday and we did it in our trusty, rusty 1940 Ford. We usually worked and traveled together, but one time he had to work the weekend and I didn't. My father went with another worker so I could use the car.

I arranged to meet Bill Highsmith that Saturday night so I got dressed and started for Turkey Hill where he still lived. I reached Rice Shire Road, made a right and almost ran over a middle-aged man considerably under the influence. I stopped to see if he was all right and he said he wasn't. "What's wrong?" I asked.

"Me and Archie got to drinking in town and first thing I knowed he and Cletis took up with one another. He wanted to use my car, but I said no. Told him if he was going to go with Cletis to get out of my car and come home the best way he could."

"He didn't leave?" I asked.

He shook his head. "Then he wanted me to take him and Cletis to Jack Bailey's house to get a jar of whiskey. So I took them to Jack's place and they bought a quart jar of moonshine whiskey and we left. They was drinking in the back and cutting up, and the first thing I knew Archie told me to stop. I did and he took the car from me and left me in the road. I walked about a mile before you come."

"How can I help you?" I asked.

"Can you take me to Ridgeland? Need to tell the sheriff."

"You gonna tell the sheriff on your own son?"

"He thirty-one years old and ain't got no business treating me this-a-way."

He cursed his son and Cletis all the way to Ridgeland. Then we had a hard time finding the sheriff because he was on duty patrolling, but we finally found him. The sheriff calmed the man and took him home.

Then I thought about it. Those two men were drunk and getting drunker, and Archie was mean enough to steal his father's car, then leave him on the road. All that happened about a mile from our house, so I tried to call Bill Highsmith and tell him I had to go home to take care of Mama and my brothers and sisters. I couldn't get Bill on the phone, but I had to do it anyway.

I got home about eight o'clock, but I didn't tell Mama why because I didn't want her to worry. Then about fifteen minutes later, Archie and Cletis drove their old car right under the overhang of the old store and began to laugh and cut up. I didn't know if they were dangerous or not, but I loaded the shotgun and waited.

They didn't come to the house, but I thought we should go for the sheriff. Mama tried to tell me it would be all right, but I persuaded her to go to the sheriff with me. We took my brothers and sisters to be sure.

The sheriff tried to make little of it, too, but I persuaded him to go and at least make them leave. He followed me to the house and store, and the car was still there. He and his deputy went over and roused Archie and Cletis who had passed out by this time and escorted them back to town. I don't know if any charges were filed, but I was concerned for my family.

HUNTING ISLAND

I was the clumsiest boy in Ridgeland when it came to social graces, but most of my friends were kind about it. Like that time during the summer of 1945. I was working at the shipyard but I had some weekends off. I spent some of these with Donald Garbade, Jack Clemmer, and Bill Highsmith.

Bill Highsmith was sweet on Martha Graham in those days and I had eyes only for Betty Ann Woods. Martha's father had died that spring so when summer came Mrs. Graham and Martha moved to Beaufort and Bill was as heartsick as a puppy. He wanted to go to Beaufort to see her. So I asked Betty Ann and the three of us drove to Beaufort.

After my clumsy remembrances with Mrs. Graham, the girls decided that we would go to Hunting Island to see the lighthouse. When we got there and walked to the stairs that went up to the light, I stepped aside for the girls to go first—you know—ladies first.

Well, they insisted that Bill and I go first. I couldn't believe this departure from good manners, but Bill jerked my arms and said we should go first. We did and when we got to the top we looked for a time at the beach and the ocean and the trees and then it was time to go down.

So I started down the stairs first since gentlemen first was clearly the watchword of the day. Well, either Betty Ann or Martha or both said no, ladies first. I looked at Bill. He nodded and followed them. I was last wondering how else the rules would change.

We took Martha home, drove back to Ridgeland, then I took Bill back to Turkey Hill and Betty Ann home. I saw Bill a few weeks later and asked him. "What was all that strange giggling and smiling about when we were going up and down the steps at Hunting Island?"

"Think, dummy," he said. "The girls were wearing full dresses so for modesty's sake, they went up last and came down first."

"What?"

"If they were above you and you looked up, you could see up their dresses."

"Oh," I said.

I was a slow learner.

THE DAY THE WAR ENDED

I was interested in science most of my life, but when I heard about the atomic bomb I couldn't understand it. It was a virtual creation of energy—an impossible event if one is to believe the fundamental theorem of science that neither energy nor matter can be created or destroyed. What I didn't know was the interchangeability of these elemental things.

When the first fragments of the science that destroyed Hiroshima and then Nagasaki came out I was worried—the essentials of my faith in science had been shattered. My father was worried about more mundane things like finding another job because our shipyard jobs would soon be terminated.

Uncle Clint and Aunt Carrie and cousins Laura and Jean had come down to visit us, but my father and I had to go to work. We had barely clocked in when the news came; the Japanese had surrendered and the shipyard would shut down for the celebration. One of our co-workers had no one to pick him up, so he asked us to drop him off at a church where he would go in, thank God for the end of the war, and call someone to come get him.

A liquor store occupied a corner near the church and the man who wanted to pray fell from grace. He asked my father to drop him off at the liquor store so he could celebrate. He would pray tomorrow.

We drove on out to U.S. Highway 17 and took it north. We hadn't gone a mile before we saw two sailors hitch hiking. These were some of the men who had brought us victory so we had to give them a ride. "We're going to Ridgeland, about thirty miles up the road," my father said. "You want to go that far?"

The sailors mumbled and one seemed to nod, so we let them in. They smelled ripe and snored with loud wheezing sounds. When we got to Ridgeland to turn off on our country road, my father stopped and told them they would have to get another ride from this point because we were going home.

No one moved and we heard no sound from the back seat. My father repeated himself. Nothing. "Drag them out," he said.

So on the day of victory over the Empire of Japan I pulled two of our fine sailors from our old 1940 Ford and leaned them against the steel pipe that held the Pure Oil sign over one of Ridgeland's service stations.

We went home to find everyone delirious and excited. The war was over and Uncle Clint and his family were there to celebrate it with us. Mama had fried chicken and we had a feast and a night off—without pay.

CATTLE JUDGING

Agricultural County Agent Davis recruited some 4-H boys for a cattle judging team and pared the numbers down based on our performance. He selected James Exley, Oswald Vaigneur, Billy Fleming, and myself. During our stay at Bee's Creek, Mr. Davis would come by for me and we would meet the others at some plantation where cattle were being fattened for market. The owners cooperated and allowed us to look at four of their animals of varying degrees of value in the cattle-judging scheme of things.

We looked first for the ideal rectangular shape. An ideal animal should be flat on top and underneath, but all have briskets and all have some up cut toward the hindquarters. We judged on the basis of the closest approximation. Likewise, when viewed from the rear, the ideal beef animal would be built like a box, and we had to pick the one closest to that configuration. Poorer cattle were rounded due to potbellies.

Finer details to look for included the fullness of the animal's rump—the animal's thickness through the pin bones. Some cattle seemed to sink in at this point and we were advised to find those with the roundest rump.

General body fullness, a healthy look, and flesh around the lower legs were telling features. The lower leg was not the most desirable meat, but a skinny lower leg indicated less time in the feed lot.

We practiced judging at Turkey Hill and Bray's Island plantations during the spring and won the district championship at a cattle show at a county fair in Ehrhardt, South Carolina. That came in April 1945 on the day President Roosevelt died. It was announced over the loudspeaker at the fair and there was a moment of silence. Everybody was sad and some men and women cried.

Mr. Davis went around the exhibit pens and auction stage where he visited with some of his fellow county agents. We were hungry and ate hotdogs. Then each smoked a cigar while we waited for Mr. Davis. While he was away the cigar taste and smell combined with the burpy hotdogs got to us. Two of the boys threw up and the other boy and I felt like it. It was not a pleasant ride back to Ridgeland.

We had more practice at other feed lots and entered the state championship at Clemson College during the summer. We won the state team championship, but a boy named Flowers won the individual title. That won us a trip to Chicago to the national 4-H Club conference in December.

James Exley couldn't go with us. He was in college at The Citadel, but Flowers and the rest of us went to Chicago with Mr. Davis and his wife. Mr. Davis drove all the way up stopping for the night twice.

In Chicago we stayed in the Stevens Hotel, then one of the largest in the world and saw some famous people. Gene Autry came by and talked to us.

In the discussion sessions we got into the inevitable talk about racial issues. A girl from Michigan wondered why there were no Negroes at the conference and a girl from Mississippi gave her reasons why she thought that was the right number. That led to a heated discussion. Otherwise Chicago was a fun place and we had a good time.

We wanted to go someplace one night so we decided to take a taxi. The driver stopped. Oswald got in, followed by Billy Fleming. I told the driver where we were going and asked how much. I don't remember the amount, but when they heard, Oswald went out one door and Billy the other. We decided to walk around instead.

We saw famous things like the Chicago Museum of Art, the Field Museum of Technology, and the stockyard. Then we took the long drive back to South Carolina.

PART FIVE

MEMORIES OF NOXBOROUGH CREEK RICE HOPE PLANTATION AT O'LEARY SIDING
(1945–1976)

GUIDE TO THE MEMORIES

THE MEMOIRS	PAGE NUMBER
THE SETTING AND THE PEOPLE:	219
THE NIGHT I THOUGHT THE WORLD CAME TO AN END.	220
MAMA'S ATTACK ON THE CHINCHES	222
ALLIGATOR HUNTING	223
TO WHOM IT MAY CONCERN	227
THE REDHORSE SUCKER	234
THE RUNAWAY MOTORCAR	238
CAVIAR!	240
THE MURDER	242
ORANGE JUICE	244
MAMA'S COOKING	245

THE SETTING AND THE PEOPLE:

When the Japanese surrendered in August of 1945 we were all jubilant, but my father worried about getting another job. He had been working in the shipyard making good money helping to build minesweepers. With the need for military things like minesweepers certain to diminish, he looked for another job. He found one and became the manager for Rice Hope Plantation, a private hunting reservation owned by Dr. Julian Chisholm.

Rice Hope Plantation consisted of about 4400 acres of woods, swamp, and duck ponds. It had a few open fields, perhaps 200 acres. My father's duties included arranging hunts, planting fields of peas and grain for quail and turkeys, duck millet for ducks and geese, and sesame or benne for doves. He also had to keep a lookout for trespassers and poachers so he was deputized by the sheriff's department.

The plantation lay between Georgia Highway 21 and the Savannah River. The house we moved to was located at O'Leary siding off the Atlantic Coastline Railroad. It had a living room, a dining room, and three bedrooms. The front screen porch looked over the O'Leary Road and the railroad beyond. On the other side of the railroad lay a place about the same size owned by Judge Solomon.

When we moved to O'Leary there was no running water and we had to use an outdoor toilet. My father slowly added to and improved the house, but it was spartan at first.

THE NIGHT I THOUGHT THE WORLD CAME TO AN END.

We relocated from Bee's Creek in Jasper County, South Carolina to Rice Hope Plantation in Chatham County, Georgia in September 1945. The house we moved into was the only one within several miles. It was situated at O'Leary Siding on the main Atlantic Coast Line Railroad about one mile from the Savannah River. The house was old and it had many features considered positive things in past years, but they became troublesome in the years following World War II. The greatest disadvantage was its proximity to the railroad.

O'Leary siding was an old railroad turnout, a little used siding off the main railroad line. It had been an important installation when the plantation produced rice. When we lived there the only use for the siding was maintenance of the railroad and the trestle over the Savannah River.

The house was on O'Leary Road and the parallel railroad ran almost in our yard, about forty yards from our front porch. Even smoothly operating trains made considerable noise. When they were in trouble or when more than one was involved, the sound could become deafening, even frightening.

The railroad had separate tracks for north and south traffic, but the trestle had only a single track for the trains to cross the river. On occasion, more than one train approached the trestle at the same time. To accommodate these situations, the railroad installed a third set of tracks in front of our house. This enabled two northbound trains to stop and wait until traffic toward the south had passed. It also permitted slower traffic like freight trains to go off line to allow a higher priority train to get in front. Train activity in front of the house could be heavy.

To add uncertainty and difficulty to such situations, traffic on the river had the right of way in those days. The railroad had to maintain a crew of bridgemen to stop the trains when a barge or boat approached the trestle. My father and brothers, Bob and John, all worked as bridgemen on that trestle.

Sometimes a slower northbound freight would stop in front of our house to let a higher priority train go ahead. These traffic situations could become tense if the bridgeman had to use the turntable to let river traffic through at the same time. Although it never happened, it was possible for the train to "go through a board," i.e., ignore a horizontal board signal that meant stop and do not proceed. It could become even more tense if the barge or boat on the river was southbound—the direction of the river flow. Northbound river traffic was against the flow and boats and barges could be stopped if necessary, but the vessel's momentum and the flow of the river could be difficult to counter if the span were not open for southbound traffic.

Other problems could develop if a train developed a "hot box" or had other mechanical problems that required stopping. If lubricant were depleted in the grease box over the rolling stock's wheels, steel would soon be wearing on steel, squealing and ruining the bearings as they became red hot. Such trains had to be put on the siding until the problem wheel was removed or repaired. In short, there were many reasons why trains could and did collect in front of our house.

The first night I slept there a number of trains must have gathered in the late evening on the south side on the trestle, i.e., in front of the house. I had fallen asleep but about midnight I heard deafening BLAM—BLAM—BLAM—BLAM clangs that went on until the sound faded in the distance. A freight engine had stopped in front and each car in tow slammed into the coupling with the one in front and each complained with that sound until they all came to rest.

I finally got back to sleep when the loudest sound I had ever heard brought me out of bed. I was sure it was Gabriel's trumpet. The end of all things had come. My heart kept pounding even after I realized it was the whistle on the steam locomotive signaling its departure. Then came the BLAM—BLAM—BLAM—BLAM metallic bangs again. The couplings were sounding off as they were pulled forward and the slack pulled out of each. It was steel pounding against steel and each coupling had to give up its slack. When a long train started up after a clangorous halt like that one, the engine could be moving at ten miles per hour while the rear cars were still at rest.

This time the engine had to stop again before proceeding over the trestle and we got the BLAM—BLAM—BLAM—BLAM complaints again. Then a southbound train roared by screaming its triumph over those stalled in front of our house. After a few minutes a higher priority northbound train also blew its deafening whistle as it streamed past the stalled freight. I was in shock by this time.

Then the stalled train in front moved again. BLAM—BLAM—BLAM—BLAM. I think it was relatively quiet after that, but I didn't know when the whole thing would start again.

I didn't get much sleep my first night at O'Leary siding.

MAMA'S ATTACK ON THE CHINCHES

When we moved to O'Leary the old frame house was in terrible condition. We spent a week cleaning it and then found to our horror that bedbugs—we called them chinches—had prior residence. Mama, already disgusted with the place, declared war.

She first took defensive measures. She poured about half an inch of kerosene in tin cans and set each bedpost in such a can. Bugs not already inhabiting crevices of the beds' springs, hardware, or wooden members would die if they tried to enter by crawling up the bedposts. She examined us for bites and the sheets for blood to see if we had killed one unaware and stained the sheets with our stolen blood.

Then Mama got tough and engaged the enemy with her own brand of chemical warfare. She threw hot water containing lye on the floors, walls, and ceilings and let it soak in. We had to be careful to wear shoes on these floors and be careful when we tossed the lye into the air or we would be casualties of Mama's chemical attack. She had already skirmished with the bugs using Gulf spray, but she was just getting started.

Mama's next assault weapons on the chinches were improvised flame-throwers. We used kerosene lamps for lighting in those days and she gave each of us a lamp without the shade. She turned the flames up high and told us to hold the flames on the springs and metal parts of the bed frames until the temperature precluded life. She put it another way. "Fry the little devils," she said.

This was before the days of innerspring mattresses, at least in my family. That was fortunate because I'm not sure how Mama would have de-chinched those. Even so, our mattresses, elongated flat bags of cotton held in ticking, presented the greatest challenge. Mama was equal to it.

She opened the ticking and spread the cotton on a scrubbed, lye-treated floor and sprayed it with Gulf spray. Then we beat the cotton for hours with forked sticks to fluff up the cotton and to make sure the alien creatures came in contact with the spray. This measure also helped the spray evaporate so its smell was not as obvious as it would have been.

The campaign seemed to work. I didn't hear of other bedbug attacks the whole time we lived at O'Leary Siding.

ALIGATOR HUNTING

This story is about an event in the lives of two young men identified only as X and Y. I am bound to protect their identities. I can't tell you their relationship to me except to say we were close.

The young men often drove through the Savannah Wild Life Refuge on U.S. Highway 17 to admire the setting and the huge flocks of ducks and other migratory birds. Both were hunters and they sometimes parked on the shoulder to watch the wild life. Lazy alligators floating in the refuge always got their attention. They seemed to be flaunting their status as protected species—hunting alligators was illegal but not uncommon. The huge reptiles tempted them for the adventure and rewards of alligator hunting. "I could kill one them gators from here with my Springfield," Y said.

"Then how would you get him out?" X asked.

Black market prices had risen to twenty dollars a linear foot for skins. A nine-foot alligator would bring more money than either X or Y's weekly salary. Finally the temptation got the best of them and they planned ways to get at the government alligators.

They knew it wouldn't be easy. At the refuge, the Savannah River separates Georgia and South Carolina in a confused way. The river divides into three streams. The state boundary is not Savannah River proper, not even Middle River, but Back River. Most of the flow of the Savannah River at this point is in Georgia, but all three streams flow through in the wildlife refuge most of which is in South Carolina.

The refuge was and is a national sanctuary encompassing many ancient rice fields that became useful parts of the refuge. X and Y surveyed the setting whenever they passed through it. One thing was certain—if they were going to get alligators out of that refuge, their plans had to be flawless.

Several highways and bridges now span the Savannah River near Savannah, Georgia, but when this happened only U.S. Highway 17 crossed it. The highway came south out of South Carolina, bore to the right and entered the refuge. Near the bend one of the ancient rice field dams had been built up to make a road that went north to a caretaker's house about half a mile from the highway. Several other rice field dams had been made into roads and connected with the highway. The caretakers used them for working and patrolling the refuge.

Highway 17 was itself a built-up two-lane highway that crossed the swampy refuge with water on either side. Thick, natural swamp vegetation flourished in the refuge and protected and sustained thousands of migratory birds every season. When guns in the area were popping off at ducks and geese, most of them simply settled down in the refuge as if they had been personally invited to the protected area. The best duck ponds in Georgia and South Carolina were those closest to the refuge because the less careful or less intelligent birds sometimes swooped down into guns when they thought they were diving into safety.

Many other wild animals found refuge in that sanctuary and multiplied into swarming numbers held in check by natural predators like the alligator. Opossums, raccoons, otter, and mink populations were also regulated by the natural appetites of wildcats and some say panthers and bears, but the latter two had not been reported for a long time. With no natural enemies except each other, the refuge teemed with alligators. Most trips through the refuge on U.S. 17 rewarded and tantalized X and Y with views of several.

The alligator is nobody's friend but naturalists consider it beneficial if not essential to a swamp's ecology. In the 1960's the population of the ugly things dropped to alarming levels, and many states including South Carolina and Georgia banned alligator hunting. They were always protected in the federal refuge and now they had been put under extra protection.

But alligator skins were still in demand for such things as shoes, boots, belts, and ladies purses. They experienced a meteoric rise in prices and the high prices caused poaching. The ban did little to protect the gators in that part of the country. Only those floating oblivious and carefree in the refuge were free from danger, and X and Y were scheming to change even that.

There being no room for error, X and Y planned the expedition with care and precision. It was simple but it would need perfect timing as well as daring and luck for successful execution. On Saturday about midnight when the caretaker would either be sleeping or hopefully in town with his family, Y would drive his pickup into South Carolina pulling X's homemade boat on a trailer. Then they would change directions and re-enter the refuge. They would stop when they saw no headlights coming north or south and put the boat in the canal north of the highway. Y would drive to Georgia, turn and return to South Carolina and wait two hours before coming through the refuge to pick up his trailer, X and his boat, and hopefully an alligator.

They stopped on the shoulder and got the boat into the water without incident or observation. Y left and X paddled the boat along the canal beside the highway, hoping the occasional headlights of a car would reflect off an alligator's eyes so he could shoot it with his old 1917 Army surplus Springfield rifle. Then he would pull the alligator into the boat with a grappling hook and line powered by a come-along winch.

Everything began according to plan. X saw some eyes, fired, threw the grappling hook into the water, and dragged it until he hooked the alligator. It was still jerking a little, but X pulled it up to the boat and got a noose around the head.

X used the come-along winch to pull the gator into the boat, but that left the gator lying on the middle seat on his belly. He was busy pulling in the gator when he noticed the lights in the caretaker's house come on. Alarmed, X shoved and pushed until the gator's head was under the front seat and bent the tail and put it under the middle seat. With the gator secured and out of view, X paddled from the back seat toward the rendezvous point.

But X got nervous. He was an hour early. Y would not come back until the appointed time. X had to hide from the caretaker in the reeds. He paddled his boat into a heavy growth hoping the caretaker would take a cursory look and go back to bed. But for half an hour, X watched him walk the dams with beams from his flashlight playing on the area where he was hidden. The lights went off and X waited. The caretaker must have given up. X felt a sense of relief, but he also felt the boat move.

X had been as still as a mouse and he was the only one in the boat except the dead alligator. Dead alligator? X reached toward the alligator with his paddle and touched it and the thing exploded. It was trapped under the front seat trying to get away. It slashed with its tail, ripping off the middle seat and barely missing X.

X had to shoot the alligator again so he held his flashlight and the rifle together with his left hand and found the alligator's head. Just as he fired the reptile moved again so he probably missed, but the light in the caretaker's cabin came on again. In a few minutes the caretaker's searchlight was exploring the reeds and swamp. X could also see the alligator by the light of a northbound vehicle so he fired again at the gator's head.

X was shaking now. He sat down on the back seat and tried to calm himself. The caretaker's light had vanished, but he didn't know what that meant. As he sat thinking he felt water rise around his shoes. The alligator had moved, but he had not rocked the boat enough to get water in the boat. But the water was rising. It's hard to think when you're that scared, but X figured it out—he had shot two holes in the bottom of the boat. He was sinking in the canal with a nine-foot alligator that was evidently alive and healthy and mad.

His only chance was to abandon his boat, try to save his rifle, and swim or wade to the road shoulder. Water had reached his ankles when he jumped into the water and started swimming toward the bank. That's when he saw red blinking lights approaching on the highway from both Georgia and South Carolina. The caretaker's pickup truck was also coming down the causeway to the highway. Then he saw Y's trailer come by and slow down, but it didn't stop. Y went on toward Georgia. X was still in the water and knew where everybody was, including the alligator.

But then the alligator splashed into the water from the boat and X thought it was the end. The reptile could swim up to him and pull him under without a sound. But by the light of a passing car, X saw the boat drifting toward him. Evidently the alligator's efforts to push off from the boat sent it the opposite way.

The boat floated up to X bow first and he felt the bottom for holes and found both of them. Cars still passed occasionally, but he had to do something. He laid his rifle against the bow and climbed into the boat. He paddled under a swamp willow and broke off several twigs he shoved into the holes.

It was hard paddling the boat because of the water load, but he went west along the canal until he came to a culvert under U.S. Highway 17 that connected the two sides of the refuge. He pulled into it and hid until the blinking red lights were gone. Then he fell asleep from exhaustion.

Next morning it was raining so he left his rifle in the boat and hitched a ride from a man going to work at one of Savannah's paper mills. "I don't usually pick nobody up on this road," the man said, "but it's raining. Git in."

So X got back to Georgia and called Y. A few days later, they went back to get X's boat and rifle using the same technique of Y leaving X off, driving to South Carolina to turn around, and coming back to pick him up. It worked that time, but the boat and the rifle were gone.

Y returned and picked X up without incident.

"Boat's gone. My rifle, too."

Y shook his head. "That's why gator hides are so expensive," he said.

"Shut up," X said.

TO WHOM IT MAY CONCERN

To whom it may concern: my father found an active moonshine project in the woods, but he didn't report it to the authorities. His reaction to the discovery made his family shudder and catch their collective breath.

At the time my father managed a private hunt club of about four thousand acres of old rice fields, woods, fields, pastures, and swamp along the Savannah River on the Georgia side. He spent much of his time in the woods patrolling the place to discourage and arrest poachers, but he usually let trespassers go with a warning. His job was to provide good, safe hunting for the owners, not to chafe the neighbors.

Like other private game reserves in the area the owners called their hunt club property a "plantation," and it had indeed grown rice in previous centuries. One of my father's responsibilities was to plant food crops for the wild life to improve their health and increase their numbers. He used the "plantation" crew that included his sons to plant the duck ponds with duck millet, the open areas with oats and peas for deer, sorghum for quail, and benne or sesame for doves. We also planted chufas, a sweet groundnut, in the wooded areas for turkeys, but squirrels ate more chufas than the turkeys. He also planted about seventy acres of corn for the plantation mules and his own hogs, but the wildlife, chiefly deer and raccoons, got most of the corn as well. Although the owners primarily wanted to keep the duck, quail, and dove numbers and the deer and turkey populations up, his policies and planning to do that increased the numbers of all wild things on the private reserve.

The "plantation" was an ideal place for us brothers to grow up. We had access to miles and miles of woods and swamps. The creek and the duck ponds gave us excellent fishing and the hunting paths and roads provided great horseback riding trails. We were not supposed to hunt deer, ducks, doves, turkeys, or quail, but we could hunt all other game animals. We sometimes killed some of the prohibited species, but the hunt club manager never reported or even acknowledged it. We often grew tired of so much venison, turkey, and duck meat, but not dove or quail—they were too small.

My father kept up with his hunting license because he was often with the owners when they hunted, but none of us boys ever bought a license. The worst illegal hunters that poached on the "plantation" lived in the club manager's house.

When there were no hunts underway, my father encouraged us to ride the horses on the hunting access roads and trails that crossed and crisscrossed the club's property to let poachers or trespassers know we were there. If we saw a vehicle, we were to get the license number and report it to him. We came to know the trails well, but no one knew them as well as my father, the poacher's nemesis. He had the uncanny ability to move through the woods like an Indian without being seen or heard. When he apprehended a poacher, he had arresting authority because he was a deputy sheriff.

He arrested many poachers who thought they were well hidden or camouflaged. He spent a lot of time in court testifying against them and other illegal hunters. He usually let non-hunting trespassers go with a warning. If they were not interfering with the game or the hunts, trespassing was a minor nuisance. For such offenses, he didn't even ask for names. He kept pads of note forms printed with the words: To Whom It May Concern. The trespassing offenders received unofficial citations suggesting that the transgression not be repeated. If he caught them again and recognized them, he might arrest them for trespassing—many trespassers came to get the lay of the land so they could sneak back in and hunt. My father was on the other side of the game laws in his earlier years and knew every trick those poachers and illegal hunters used and some they didn't.

Most trespassers were not involved in hunting—the most common type of simple trespassing he encountered was use of the hunting roads and trails as lover's lanes. Both the local boys and the service men from the military installations in the area seemed to know about the place. They took advantage of the isolation of the private game reserve, and some even used the secluded woods in the daytime. With his intelligence network, my father found most of them.

He encountered more parked cars at night. He left nocturnal and daylight trespassers of the amorous sort alone except for the "To Whom It May Concern" warnings that he left under the windshield wipers. In these instances, he wrote down the vehicle license number so that he would be able to identify repeat offenders.

My father could move unseen and unheard through the night woods, and the people in the love cars and trucks didn't often know when he placed the warning note. Perhaps they didn't hear him because they were concentrating on something else. He sometimes heard laughter and female sighs and giggles and sometimes heavy male breathing.

Some boys or men would roll down a window, feign ignorance about where they were and apologize, but most didn't show themselves. They found out later from the note that they were among those who should be concerned.

My father's intelligence network included the plantation workers and friends at the railroad trestle who could see boats enter the creek that penetrated the "plantation." Some hunters would try to sneak into the duck ponds that bordered the creek, shoot at rafts of duck sitting on the water, collect them, and disappear down the creek to the river. Several were amazed to find my father waiting for them when they landed. He kept himself hidden until they had their guns and equipment on the "plantation" property before he confronted them.

Friends and neighbors helped in similar ways by letting him know when unknown vehicles went by their houses or small farms. He caught deer hunters with their weapons and some without. Some of them protested they were lost and had no weapon and he let them go with the warning as innocent trespassers. When he was sure they were gone, he went back and searched the areas where he apprehended them. That way he found several expensive rifles and shotguns that he kept because they lied to him. There was no way they could make a claim on the guns without seriously exposing themselves as violators of the state's game laws.

Some of these friends did some poaching of their own and my father knew it. He tried to discourage it by his presence when he found out where they were and what they were doing. They even told on each other so that the "plantation" would not be over-hunted. He usually said nothing when he found them because they were essential elements in his warning apparatus. He just stared at their guns and kills if any. They knew that he knew what they were doing. They didn't do it often.

He found everything from discarded trash and garbage to worn out tires and junk cars along the trails and paths. He found a few stolen and abandoned vehicles. Cleanup of the hunt trails was a major problem, and he had to hire help to get it done at times. He found deserted women who had not been as cooperative as their escorts demanded so they left them in the woods. Over the years he had to call their friends to come for three different women with separate experiences of abandonment.

My father thought he had seen it all until he found the illegal distillery deep in the woods near the river. He evidently felt a mixture of emotions beyond simple outrage that a moonshine enterprise was operating in the area for which he was responsible. It also surprised him—he had passed the place only a few weeks earlier without seeing anything suggestive of the operation.

The size of the venture amazed him. He found twenty-one rusty steel drums of corn mash fermenting under lids and covered by large plastic film sheets like painters' dropcloths. From the penetrating odor of alcohol mixed with the sour smell of the fermentation, he knew the stuff was already strong, and the trespassing moonshiner would soon use the boiler and condenser also lying under plastic.

The moonshiner was violating federal and state laws so the offense was a serious crime, but since it didn't harm or jeopardize the "plantation" my father didn't think it all that significant. The still would not interfere with hunting unless it started a forest fire, and that was the major reason he wanted it gone. He decided to follow his live and let live philosophy so he took out his pad and wrote this note: "To Whom It May Concern: get this operation off this private game reserve by Saturday or you will lose it."

He left the note under a small stone on top of one of the drum lids and covered it again with the plastic film sheet. To make sure the moonshiner saw the note, he placed a rusty hatchet and a dull axe he found at the site on top of the same barrel and leaned a shovel and bush hook against it. Yes, he should have called in the sheriff or federal agents but he didn't.

The Saturday deadline came three days later. My father went to the site and found the mash still fermenting and the illegal distillation equipment erected for use. He also found the note, crumpled and wadded on the ground. He saw red—his friendly warning had been ignored. If the offender had known my father, he would have moved the project to some other place—any other place—because my father never broke his promises and always kept his ultimatums.

He fumed at being ignored and went back to the house for a shotgun—he didn't patrol with a weapon because he didn't want to shoot anybody. But on that Saturday morning, he loaded a 12-gauge pump gun with buckshot. Then he went to the barn for the tractor and trailer and recruited one of my brothers to help him. "Bring all the rope you can find and get your rifle, son," he said.

"We going hunting, Daddy?'

"We might."

My brother said he uttered not a word until they got to the site. "What's that, Daddy?" my brother asked him.

"Moonshine mash and still. We gonna take it to the barn."

"Everything? Them drums, too?"

"Especially them drums."

So they grunted, sweated, and lifted the drums of mash onto the trailer bed. Then they loaded the boiler, the condenser, and the few tools they found on the site. "I was plumb wore out and my back hurt," my brother told me afterwards.

He also told me that the mash barrels made the heaviest load they ever put on that old trailer. They didn't have enough rope to secure the drums well so my father was worried they would tip over. The tires were several years old and under the heavy load they all looked like they needed air. But he was ready to leave with the smelly load.

He took out his pad and wrote another note that read: "To Whom It May Concern: maybe you will believe me now. If you want them, come down the old logging road to the barns and stables and pick up your drums, tools, and still, but don't come for a week. It will take me that long to empty the drums. I'm going to feed the mash to my hogs."

Daddy left the unsigned note nailed to a tree where the still had been.

My father could be daring—even impetuous, but this may have been the most audacious of his many exploits. He didn't know anything about the moonshiner such as how violent he might become when he found his project destroyed and his equipment moved—just as the moonshiner was evidently ignorant of my father and his nature.

After loading the aromatic contraband, my father faced some major problems. The hunting trails and paths were rough with puddle holes from past rains and sticks, branches, and even logs that lay across the way. Because the mash would slosh about in the barrels and spill out, he hauled the barrels at a snail's pace along the hunting access trails. My brother cleared the forest debris as they proceeded the shortest way to the nearest paved road—a major state highway. My father needed a smooth paved surface to avoid excessive sloshing of the mash and spillage. He reached the highway with minimal spillage and hauled twenty-one fermenting, odoriferous barrels with the distillation equipment along that highway in the open trailer in broad daylight.

To Whom It May Concern: possession of fermenting grain products containing ethyl alcohol without proper licensing is a federal offense, and concurrent possession of unlicensed distillation equipment compounds the felony.

To minimize agitation and spillage of the mash, my father maintained a constant but low speed on the highway. Hundreds of cars went around the tractor and trailer and hundreds more saw them coming the other way. Many drivers behind the trailer blew their horns at the inconvenience—it was Saturday and they didn't want to be delayed by some old farmer with his tractor and dilapidated equipment.

The tractor and trailer, always a nuisance on the highway, was for that undertaking a spectacle as well. The appearance was unusual and the smell was also sure to attract interest especially among those that had tasted and smelled "corn likker" or homemade sour mash whiskey.

To Whom It May Concern: my brother estimated that they met four highway patrolmen and as many went around the slow-moving wagon. None of them stopped even when they had to pull off to the side for twenty minutes to change a flat tire.

We still wonder about my father's motivation and determination that day. Was he aware of what the various state and federal law officers would say about that load? He and my brother were on that highway for two and a half miles with this fragrant contraband because he wanted to give the illegal mash to his hogs.

To Whom It May Concern: my father would feed almost anything to his hogs.

Whenever he passed the commercial bakery, he stopped to see if they had bread too old for charity disposition, and he often came home with the back seat of the old car full of old bread. He never got into garbage pick-up like some pig farmers did, but he used our kitchen waste. When he killed chicken snakes or rattlers, he brought them to the hogs that accepted them as fast food items—almost everything is fast food for a hog.

Several of my father's off-duty activities also produced food for the hogs—like trash fish. When he went fishing, he went food fishing, but he usually caught more trash fish than table fare. His seining operations in salt-water creeks and rivers yielded a few mullet, croakers, drum, and channel bass with larger numbers of stingrays, sharks, and crabs. Fresh water netting expeditions provided more garfish and mudfish than it did bass and bream. By the time he got home and cleaned and prepared the food fish, all the trash fish except the mudfish and crabs would be dead. That was a good thing because even hungry pigs might have trouble with live sharks.

My mother didn't cook the crabs because it was too difficult to pick out the meat so my father carried them with the dead fish to the hog lot because hogs will eat anything. He had about seventy pigs at the time and he was always looking for things containing protein to feed them—like trash fish. He would shake out the bags and baskets of mudfish, garfish, sharks, stingrays, dogfish, and crabs and distribute them throughout the feeding lot. Then the swine went after their seafood with enthusiasm they seldom exhibited. They gorged themselves on the fish but saved the crabs for last—not because they were the least tasty, but because eating live crabs can be a challenge when all you have is an appetite and a snout.

When the time came to feast on the live crabs, the porcine thespians gave us several spectacular performances with unforgettable audio effects. When the pigs approached the crabs with their snouts, the crabs seized clawfulls of pig nose, and the pigs squealed and ran about shaking their heads to dislodge them. Soon the barnyard reverberated to sounds like shrill voices of untalented sopranos struggling toward high C. The hogs did eat the crabs, though. Hogs will eat anything.

When my father parked the trailer load of moonshine mash under the shed, the hogs were reclining all around the feeding lot on their lazy sides and haunches unaware of the banquet they were about to receive. Everything changed when he entered the lot with two large buckets of mash—they almost trampled him down to get to the strange smelling stuff. Then he filled the water troughs with the still fermenting mash and the pigs went after it with a passion—the swine made pigs of themselves grunting *bon appetit* in piglish to each other and *le roi le veut* at my father.

But about two hours later, some hogs were wobbling about, and others tripped on their own feet. Some were lying down unable to get up so my father waited two days before he gave them more. During that time, he had a smelly commodity under the shed that would have been of interest to lawmen of any jurisdiction, especially with the boiler and copper condenser lying on the same trailer that now had another flat tire.

The mash kept the hogs happy and us entertained for about a week, but when it was all gone, the drunken swine wouldn't leave the troughs to feed on ground corn and meal he kept in the feeders. Then they reluctantly resumed feeding on the ground feed products, but for several days after the mash was gone, they stayed near the troughs for more sour mash.

To Whom It May Concern: The hogs sobered up, dried out, and returned to sobriety giving hope to all pigs on drugs or booze—it's awful for a few days but it can be done.

About a week later, a man drove up in an old truck and hemmed and hawed. "This your place, Cap'n?" he asked.

My father shook his head. "I run it for the club owners. Who might you be?"

"Name don't matter," he said and produced the note to Whom It May Concern. "I got permission to come here and pick up some barrels and some equipment."

The man had the note so he must have been the moonshiner. We assumed he had concluded that my father was not a lawman and had risked coming to get the barrels and still. My father was in fact a deputy sheriff although he restricted his law duties to control poachers and trespassers. He told this gentleman about that and added as he departed. "Mr. To Whom It May Concern, this whole business has been a lot of trouble. If you ever put up your operation on this hunt club property again, I'll get the sheriff or the U.S. Marshall to help me feed my hogs the next time."

We were glad and relieved to hear that. The last thing we wanted was our father administering his own concepts of justice again no matter how vile the crime or how richly deserved the punishment might be. Especially when we later found out to our horror that our father had been in error about the boundary of the hunt club's land.

To Whom It May Concern: the offensive moonshine site was more than a hundred yards outside the hunt club's property.

It was in the swamp where boundaries are more obscure than most places, so it was easy for my father to make the mistake. We found out later that the land belonged to the unidentified man who came for the drums and "the equipment." The man was in no position to make any protest, personal or official, to my father's intrusion on his property and the loss of his fermenting treasure.

To Whom It May Concern: My father never saw or smelled any evidence of white lightning production in that section of the swamp or anywhere on the hunt club property again.

THE REDHORSE SUCKER

My heart raced as my cork bobbled and then bobbled again. Then it plunged and I pulled back and felt the struggling fish on the end of the line. The cane pole was flexing with the escape efforts of the fish, but I pulled the pole to a vertical position and swung in a fish I didn't recognize. My brother Richard stared at it and waved his head. "If I didn't see it, I wouldn't have believed it. You can't catch no redhorse sucker with a hook and line."

Richard and I were enjoying ourselves. Our father liked fishing, craved fish, and bestowed both loves on his sons. When he got fish-hungry nothing else would satisfy him and he was in a good position to get satisfied. He managed a hunt club property with several duck ponds separated by a dam from Noxborough Creek, a fresh water tidal tributary that entered the Savannah River about fifteen miles upstream from Savannah.

The duck ponds were made centuries ago for use as rice fields and then as now the water levels in the ponds were controlled by watergates using the tide to flood or drain the fields as necessary. My father had to get the soil dry to plant duck millet just as the early ones had to plant rice in dry soil. Then the ponds had to be flooded so the seeds would soak and sprout. After the plants sprouted, water was an effective way to control weeds—the weeds could be drowned, but both duck millet and rice thrived in standing water.

Canals for drainage and flooding surrounded each field and these canals were full even when the fields were in the dry state. but they had to be drained frequently and refilled to "freshen" them, i.e., to keep the water from becoming stagnant. Fish came and went through the water gates to spawn and to feed. The canals provided us with easy access to good fishing.

My father also kept two boats moored on the creek side of the dam when we wished to fish in the creek that wandered for miles through swamps and beneath water-loving trees like cypress, gum, and bay trees. Even after we were grown, we brothers would often plan or gravitate to fishing when we visited my mother and father together. After we had visited for a while someone was sure to suggest fishing.

On this occasion, the urge to fish smote my brothers Richard, Bob, Mike, and I. We found fishing poles, dug some worms, and went to the duck ponds. The canals had been recently "freshened" so we expected pole fishing to be good— large mouth bass, bream, and red breast were bedding. We were disappointed. After fishing for half an hour we had caught nothing. No one had so much as a bite. Bob summarized the situation. "Ain't no dern fish in these dern ponds."

"Tide's going out. Let's go down creek to the fishing holes," Mike said

So we loaded our equipment and ourselves into my father's boats—Bob and Mike were in one boat and Richard and I in the other. Then we paddled down Noxborough Creek as happy as kids without a care in the world and without a fishing license among us.

We drifted down the creek under the shade of giant cypress and gum trees under a cloudless blue sky. It was a hot but perfect day for fishing—gentle breezes blew up the red water creek and kept us comfortable. We decided to separate the boats so we could fish the known productive drops until one boat found fish. Then the other would join in. We fished at several drops and had little luck so we continued to fish separately. "We might have to lie to make this fishing trip sound exciting," Richard said, "but the fellowship is fine."

Then we found a spot where the fish favored Richard's hook and ignored mine. I had far more fellowship than success. "It doesn't get any better than this," Richard said, landing another large bream.

"It could get a lot better for me," I said. "I've caught only two small breams and that redhorse sucker."

"Quit rocking the boat," Richard said. "You'll scare the fish."

When the fish stopped biting Richard's worms we joined the other boat and started for home. "We got about two dozen," Mike said, "How about you?"

"Twenty eight," I said, "and one's a redhorse sucker."

"Y'all put out a net?" Bob asked.

Richard shook his head. "We didn't bring no net."

"Then how did y'all get a redhorse sucker?" Bob asked. "You can't catch no redhorse sucker with a hook and line."

"George did. I seen him do it," Richard said.

Bob waved his head and we paddled with the incoming tide back to the duck pond dam. We all looked and gave unspoken praise to the beauty of the swamp and the creek, but Mike noticed an airplane flying low over the swamp. "Some Saturday pilot out learning how to fly," Mike said.

We gave the plane no further thought. We reached the dam and were unloading when we heard an outboard motor in the swamp. We didn't worry about it either because many people fished the creek. We pulled up to the dam and began to unload the boat, but before we got everything out, a boat rounded the curve and came upon us. Bob recognized the man—he was a game warden. "We're caught," Richard said.

"Now it's going to get exciting and we won't have to lie," I said.

"Ain't it hot?" the game warden asked. "What y'all fellas doing?"

"We sweating and tying up and going home," Bob said

"Well, I need to look in y'all's boats."

He looked and found the poles, fish, and bait. "Lookee here," he said. "Y'all got a redhorse sucker. How'd y'all catch him? You can't catch no redhorse sucker with a hook and line."

"Everybody seems to know that but me and that fish," I said.

"Don't make no difference," the warden said, "but I need to see four fishing licenses."

"Licenses?" Mike bluffed. "You don't need no license for pleasure fishing in Georgia."

"That's true for salt water but this here's fresh water. Gotta have a license."

We had none so he wrote tickets for each of us then looked at his watch. "Let me see. It'll take me three hours to get back, eat, and get over to the judge on duty. He's the one named on y'all's tickets. I can meet y'all at the courthouse at three o'clock or I can take you with me."

"We'll meet you at the judge's place," Richard said.

The warden took the fish and left in his boat and we went home to tell our father we got caught. He didn't say much but we could see the thing embarrassed him. He knew that judge well because he had been before him many times with poachers he arrested on the club property. He said the judge was a blind man and a little harsh, but he liked to fish himself so he might go easy on us.

At three o'clock we entered the blind judge's chambers and our father made a few introductory remarks. "We got fish-hungry and the boys (I was thirty-five years old) decided to go get a mess of fish. I thought the boys were going to fish in the duck pond canal where they wouldn't need no license. Guess they couldn't catch nothing so they went out in the creek."

"They went two miles down the creek. And you should be ashamed. You bring so many men in here and now your own family has broken the game laws. Read the charge."

"We combined the charges on one docket, Judge," the warden said.

"Read it then," the judge said.

"The State of Georgia versus the Youngbloods. Whereas the following named men are charged with fishing in Georgia fresh water streams without a license—"

The document went on to name us and list the fish we caught. The judge interrupted. "Wait a minute, Warden. You sure that was a redhorse sucker?"

"I got the fish right here."

"Well, I can't see so I take your word for it. But you can't catch redhorse suckers with a hook and line. Were they fishing with a net?"

"No, sir. There was no net in the boats and the charge would have been the same anyhow."

"Never heard of anybody catching a redhorse sucker on hook and line," the judge said, "but strange things happen in fresh water. That's why I fish in salt water where the law doesn't bother sport fishermen too much. Fresh water fishing's got too many laws, rules, and limitations, so I leave it alone. Too much trouble."

We smiled and nodded at each other—the judge seemed to be softening. "So many rules and so much to remember, I sympathize with you, but gentlemen, the need for a license—that's fundamental. I'm going to fine each one of you twenty dollars."

We frowned and paid up and the judge took the money. "But I understand fish-hunger," he said, "so you can keep the fish. Now tell me how you caught that redhorse sucker."

THE RUNAWAY MOTORCAR

My father and my brothers, Bob and John, worked as bridge men for the Atlantic Coast Line and after it merged with the Seaboard Coast Line to become part of CSX, Inc. Their job was to watch the Savannah River trestle and stop the trains if river traffic needed to pass—water traffic had the right-of-way. Then they would open the bridge to the boat or barge until it passed, close it again, and open the trestle to train traffic again.

My father lived at O'Leary Siding, only a mile from the bridge. The railroad provided a gasoline-powered motorcar for transportation from O'Leary Siding to the bridge. My father was conveniently located for the job. When they were on duty, Bob and John drove to our house and took the same motorcar down to the bridge. When they reached the trestle bridge, the relieved bridge man would take the motorcar back to O'Leary Siding. When my father retired and moved, Bob and John stopped at the railroad crossing on O'Leary Road about three miles from the bridge where the motorcar was kept.

Safety regulations required the bridge men to alert the section dispatcher when they were going to use the motorcar. He would advise them if it was safe to do so or if a train was too close. If the situation provided enough time, the dispatcher gave permission to use the motorcar. A telephone to communicate with the watch shack at the bridge and the dispatcher was provided on a post near the motorcar parking spot.

One day, John started the motorcar for the ride to work and went to the telephone to call the dispatcher. While he was on the phone, the motorcar's vibration caused it to slip into gear and start toward the bridge. John saw the thing moving toward the trestle. He had it on idle speed so he tried to run it down, but he lost the race.

John called the dispatcher and told him that the motorcar got away from him and was headed for the bridge. He also called the bridge man he was supposed to relieve and told him the situation. "Don't worry about nothing," the bridge man said, "when it comes by, I'm gonna lasso it."

John worried about his fellow worker trying to catch a moving motorcar with a rope. Then he learned from the dispatcher that the motorcar got past the bridge man because his lasso attempt missed. Then the motorcar crossed the Savannah River on the trestle and entered South Carolina. By this time the entire section was on alert for the runaway motorcar.

Telephone wires buzzed with suggestions on what to do about the truant motorcar. Some said the thing had to be derailed by a locomotive so it wouldn't endanger workers on the railroad. Others said get all northbound traffic off the rails and just let it run out of gas. The idea that worked was to run it down with another motorcar and short out the ignition wire with a screwdriver tied to a long stick. "They finally stopped the dern thing in Hardeeville," John told us afterwards.

CAVIAR!

Two people identified only as Q and Z are the principals in this story. Any relationship to me will also go undeclared lest they be somehow identified.

When my family lived on Rice Hope Plantation, laws and regulations for shad fishing were strict and strictly enforced. To make matters worse, the Savannah River was the boundary between South Carolina and Georgia, and the two states had different rules. But my father and brothers still fished the river for shad during the spring run. "You got be a dern lawyer to fish this dern river," Joe said.

"It would help to be a surveyor, too," Bob said. "Both states allow you to fish only half the river."

Bob alluded to the regulation limiting the length of the drifting nets to no more than the half the width of the river. The trouble was, the river varied in width, so they had to use nets only as long as half of the narrowest run they would fish.

But my family did very well with the shad fishing for a while, but the regulations became ever more restrictive. It could be profitable if the prices were good and the sow shads were running. The females carried large sacs of roe and these fish eggs were considered delicacies by many. The shad flesh also had a market, but prices fluctuated widely depending on the catches, the demand, and the amount of fish being taken in other southern rivers.

Another fish much larger than the shad also swam these streams. The females of that species also carried eggs and it was even more valuable than shad roe. The river sturgeon was not as highly prized as its relative in the Black Sea streams, but its roe could bring as much as thirty-five dollars a pound, and a large sow sturgeon might carry as much as thirty-five pounds. The only problem was the closed season. The river sturgeon was a protected species.

One night when the subjects of this story, Q and Z, were shad fishing with limited luck, something large got caught in the net. They thought it was an alligator, but Q quickly found that it was a large sow sturgeon whose belly was swollen. He became excited and so did Z because he found another sow sturgeon on the other end of the net. There were several holes in the net, so they must have drifted into a school of sturgeon.

Q tried to work the sturgeon into the boat by pulling in the net, rolling it up, and trying to find a way to get a handle on the fish. All failed. He was getting tired and the fish was fighting to get away. He called Z to come help him and then Q managed to get a loop around the sturgeon's tail and worked it free from the net.

Then the fish took Q and Z for a joy ride up Savannah River for about a mile before it became exhausted. The two men were then able to pull the fish into the boat. "Let's go get the other one," Q said.

"Let's don't and say we did," Z said. "We in trouble enough if the law comes."

"If we get caught, the fine will be the same. Might as well go for broke."

"If I get caught, I'll be broke all right."

But Q was persuasive. They loaded the other fish in the second boat, covered both with netting, bags, coats and whatever they could find and headed for the landing. "If a game warden catches us, we'll lose everything," Q said. "I mean our licenses, the pickup, and a lot of money in the fines."

"Let's don't get caught, then," Z said.

They managed to get to Q's pickup truck and load the two monster fish into the truck bed. They covered them and left the landing. Their efforts had only begun. Now what were they going to do with two live sow sturgeons, both swollen with roe?

Q got on the telephone and investigated the situation with men he knew and learned a man near Brunswick, Georgia was not too inquisitive about the source of roe sturgeon—he only stipulated they be alive.

Although near exhaustion, they drove to Brunswick and found the man's fish camp. They bargained and disposed of the fish and came home with the money. The money was much easier to hide than the fish. "And easier to get rid of, too." Z said.

THE MURDER

O'Leary Siding branched off the railroad about a mile south of the Savannah River. Our house stood only fifty yards from the siding and the barns and sheds were even closer. There were only three ways to get to O'Leary Siding: the railroad itself, Buried Treasure Road that went through Rice Hope Plantation, and O'Leary Road. No one except the Chisholm family and friends and my father and his family used Buried Treasure Road. The name came from local legends that suggested a cache of gold was buried somewhere along the road.

It was possible for hobos to ride the rails and jump off at O'Leary Siding, but who in the world would want to jump off so near the swamp? O'Leary Road was semi-private—the plantation maintained it, but the railroad crews and bridge men used it to go to work. These observations may seem irrelevant, but one day the sheriff came and asked those and many other questions because of the murder.

One day about mid-morning my father was at home getting ready to go to town via O'Leary Road when he heard two sharp cracks. He thought it was a backfire from one of the motorcars the railroad used to go to the trestle, so he gave it no further thought.

A few days later Richard went to see our father and used Noxborough Creek Road entrance and took it to Buried Treasure Road, through the plantation, and came up to the barn and shed complex. He was shocked to see an armed man guarding the gate and asked what it was all about.

"Who are you and what are you doing here?"

"I'm Richard Youngblood. My father lives in that house yonder and I come to see him."

"Why?"

"He's my father and I come to see him so what are you talking about?"

"Your father Herbert Cecil Youngblood, Sr.?"

"He is."

"Well, he's in a lot of trouble. This is a crime scene so I can't let you come any further."

"I can't go see my father?"

The man hesitated and got on the radio and Richard got permission to go on to the house. There he found my father and mother in a state of unbelief. My father was under virtual house arrest for murder, but he had not been charged with anything.

"Woman got killed right off O'Leary Road," my father said. "Sheriff said she had been raped and shot twice with a .22 pistol. They found the body by watching the area for buzzards. She was lying off one of the deer hunting trails on the other side of the pasture yonder."

The woman had been killed about half a mile from our house and the backfire my father thought he heard earlier in the week was really the pistol.

The sheriff came by later that day with news they had caught a suspect. The woman had operated a panel truck loaded with breakfast sweets, coffee, and juice for working crews she sold to along her daily route in Port Wentworth and Garden City. On a normal day, she would have sold those things and gone back for lunch items. But that was not a usual day and her employer reported her absence to the police when she didn't show up with the panel truck.

The man evidently walked up to her truck pretending to want to buy something and abducted her at gunpoint. Witnesses saw him driving the truck along Georgia Highway 21 going away from her trading area. Ballistics identified a gun he owned as the killer weapon. The evidence was strong, but he never confessed. He was sentenced to life imprisonment.

ORANGE JUICE

In 1955, I was doing graduate work in chemistry for my Ph.D. My lab work gave me access to many chemicals, among them absolute ethanol or pure ethyl alcohol. Since that is the drinking variety, some of the graduate students used it for things other than its intended use as a solvent. One of my fellow researchers distilled the ethanol with juniper berries. He added some water to the distillate and made a fair gin and that in turn made a good Tom Collins.

Absolute ethanol was not a good solvent for the things I was working on, but I did find a use for it. Orange juice has a commonly known limitation; it needs to be fortified. I did some investigative experimentation and verified my theory that absolute alcohol blends well with orange juice in all proportions. That made it possible to make drinks as potent as anyone could wish.

During the summer of that year the time for our family reunion arrived and I took a liter of the absolute alcohol with me. That's equivalent to more than two quarts of 100 proof whiskey.

Pat and I stayed with Joe and Betty who lived in an apartment in Port Wentworth. When we arrived, a close friend of Betty and Joe was there with his wife and they were having good fellowship. We were introduced around and the other guest mentioned that he wished we had something stronger than coffee and cokes. I asked Joe if he had any frozen orange juice concentrate. He found some and we all had some of the concoction. The friends left praising the great orange juice that Joe served.

The next day we all visited the family at O'Leary Siding and we had one of Mama's great dinners. We stayed bloated most of the afternoon. That evening after supper Joe mentioned how good orange juice could be when properly treated. So my father, Richard, Joe, and I enjoyed orange juice and even the ladies commented on how good it tasted.

"Give me some more of that orange juice," Joe said.

Soon everyone had another round and the conversations became livelier.

"Orange juice sure makes for friendly talk," my father said.

We all laughed and commented on the sagacity of that profound statement. We also commented on many other things that made no sense and I don't even remember what they were.

Orange juice was the hit of that homecoming.

MAMA'S COOKING

Mama could cook. She could take various meats and plain garden produce and prepare a feast. We were dirt poor most of the time. That gave Mama a real challenge and made her successes even more remarkable. My father hunted and fished a lot and raised hogs for meat, chickens for meat and eggs, and cows for milk. Using these things with a few store-bought items like corn meal, flour, rice, sugar, and tea, Mama made great dinners.

We had a lot of pork because we raised our own hogs. At hog killing time, she made fresh liver, brains and eggs, and backbone and rice while she was making sausage and liver pudding. She scraped the intestines for sausage and pudding casings, but she balked at chitterlings. Sometimes my father wanted chitterlings and our neighbor, a colored lady who knew soul food, would fry the chitterlings for my father and her family. Thus did my father remember his heritage.

A few days after the great effort of butchering, we started to enjoy Mama's handiwork even more. I remember her getting up early in the morning and putting on a pot of grits. Then she would fry sausage and bake liver pudding to go on the grits. The smell of that woke us all and it woke our appetites. Joe and Helen didn't care for the pudding, but we all loved her sausage. It was so good Jeremiah Milbank, owner of Turkey Hill/Cypress Woods Corporation had been ready to set her up and produce her sausage on a commercial basis. He knew a good thing when he tasted it.

When the "fresh," that's what we called the liver pudding and sausage, was gone, Mama attacked the cured pork shoulders. She would slice off pieces and have eggs and grits with the meat. She also cooked thick bacon slices that were cholesterol bombs, but we didn't know and we didn't care. It was good. She used the hams for Sunday meals and for breakfast. When the slices became small, she made ham pie.

Mama's roast beef and gravy filled the house with delicious smells and our stomachs with the best rendition of that dish known to man. She was equally good with beef stew using the fatty beef rib plates. It came piping hot over rice with about five thousand calories per serving and a flavor out of this world.

She made several outstanding chicken meals like baked hen, fried chicken, chicken pie, chicken pilau, and chicken stew with dumplings. Her turkey was just turkey, but her turkey dressing made that a celebration, too. It's hard to make wild duck into a feast, but she did with her stuffing. Even her baked coon tasted good if you concentrated on the dressing. She fried venison, squirrel, rabbit, quail, and dove to perfection.

As to her vegetables, what can I say? They were hearty and delicious, like her field peas made with a piece of fatback, whole okra, and corn on the cob, often in one large pot and served over rice with her hoecake cornbread, sliced tomatoes, green and hot peppers, and sliced onions. As good as that was, it didn't surpass her collards or rutabaga turnips made with hog jowl meat and spiced up with my father's pepper vinegar. Butter beans and Kentucky Wonder beans were staple vegetables, but they danced when Mama made them. Even her "garden peas" floated in cream and tasted great.

I challenge anybody to match her candied sweet potatoes and sweet potato pie. Even her boiled white potatoes were seasoned and thickened so that you really needed nothing else. Her potato salad looked like mashed potatoes, but they were seasoned with her unique hand. Nobody made yellow squash like Mama, nor could anyone match her fresh creamed corn.

Deserts? Only the world's best. With her skill with toppings, she converted her workhorse 1,2,3-cakes (1 cup of butter, 2 cups of flour, and 3 cups of sugar) into masterpieces like caramel cake, banana cake, pineapple cake, coconut cake, and chocolate fudge cake. Her peach cobbler and pie, coconut pie, sweet potato pie, blackberry pie, huckleberry pie, banana pudding, lemon meringue pie were as good as you could find anywhere. Her special pound cake and fruitcake were appreciated by many and duplicated by none.

Sometimes we ran out of our own meat and produce, but all was not lost. Mama could make chicken fried steak, breaded pork chops, pork loin roast with anybody, and beat their pants off with things like her salmon patties,

But Mama backed away from some dishes like catfish stew. She gave my father free reign in the kitchen for most fish dishes and he did himself proud, but he was always ready to yield the kitchen back to Mama. He knew when he had a good thing going.

EPILOGUE

MEMORIES OF ROSEMARY CREEK THE HELEN GLADYS JOWERS YOUNGBLOOD CORPORATION (1976–)

The area around Mama's birthplace was called Rosemary Township for the creek that flowed through it on its way to join Buck Creek where the two formed the Saltchehatchie River. Here her people put down their roots in the eighteenth century and helped to establish the community.

The towns of Elko and Williston can be visualized as two points that with Mama's old home place made a triangle. The towns were three miles apart making the shortest side of the triangle. The distance from Williston to Mama's old home place was four miles and formed the second side of the triangle. It was five miles from the old home place to Elko and that formed the third side.

Mama's old place was only eight miles from Grandma Youngblood's place so when Mama and my father moved back in 1976, they were both coming home. Helen was born there so she was also returning to her roots.

But it had changed. Barnwell County has seen much of the history of this country from the Desoto's March and Indian wars to the hydrogen bomb. It was attacked and burned by the Indians, the Tories, the British, and the Hessians. Sherman was even more thorough, and the Depression destroyed hope as well as property. That's why my father and mother moved away.

Not even the wartime economy brought the area back to prosperity, but then came the hydrogen bomb. The "Bum Plant" made the area boom with hasty and sub-standard construction. The government bought the whole area and closed down entire towns like Dunbarton and Ellenton. They relocated the people and paid for or relocated their houses. They also relocated church buildings and cemeteries if the people wanted it done.

Everything changed. Migrant construction workers outnumbered the indigenous people for a while and helped create a boomtown. When the plant was completed, they moved away and left many areas little more than deserted shanty towns, but when the plant started operating, many local people found jobs as plant workers and as security and clerical staff. Scientists, engineers, and management moved in and things became stable and prosperous. Then they stopped making bombs and most people left or were terminated.

To make matters worse, the plant became a dump for spent radiation material that was still radioactive. Not only is national nuclear waste being deposited there, they are importing it from other countries. Many in the area opposed the storage of the radioactive waste. It is still under investigation by several groups pursuing programs to determine the psychological effects of forced mass re-location and the health risk of such concentrated radioactivity.

My parents had lived on Hardemore Creek for twelve years, on Bee's Creek for three years, Black Mingo Creek for five years, Bee's Creek again for one year, and Noxborough Creek for thirty-one years. When my father retired from Rice Hope Plantation and the railroad, he, my mother, and Helen moved back "up home" to a farm near Rosemary Creek that Mama inherited from her father. Mama and Helen built their dream house on the site of the house where Mama was born. Mama deeded the place to Helen with the consent of all her brothers and sisters who, by this time, were all married and living in several states with their own children and grandchildren. So we gave Helen a housewarming and celebrated my parents' golden anniversary at the same time.

They melded back into Williston/Elko society, especially Pleasant Hill Baptist Church. The building had been relocated out of the Bomb Plant site to a location only two miles from the new house. There Mama played the piano, Helen taught Sunday School, and my father was a deacon.

My father's brother, Norman, and he spent a lot of time together, and Mary Katherine, Norman's daughter, visited Mama often and Mama was only two miles from her Aunt Lois. Uncle Alvin "Money" Youngblood came from Arizona to visit often, and my father's nephew, Clinton Stansell Youngblood, Jr., or, Bo, as we called him, visited my father as well. My father visited Bub Waters, the deaf mute, who was still living.

They resumed things they had forgotten. My father again attended the Chitterling Strut Festival in Salley, SC until it closed and the Collard Festival in Gaston, SC until he died. He sometimes made it to the Catfish Stew Cook-off in Santee, SC and the Watermelon Festival in Hampton, SC. Mama was content to enjoy her surviving relatives like her aunts Essie and Lois, and everything was new to Helen who was only four years old when we moved away.

My father and mother had been in their Babylonian captivity away from Barnwell County for thirty-eight years and found many things changed. Some relatives remained and they found a few old friends, but most of them had passed on by the time they came back. Shortly after the Return, the death angel started another campaign on the family. Uncle Norman died in 1977, Mama died in 1983, Uncle Money died in 1987, and my father died in 1989. Then the next generation was hit. Laura Virginia died in 1889, Helen died in 1996, Bo died in 1998, Mary Katherine in 2003, and Joe in 2004.

Nell and Lang Roland are also dead. So is Lang, Jr. who was almost totally blind when I last saw him. It was heartbreaking, but he still had that grin that had warmed my heart many times. He later regained some of his sight and ran a cafe in Coosawhatchie before he died. I never got to see him since that time I saw him totally blind.

I don't remember the last time I saw Big Lang, but he was still alive when we left Turkey Hill. I saw Nell for the last time when Joe Graham, superintendent of Turkey Hill died. She was helping in the Graham home that night I went with several boys to pay respects to Mrs. Graham and daughters.

When my father died, Bub Waters came to his funeral—the only black person who did. All the others who knew my father were themselves all dead. Bub's appearance was affirmation of the relationship they had more than a half-century before.

The afternoon before Brother Joe died, I sat with him and we talked about the Rolands and he remembered Big Lang, Lang, Jr. and Nell with affection and humor because of all the scrapes we got into.

God still owns Healing Springs. I have heard nothing more about the government trying to take it from Him. Maybe they've figured out what the word "domain" really means.

Helen wanted Mama's birthplace to be shared by her brothers and sisters and devised the "corporation plan." On her death, we all deeded our shares of her estate into an S-corporation called the Helen Gladys Jowers Youngblood Corporation. We meet frequently at her dream house for corporation meetings and we also have an annual family reunion there with relatives and friends. This corporation or rather its architect, Helen, has kept this family close, and that's just what she had in mind. She was the finest person I ever knew and that's saying a lot because all my people are or were wonderful.

These stories are memories of childhood, adolescence, and a few of adulthood. I confess—my memory is incomplete and at times it may be inaccurate. Others have helped with the memory and sometimes I have given my memory some designed assistance and some of these stories are best defined as creative non-fiction.

We have aged and our brother Joe has passed on. Gone are the vigor of youth and the strength of young bodies. The streams of memory have become like the tired old river in Swinburne's The Garden of Proserpine that seeks its rest.

"—even the weariest river
Winds somewhere safe to sea."

Algernon Charles Swinburne (1866)

I remember things that scared, amused, disgusted, embarrassed, surprised, pleased, warmed, and impressed me. Usual and commonplace things no longer come to mind. If I got things a little mixed up, these stories are still the way I want to remember them. Life was probably more mundane, tedious, and difficult than these pages indicate, but these are the things I remember and want to remember.

The End.

978-0-595-39512-5
0-595-39512-0

Printed in the United States
63791LVS00002B/154-252